Lesson Masters A

W9-BFR-214

THE UNIVERSITY OF CHICAGO SCHOOL MATHEMATICS PROJECT

ADVANCED ALGEBRA

INTEGRATED MATHEMATICS

Further practice on
SPUR objectives

Scott Foresman
Addison Wesley

Editorial Offices: Glenview, Illinois • Menlo Park, California
Sales Offices: Reading, Massachusetts • Atlanta, Georgia • Glenview, Illinois
Carrollton, Texas • Menlo Park, California

http://www.sf.aw.com

Contents

ISBN: 0-673-45809-1

3456-BI-00999897

LESSON MASTER

1-1
A

Vocabulary

1. Name all the *variables* in $\pi r^2 h$. _____

2. Give an example of a sentence that is an *equation* but not a *formula*. _____

Skills Objective A

3. The formula for the surface area of a sphere is $A = 4\pi r^2$. Find the surface area if $r = 5$m. _____

4. In the formula $E = \frac{1}{2}mv^2$, find E if $m = 4$ kg and $v = 9\ \frac{m}{s}$. _____

In 5–7, evaluate the expression $4n^3 + 3n - \frac{1}{2}$ for the given value.

5. $n = 3$ _____   6. $n = -4$ _____   7. $n = \frac{1}{2}$ _____

8. To evaluate $30 \div 2 \cdot 5$, Martina stated that the first step was $2 \cdot 5$. Do you agree with Martina? Why or why not?

_____

_____

9. Evaluate $5 \cdot 8 - 3^4 + 24 \div 4$. _____

Uses Objective I

10. Ruby drove M miles in h hours. Write an expression for her average speed. _____

11. An airplane is traveling at P miles per hour. Write an expression for the distance the airplane travels in t hours. _____

12. In the downtown area of a city are G parking garages, each accommodating c cars, and S street parking spots, each accommodating one car. How many cars can be parked in the downtown area? _____

13. R ounces of juice sell for c cents. What is the price of one ounce of juice? _____

LESSON MASTER 1-2 A

Vocabulary

1. The equation $h = 2t$ gives the number of inches h of new snow after t hours if snow falls during a storm at the rate of 2 inches per hour. Identify the *independent* and *dependent variables*.

_____

In 2–4, give an example of a number satisfying the given conditions.

2. an integer that is *not* a natural number _____

3. a real number that is *not* an integer _____

4. an integer that is *not* a real number _____

Skills Objective A

5. Evaluate the function $p = \dfrac{4y}{y^2 - 3}$ if the independent variable has a value of 5. _____

6. Evaluate $t = 450(3)^n$ when $n = 4$. _____

Properties Objective G

7. Determine whether or not the table below describes r as a function of s. Justify your answer.

s	1	1	2	2	3	3
r	3	-3	6	-6	9	-9

_____

_____

ADVANCED ALGEBRA © Scott, Foresman and Company

▶ **LESSON MASTER 1-2 A** *page 2*

8. The table at the right gives the high
   school enrollment, in millions, in the
   United States from 1985 to 1991. Is the
   female enrollment a function of the
   year? Explain your answer.

Year	Male	Female
1985	7.2	6.9
1986	7.2	7.0
1987	7.0	6.8
1988	6.7	6.4
1989	6.6	6.3
1990	6.5	6.4
1991	6.8	6.4

_____

_____

_____

Properties Objective H

9. If y is a function of x, what real numbers are

   not in the domain of $y = \dfrac{1}{x^2 - 64}$? _____

In 10 and 11, identify the domain and the range for the function.

10. $\{(2, 4), (7, 11), (9, 13), (8, -4)\}$

   Domain _____   Range _____

11. $y = x^4 - 3$

   Domain _____   Range _____

Uses Objective J

12. The volume of a sphere is given by $V = \frac{4}{3}\pi r^3$.
    How much air does it take to blow up a beach ball
    to a radius of 8 inches? _____

13. Near the surface of Jupiter, the distance d that an
    object falls in t seconds is given by $d = \frac{1}{2}gt^2$,
    where $g = 84.48 \frac{ft}{sec^2}$. Find the distance
    an object falls in 3 seconds. _____

14. Sara recently bought a house. She made a down payment of
    $10,600 and will make payments of $369.35 each month.

    a. Write a formula that gives the total amount
       p she has paid as a function of the number of
       months n she has been making her payments. _____

    b. Find the total amount she will pay if she pays
       the house off in 15 years. _____

ADVANCED ALGEBRA © Scott, Foresman and Company

LESSON MASTER

1-3
A

Vocabulary

In 1 and 2, use the function g defined by $g(p) = p^4 + 1$.

1. Identify the *argument* of the function. _____

2. Rewrite the function in *mapping notation*. _____

Skills Objective B

In 3–5, let function r be defined by $r(x) = 3x^2 - 5$.

3. Find $r(7)$.   4. Find $r(\pi)$.   5. Find $r(c)$.

_____   _____   _____

6. Consider the function d defined by

   $d{:}n \to \frac{1}{2}n^3 + \frac{1}{3}n^2$. Then $d{:}$ -4 → ____?____.   _____

7. Let the table
   define function s.

a	0	1	2	3	4
$s(a)$	3	7	14	15	19

   Evaluate $s(4) - s(1)$.   _____

Uses Objective J

In 8–10, $C(x)$ is the number of cellular-phone subscribers, in thousands, in the United States in year x.

x	1984	1985	1986	1987	1988	1989	1990	1991
$C(x)$	92	340	682	1231	2069	3509	5283	7557

8. a. Find $C(1986)$ _____

   b. Tell in words what $C(1986)$ means. _____

   _____

9. Calculate $C(1991) - C(1984)$. _____

10. a. Calculate $\dfrac{C(1990) - C(1985)}{1990 - 1985}$. _____

    b. Tell in words what the calculation in Part **a** represents.

    _____

    _____

11. Marlene makes \$4.75 an hour. The function P, defined
    by $P(h) = 4.75h$, gives her gross pay as a function of the
    number of hours worked, h. Find Marlene's gross
    pay when she works 15 hours in one week. _____

ADVANCED ALGEBRA © Scott, Foresman and Company

LESSON MASTER 1-4 A

Uses Objective J

1. The graph at the right gives the number of deaths due to AIDS from 1984 to 1991 in the U.S.

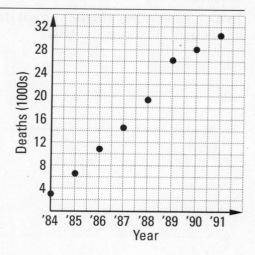

   a. If $D(x)$ represents the number of deaths in year x, estimate $D(1988)$.

   _____

   b. Estimate $D(1991) - D(1990)$ and write a sentence that describes what this result means.

   _____

   _____

Representations Objective L

In 2 and 3, a function is graphed.

2.

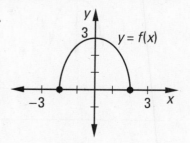

   a. Give the range. _____

   b. Give the domain. _____

   c. For what values of x is $f(x) = 0$? _____

3.

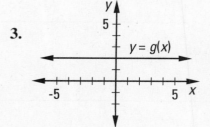

   a. Give the range. _____

   b. Give the domain. _____

   c. Find $g(-3)$. _____

▶ **LESSON MASTER 1-4 A** *page 2*

Representations Objective M

In 4–7, determine whether or not the graph represents a function. How can you tell?

4.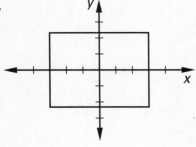

_____

_____

_____

_____

5.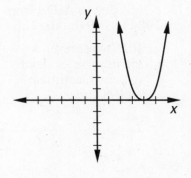

_____

_____

_____

_____

6.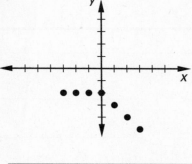

_____

_____

_____

_____

7.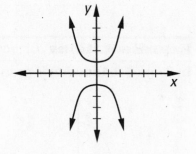

_____

_____

_____

_____

8. Explain why a horizontal line can be the graph of a function, but a vertical line cannot.

_____

_____

_____

_____

LESSON MASTER

1-5
A

Skills Objective C

In 1–4, solve and check the equation.

1. $\frac{3}{5}x = 12$

2. $\frac{3}{4} = \frac{2}{3}(z - 15)$

_____

3. $\frac{1}{2}x + \frac{1}{4}x + \frac{1}{8}x = 84$

4. $.03(2000 - y) + .05y = 90$

_____

5. Suppose $h(x) = \frac{4}{3}x + 9$. For what value
of x is $h(x) = 65$? _____

Uses Objective K

6. Devin plans to drive from Tampa to Chicago, roughly
1240 miles. At 60 miles an hour, $d(h) = 1240 - 60h$
gives his distance from Chicago after h hours of driving.

   a. How far is Devin from Chicago after
   10 hours of driving? _____

   b. About how long has Devin driven when he
   is 490 miles from Chicago? _____

7. When Ms. Jones's students asked her age, she gave them
the following problem to solve: "I spent $\frac{1}{8}$ of my life

   before entering school, $\frac{3}{10}$ of my life in elementary and

   secondary schools, and $\frac{1}{5}$ of my life in college and grad-

   uate school. Since completing my degrees, I have been
   teaching 15 years." How old is Ms. Jones? _____

8. For electrical service, Lynne pays a fixed cost of $8.12 a
month plus a charge for electricity used. If $k =$ the number
of kilowatts of electricity used, then $C(k) = 8.12 + .07k$
represents the amount of her bill.

   a. Find the amount of Lynne's bill if she used
   1000 kilowatts during the month. _____

   b. If her November bill was $200.62, how much
   electricity was used during the month? _____

LESSON MASTER 1-6 A

Skills Objective D

In 1 and 2, use the formula $w = \frac{v}{r}$, which gives the angular velocity w for an object traveling at a velocity v along a circle with radius r.

1. Solve this formula for r. _____

2. Solve this formula for v. _____

3. The formula $F = ma$ describes the force on an object with mass m and acceleration a. Solve this equation for m. _____

4. **a.** Solve $r = a + (n - 1)d$ for d. _____

   b. Use your result in Part a to find the value of d when $r = 15$, $a = -6$, and $n = 4$. _____

5. Solve the formula $r = 2p + ps$ for p. _____

6. The current I, in amps, needed to operate an electrical appliance is given by the formula $I = \frac{P}{V}$, where P is the power in watts and V is the voltage in volts.

   a. Solve this formula for the power. _____

   b. How many watts of power are needed by a slow cooker that uses 1.5 amps of current and runs on 115 volts? _____

7. The volume V of a pyramid is given by $V = \frac{1}{3} Bh$, where B is the area of the base and h is the altitude. Solve this formula for Bh. _____

Uses Objective K

8. When engineers design and build roads, they must allow for expansion so that the road does not buckle and crack. The formula $I = k\ell(T - t)$ gives the expansion I (in feet) that should be allowed for a road of length ℓ (in feet), at a temperature T (in Fahrenheit) if the road were built at temperature t. (k is a constant.)

   a. Solve this formula for T. _____

   b. Find the temperature on a day when a 1 mile (5280 ft) stretch of road built at 65° expands 0.5 feet. Use $k = .000012$. _____

ADVANCED ALGEBRA © Scott, Foresman and Company

LESSON MASTER

Vocabulary

1. Write the notation for "*s* sub 4 equals 81." _____

2. Write the notation for the eighteenth term
   of a sequence *p*. _____

3. Tell how the equation "$r_3 = -7$" should be read.

   _____

   _____

Skills Objective E

4. Give the first 6 terms of the sequence
   defined by the formula $b_n = 3n^2 + 1$. _____

5. If $p_n = 4^{n-1}$, find p_7. _____

6. **a.** Draw the next term in the sequence.

   b. Give a formula for T_n, the number
   of dots in the nth term. _____

7. Write the third, fourth and fifth
   terms of the sequence whose
   explicit formula is $a_n = \dfrac{n+1}{n+2}$. _____ _____ _____

8. *Multiple choice.* Which is an explicit formula for the
   *n*th term of the sequence 3, 6, 11, 18, 27, . . . ? _____

   (a) $t_n = 3n$ (b) $t_n = 2n + 2$ (c) $t_n = n^2 + 2$

Uses Objective J

9. At the end of each week at a discount store, the price of all
   remaining items is reduced 10%. So after week *n*, the price of
   a $60 jacket is given by $p_n = 60(.9)^n$. Find the price
   of the jacket after 3 weeks if it remains unsold. _____

10. A group of students took a bike trip across the country,
    averaging 60 miles of riding each day. The sequence
    $d_n = 60n$ gives the distance they have biked after *n*
    days. How far has the group biked after 7 days? _____

LESSON MASTER

1-8
A

Questions on SPUR Objectives
See pages 66–69 for objectives.

Skills Objective E

In 1–3, write the first six terms of the sequence defined by the recursive formula.

1. The first term is -3; each term after the first is 7 less than the previous term.

   _____

2. $\begin{cases} a_1 = 9 \\ a_n = (3 \cdot \text{previous term}) + 11, \text{ for integers } n \geq 2. \end{cases}$

   _____

3. $\begin{cases} s_1 = 1 \\ s_n = \boxed{\text{ANS}}^2 + 1, \text{ for integers } n \geq 2. \end{cases}$

   _____

Skills Objective F

4. Consider the sequence 9, 7, 5, 3, ...
   a. Use words to describe this sequence recursively.

   _____

   _____

   b. Use symbols to write a recursive formula for the sequence.   _____

5. Consider the sequence defined explicitly as $t_n = 3n + 18$.
   a. Give the first six terms of the sequence.

   _____

   b. Write a recursive definition for the sequence.   _____

Uses Objective A

6. Debbie has 520 books in her library. Each year she buys an average of 50 new books.

   a. Write a recursive formula that gives the number of books b_n in Debbie's library in year n.   _____

   b. How many books will Debbie have in her library ten years from now?   _____

LESSON MASTER   1-9 A

Vocabulary

1. **a.** If t_n represents the nth term of a sequence, what notation is used to denote the previous term?   _____

   b. What notation denotes the term following t_n?   _____

2. With a sequence a, would you use an *explicit* formula or a *recursive* formula if you wanted to find a_{200}? Explain your choice.

   _____

   _____

   _____

   _____

   _____

Skills Objective A

3. Write the first four terms of the sequence defined by the following recursive formula.

$$\begin{cases} w_1 = 81 \\ w_n = \frac{1}{3}w_{n-1} + 9, \text{ for integers } n \geq 2. \end{cases}$$ _____

4. Find p_6 if $\begin{cases} p_1 = 3 \\ p_n = 5p_{n-1}, \text{ for integers } n \geq 2. \end{cases}$ _____

5. The formula $\begin{cases} a_1 = 1 \\ a_2 = 3 \\ a_n = 2a_{n-1} + a_{n-2}, \text{ for integers } n \geq 3 \end{cases}$

   describes a sequence recursively. Find the first seven terms of this sequence.

   _____

▶ **LESSON MASTER 1-9 A** *page 2*

Skills Objective F

6. Consider the sequence 7, 35, 175, 875, ...

   a. Describe this sequence recursively using words.

   _____

   _____

   b. Write a recursive formula
   for this sequence.

   _____

7. Consider the sequence 1, 16, 81, 256, 625, ...
   Write an appropriate formula for the sequence.   _____

8. **a.** Write a recursive formula for
   the sequence -2, 6, 14, 22, ...

   _____

   b. *Multiple choice.* Which explicit formula also
   describes the sequence in Part **a**?   _____

   (i) $t_n = (-2)^n$ (ii) $t_n = 8n - 10$ (iii) $t_n = -4n + 2$

Skills Objective A

9. A new company projects that its annual revenue
   will grow by roughly 10% each year. The company's
   projected annual revenue for the first year is $100,000.

   a. Let r_n be the company's projected annual revenue
   in year n. Find $r_1, r_2, r_3, r_4,$ and r_5.

   _____

   _____

   b. Write a recursive formula
   for the sequence.

   _____

   c. *Multiple choice.* Which of the following is
   an explicit formula for the sequence?   _____

   (i) $t_n = 100,000(.1)^n$ (ii) $t_n = 100,000(1.1)^n$ (iii) $t_n = 100,000(1.1)^{n-1}$

   d. If you wanted to find the projected annual revenue
   in the company's fifteenth year, which formula, explicit
   or recursive, would you use? Explain your choice.

   _____

   _____

ADVANCED ALGEBRA © Scott, Foresman and Company

LESSON MASTER  **2-1 A**

Skills Objective A

In 1–5, translate into a variation equation.
Let k be the constant of variation.

1. m varies directly as the fourth power of n.　　　　　　_____

2. y is directly proportional to the fifth power of x.　　_____

3. The height h of a cottonwood tree varies directly as the
   square of its circumference C.　　　　　　　　　_____

4. The distance d a star is from the earth is directly proportional
   to the length of time t it takes for its light to get here.　_____

5. The volume V of a cylinder with constant height varies
   directly as the square of the diameter d of its base.　_____

Skills Objective B

6. y varies directly as x. If $y = 8$ when $x = -3$,
   find y when $x = 16$.　　　　　　　　_____

7. c is directly proportional to d^4. If $c = -13,824$
   when $d = 12$, find c when d $= 6$.　　　_____

Uses Objective F

In 8 and 9, _true or false_.

8. The cost of filling a car's gas tank with gas
   varies directly as the volume of the tank.　　_____

9. The outdoor temperature varies directly as the
   time of day.　　　　　　　　_____

Uses Objective G

10. The number of volts across an electrical circuit with
    constant resistance varies directly as the strength of
    the current in amps. There are 500 volts across a
    circuit of 25 amps. What would be the voltage across
    a circuit of 60 amps?　　　　　　_____

11. The surface of a sphere is directly proportional to
    the square of its radius. The surface area of a sphere
    with radius 3 cm is 36π cm^2. What is the surface
    area of a sphere with radius 12 cm?　　_____

LESSON MASTER

2-2 A

Vocabulary

1. Explain how *direct* and *inverse variation* differ.

   _____

   _____

   _____

   _____

   _____

Skills Objective A

**In 2–6, translate into a variation equation.
Let k be the constant of variation.**

2. y is inversely proportional to x.   _____

3. F varies inversely with the square of r.   _____

4. The gravitational pull F of the earth on a
   spaceship varies inversely as the square of the
   distance d of the spaceship from the earth.   _____

5. In a spherical balloon with a constant mass
   of air, the pressure varies inversely as the
   cube of the radius.   _____

6. In photography, the exposure E is inversely
   proportional to the square of the f-stop f.   _____

7. Write the variation equation $y = \dfrac{k}{x^5}$ in words.

   _____

   _____

Skills Objective B

8. y varies inversely as the cube of x. If $y = 5$
   when $x = 2$, find y when $x = 6$.   _____

9. y varies inversely as the fourth power of x.
   If $y = 5$ when $x = \frac{1}{2}$, find y when $x = \frac{1}{3}$.   _____

ADVANCED ALGEBRA © Scott, Foresman and Company

▶ **LESSON MASTER 2-2A** *page 2*

Uses Objective F

In 10–14, complete with "directly," "inversely," or "neither directly nor inversely."

10. The perimeter of a square varies
    __?__ as the length of the side.   _____

11. A telephone bill varies __?__ as the
    number of telephone calls made.   _____

12. The temperature in a house varies __?__
    as the setting on the thermostat.   _____

13. The intensity of light from a lamp varies
    __?__ as the square of the distance one
    sits from it.   _____

14. The time required to fly from Charlotte
    to San Antonio varies __?__ with the
    speed at which the airplane flies.   _____

Uses Objective G

15. The length of an organ pipe varies inversely as its
    pitch. If the pipe is $5\frac{1}{3}$ ft long, its frequency is
    96 cycles per second. What is the frequency of
    a pipe which is 8 ft long?   _____

16. The number of spans of steel needed to construct a
    bridge over a river varies inversely as the length of
    each span. If 10 spans are used, each span is 18 ft
    long. How long would each span be if 12 spans
    were used?   _____

17. The resistance in a certain electrical circuit varies
    inversely as the square of the current through it.
    The resistance of the circuit is 10 ohms when the
    current is 15 amps. What is the resistance in
    the circuit when the circuit is 20 amps?   _____

18. The force needed to keep a car on the road varies
    inversely as the radius of the curve. It requires
    1286 N of force to keep a 1000-kg car traveling
    at 50 km/hr from skidding on a curve of radius
    150 m. How much force is necessary to keep the
    same car traveling at the same speed from skidding
    on a curve of radius 750 m?   _____

LESSON MASTER

2-3
A

Properties Objective D

In 1–4, suppose that in a variation problem the value of x is tripled. How is the value of y changed if

1. y varies directly as x? _____

2. y varies inversely as x? _____

3. y varies directly as x^2? _____

4. y varies inversely as x^3? _____

In 5–8, suppose that m varies directly as the fourth power of q. How does the value of m change if

5. q is doubled? _____

6. q is quadrupled? _____

7. q is multiplied by 6? _____

8. q is multiplied by $\frac{1}{3}$? _____

In 9–12, suppose that p varies inversely as the fifth power of n. How does the value of p change if

9. n is doubled? _____

10. n is quadrupled? _____

11. n is multiplied by 6? _____

12. n is multiplied by $\frac{1}{3}$? _____

13. If $w = kz^n$ and z is multiplied by a constant c, what happens to w?

_____

14. If $w = \dfrac{k}{z^n}$ and z is multiplied by a constant c, what happens to w?

_____

ADVANCED ALGEBRA © Scott, Foresman and Company

LESSON MASTER

2-4
A

Skills Objective C

In 1–3, find the slope of the line through the two points.

1. (9, 12), (15, 21)   **2.** (-3, 8), (-5, -7)   **3.** (6.3, -7.1), (-7.1, 6.3)

_____   _____   _____

Properties Objective E

4. The graph of the equation $y = 0.13x$ is a line with slope _____ .

5. The graph of the equation $y = -17x$ is a line with slope _____ .

Representations Objective I

In 6 and 7, graph the equation.

6. $y = \frac{2}{5}x$ **7.** $y = 4x$

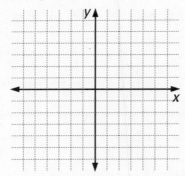

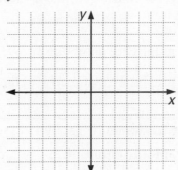

Representations Objective J

8. Match each graph
with its equation.
The x- and y-axes
have the same scale.

i. $y = 1.5x$

ii. $y = -1.5x$

iii. $y = \frac{2}{3}x$

iv. $y = -\frac{2}{3}x$

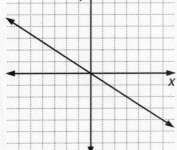

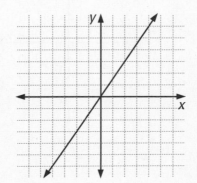

a. _____   **b.** _____

LESSON MASTER 2-5 A

Skills Objective C

In 1 and 2, $y = 3x^2$.

1. Find the rate of change between $x = -2$ and $x = -1$.

_____

2. Find the rate of change between $x = 1$ and $x = 2$.

_____

In 3 and 4, $y = -8x^2$.

3. Find the rate of change between $x = 2$ and $x = 4$.

_____

4. Find the rate of change between $x = 4$ and $x = 6$.

_____

Properties Objective E

In 5 and 6, refer to the graphs of these equations.

(a) $y = 5x$ (b) $y = -5x$ (c) $y = 3x^2$ (d) $y = -7x^2$

5. Which graphs are parabolas? _____

6. Which graphs are symmetric to the y-axis? _____

Representations Objective I

In 7–10, graph the equation.

7. $y = 4x^2$

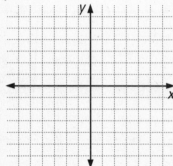

8. $y = -4x^2$

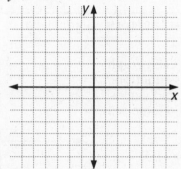

ADVANCED ALGEBRA © Scott, Foresman and Company

Name _____

► **LESSON MASTER 2-5A** *page 2*

9. $y = \frac{1}{4}x^2$

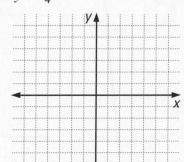

10. $y = -\frac{1}{4}x^2$

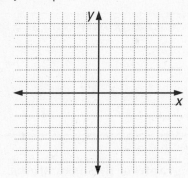

Representations Objective J

Multiple choice. In 11 and 12, select the equation whose graph looks most like the one shown. Assume the scales on both axes are the same.

11.

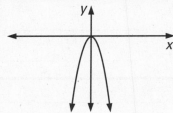

    (a) $y = 3.5x$

    (b) $y = 3.5x^2$

    (c) $y = -3.5x$

    (d) $y = -3.5x^2$

_____

12.

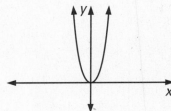

    (a) $y = 5x$

    (b) $y = -5x$

    (c) $y = 5x^2$

    (d) $y = -5x^2$

_____

Representations Objective K

14. *Multiple choice.* Which of the following graphs could be the graph of the equation $y = -4x^2$? Explain why.

(a)

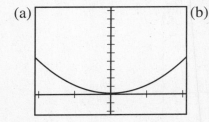

(b)

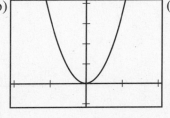

(c)

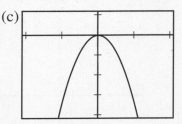

$-1 \leq x \leq 1$, x-scale = 1
$-2 \leq x \leq 10$, y-scale = 5

$-2 \leq x \leq 2$, x-scale = 1
$-1 \leq y \leq 4$, y-scale = 1

$-2 \leq x \leq 2$, x-scale = 1
$-4 \leq x \leq 1$, y-scale = 1

ADVANCED ALGEBRA © Scott, Foresman and Company

19

LESSON MASTER 2-6 A

Skills Objective C

In 1–4, find the rate of change between $x = 3$ and $x = 4$.

1. $y = \dfrac{16}{x}$ _____

2. $y = \dfrac{16}{x^2}$ _____

3. $y = -\dfrac{16}{x}$ _____

4. $y = -\dfrac{16}{x^2}$ _____

Properties Objective E

In 5–8, refer to the graphs of these equations.

(a) $y = kx$ (b) $y = kx^2$ (c) $y = \dfrac{k}{x}$ (d) $y = \dfrac{k}{x^2}$

5. Which graphs have two symmetry lines? _____

6. Which graphs have asymptotes? _____

7. When $k < 0$, which graphs have some points in the first quadrant? _____

8. Which graphs are hyperbolas? _____

Representations Objective I

In 9–12, graph the equation.

9. $y = \dfrac{24}{x}$

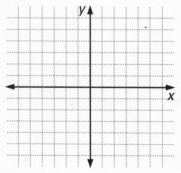

10. $y = -\dfrac{24}{x}$

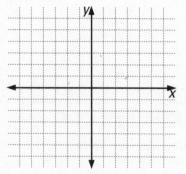

11. $y = \dfrac{24}{x^2}$

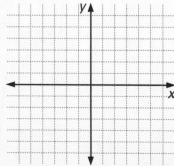

12. $y = -\dfrac{24}{x^2}$

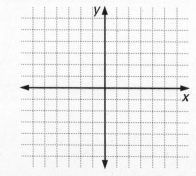

▶ **LESSON MASTER 2-6A** *page 2*

Representations Objective J

In 13–16, *multiple choice.* Select the equation whose
graph is most like that shown.

13.

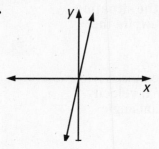

(a) $y = \dfrac{5}{x^2}$ (b) $y = 5x$

(c) $y = \dfrac{5}{x}$ (d) $y = 5x^2$

_____

14.

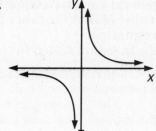

(a) $y = -\dfrac{2}{x}$ (b) $y = 2x^2$

(c) $y = -\dfrac{2}{x^2}$ (d) $y = \dfrac{2}{x}$

_____

15.

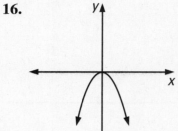

(a) $y = \dfrac{12}{x^2}$ (b) $y = -12x^2$

(c) $y = -\dfrac{12}{x^2}$ (d) $y = 12x^2$

_____

16.

(a) $y = x^2$ (b) $y = -x^2$

(c) $y = \dfrac{1}{x^2}$ (d) $y = \dfrac{1}{x}$

_____

17. In the graph of $y = \dfrac{k}{x^2}$ below,
what type of number is k?

_____

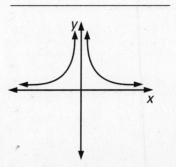

18. In the graph of $y = \dfrac{k}{x}$ below,
what type of number is k?

_____

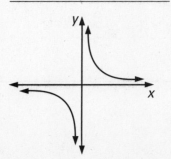

LESSON MASTER

2-7
A

Questions on SPUR Objectives
See pages 134–137 for objectives.

Uses Objective H

In 1 and 2, do Steps a through d.

  a. **Draw a graph to represent the situation.**
  b. **Write a general variation equation to represent the situation.**
  c. **Find the value of the constant of variation and rewrite the variation equation.**
  d. **Answer the question stated in the problem.**

1. A science class investigated the relationship between the horizontal range an object would travel and the initial velocity at which it was shot. The object was shot at a constant angle of 40° to the ground. The class collected these data.

Velocity (m/s)	10	20	30	40	50	60
Range (m)	10	40	90	161	251	362

How far would the object travel if it were shot at 100 m/s?

  a.

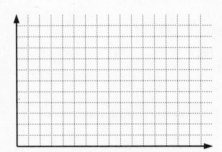

  b. _____

  c. _____

  d. _____

2. A group studied the relationship between the resistance and the strength of the current in an electrical circuit. The power of the circuit remained constant. The group obtained these data.

Current (amps)	10	20	30	40	50
Resistance (ohms)	.150	.0375	.0167	.00938	.00600

What would the resistance be if the current were 75 amps?

  a.

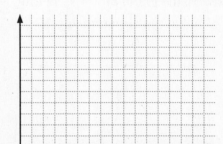

  b. _____

  c. _____

  d. _____

LESSON MASTER

2-8 A

Uses Objective H

1. An automotive engineer performed tests on a new tire to find the relationship between the air pressure P in pounds per square inch, the volume V in cubic inches, and the temperature T in degrees Kelvin. The engineer obtained the graph on the left by measuring pressure and volume when the temperature was 280°K. The graph on the right was obtained by measuring the pressure and the temperature when the volume was 2200 in³.

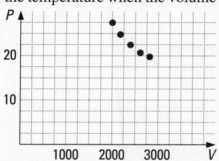 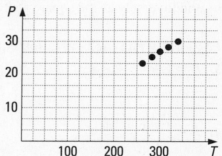

Write an equation relating P, V, and T. Do *not* find the constant of variation.

_____

2. Jeremy and Jenny performed an experiment to discover the relationship between the power of an electric light and the resistance in the circuit and the voltage supplied. They first collected the following data relating the power P and the resistance R on circuits with 2 volts.

I.

Resistance (ohms)	50	100	150	200	250
Power (watts)	800	400	267	200	160

Then they collected data when the resistance in the circuit was 200 ohms. These data relate the power P and the voltage V.

II.

Voltage (volts)	1	2	3	4	5
Power (watts)	50	200	450	800	1250

a. Graph the points from Table I.

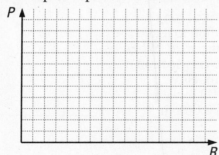

b. Graph the points from Table II.

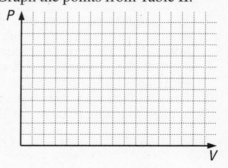

c. How does P vary with R?

_____

d. How does P vary with V?

_____

e. Use the Converse of the Fundamental Theorem of Variation to write an equation relating P, R, and V. Do *not* find the constant of variation. _____

LESSON MASTER 2-9 A

Skills Objective A

In 1 and 2, translate into a variation equation.

1. The volume V of a rectangular prism varies jointly as its length L, its width W, and its height H.

   _____

2. R varies directly as the square of P, directly as L, and inversely as the square root of A.

   _____

In 3 and 4, write each variation equation in words.

3. $P = kIRT$

   _____

4. $E = \dfrac{2(V_1 - V_0)}{X}$

   _____

   _____

Skills Objective B

5. w varies directly as the square of x and inversely as y. When $x = 5$ and $y = 2$, $w = 23.75$. Find w when $x = -3$ and $y = -6$.

   _____

6. z varies jointly as the square root of x and the cube of y. When $x = 9$ and $y = 2$, $z = 4$. Find z when $x = 25$ and $y = -5$.

   _____

Uses Objective G

7. The amount that a piece of copper wire 50 ft long stretches varies directly as the force applied to it and inversely as the cross-sectional area of the wire. When a 250-lb force is applied to a wire with cross-sectional area 0.0032 in², the wire stretches 1.08 in. How far would the wire stretch if a force of 300 lb were applied to a wire of cross-sectional area 0.005 in²?

   _____

8. The kinetic energy of an object varies jointly as its mass and the square of its velocity. The kinetic energy of an object with mass 12 kg moving at 8 m/s is 384 joules. Find the kinetic energy of an object with mass 8 kg moving at 12 m/s.

   _____

ADVANCED ALGEBRA © Scott, Foresman and Company

LESSON MASTER 3-1 A

Vocabulary

1. Write the *slope-intercept* form of an equation of a line. _____

Skills Objective A

In 2–4, complete the table.

	Equation	Slope	*y*-intercept
2.	$y = 5x + 2$		
3.	$y = -\frac{7}{3}x$		
4.		$\frac{2}{3}$	$\frac{1}{4}$

Properties Objective E

5. *True or false.* If $m > 0$, the equation $y = mx + b$ models a constant-decrease situation. _____

6. In the equation $y = mx + b$, the initial value of the dependent variable occurs when ___?___ . _____

Uses Objective G

7. Dolores bought a box of 200 plastic garbage bags. She uses an average of 3 bags a week.

   a. Write an equation relating the number of bags b left after w weeks. _____

   b. How many bags are left after 15 weeks? _____

   c. Will the box of bags last Dolores for an entire year? Justify your answer.

   _____

   _____

8. A postal container weighing 29 oz when empty is filled with letters averaging 4 oz each.

   a. Write an equation relating the total weight of the container w when it is filled with r letters.

   b. Will 200 letters fit in the postal container without _____ exceeding a 50-pound weight limit? Justify your answer.

   _____

   _____

Uses Objective K

9. Graph this situation. The temperature in a freezer is initially 0.8°C. It rises at a rate of 0.2°C an hour over a period of 6 hours, after which it holds constant for 2 hours. It then falls at a rate of 0.5°C over a period of 6 hours.

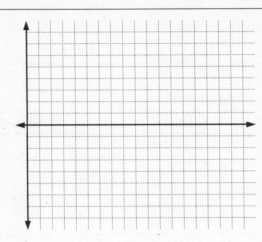

Representations Objective M

10. Refer to the graph below. Anita drove from school to her dentist's office, where she stayed 35 minutes, and then she drove home.

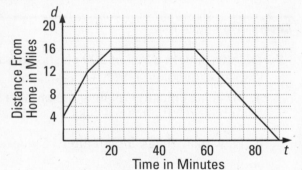

   a. How far is the dentist's office from Anita's school?

   _____

   b. How fast was Anita traveling on the last 4 miles of the trip to the dentist?

   _____

   c. How fast was Anita traveling on her trip from the dentist's office to her home?

   _____

   d. What was the total distance Anita traveled? _____

LESSON MASTER 3-2 A

Skills Objective A

In 1–4, give the slope and the *y*-intercept of the
line with the given equation.

1. $y = 7x - 2$

_____ _____

2. $4x + 5y = 11$

_____ _____

3. $y = -9$

_____ _____

4. $2x - y = 15$

_____ _____

Skills Objective B

In 5–7, write an equation for the line described.

5. line with slope $\frac{2}{5}$ and *y*-intercept 7   _____

6. horizontal line through (-8, 17)   _____

7. line with *y*-intercept 6 and parallel to $y = -\frac{1}{2}x + \frac{3}{8}$ _____

Properties Objective E

8. A line has a slope of $-\frac{4}{3}$. Fill in the blanks.

   a. As you move one unit to the right, it ___?___ $\frac{4}{3}$ units.   _____

   b. As you move ___?___ units to
      the right, it drops ___?___ units.   _____ _____

9. Give the domain and the range of
   the function *f* when $f(x) = 10$.   _____ _____

Representations Objective L

In 10–13, on the grid at the right, graph the line
described. Label each graph.

10. $y = \frac{2}{5}x + 3$

11. slope = -3 and *y*-intercept = 4

12. *y*-intercept = -3 and parallel to
    $y = \frac{1}{2}x + 16$

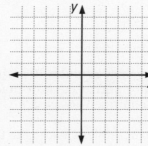

LESSON MASTER

3-3
A

Vocabulary

1. Write an expression that is a *linear combination* of *R* and *S*.   _____

Uses Objective H

2. In football, touchdowns are worth 6 points, extra points are worth 1 point, and field goals are worth 3 points. Suppose the Manatee Cougars earn *T* touchdowns, *P* extra points, and *F* field goals.

   a. Write an expression that gives the total number of points earned.   _____

   b. Suppose the Cougars scored 44 points and had 3 field goals. If they made an extra point on each touchdown, how many touchdowns did they make?   _____

3. Ivan bought *P* pounds of peaches at 79¢ a pound and *G* pounds of grapes at $1.99 a pound.

   a. Write an expression that gives the amount Ivan paid for the peaches and the grapes.   _____

   b. If he paid $7.55 and bought 3 pounds of grapes, how many pounds of peaches did he buy? _____

4. A chemist mixed *A* ounces of a 30% chlorine solution with *B* ounces of 40% chlorine solution. The final mixture contained 18 ounces of chlorine.

   a. Write an equation to model this situation.   _____

   b. Graph the solutions to the equation.

   c. Give three pairs of integer values for *A* and *B* that satisfy this equation.

   _____

   _____

   _____

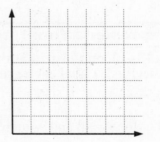

   d. If 18.6 ounces of the 40% chlorine solution were used, how much of the 30% chlorine was used?   _____

5. Make up a problem leading to the expression $12.99P + 8.99T$.

   _____

   _____

ADVANCED ALGEBRA © Scott, Foresman and Company

LESSON MASTER

3-4 A

Skills Objective A

In 1–4, complete the table. All equations should be in standard form with integers for A, B, and C.

	Equation	Slope	y-intercept	x-intercept
1.	$2x + 5y = 20$			
2.		$-\dfrac{4}{3}$	7	
3.			12	none

Properties Objective E

In 4–6, determine whether each line is *oblique*, *horizontal*, or *vertical*.

4. $12y = 18$ **5.** $4x + 9y = 27$ **6.** $-7x = 21$

_____   _____   _____

7. Identify the domain and the range of $y = 3x + 2$. _____ _____

8. For what values of A, B, and C is $Ax + By = C$ a horizontal line? _____

Representations Objective L

9. Graph $5x = 30$.

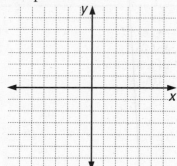

10. Use intercepts to graph $3x + 5y = 30$.

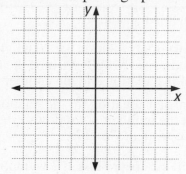

In 11–13, tell whether the slope of the line graphed is *positive*, *negative*, *zero*, or *undefined*.

11.

12.

13.

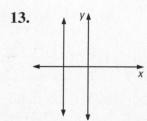

_____   _____   _____

ADVANCED ALGEBRA © Scott, Foresman and Company

LESSON MASTER 3-5 A

Skills Objective B

In 1–7, write an equation for the given line in standard form with integers for A, B, and C.

1. slope $\frac{7}{5}$, through (-2, 9) _____

2. slope -4, through (8, 11) _____

3. through (12, 7) and (-4, 5) _____

4. through (6, 8), parallel to $3x + y = 9$ _____

5. through (5, 6), y-intercept -2 _____

6. x-intercept 10, parallel to $3x - 2y = 5$ _____

7. through (15, 20) with undefined slope _____

Properties Objective E

In 8 and 9, *true* or *false*. Justify your answer.

8. The point (7, 2) lies on the line with equation $y - 7 = 3(x - 2)$.

_____

9. A line parallel to $8x = 9$ has a slope of 0. _____

_____

Uses Objectives I and K

10. The cost of installation for 10 windows is $800 and for 12 windows is $1000. Assume the relationship between the cost of installation and the number of windows is linear.

    a. Write an equation for the relationship. Let the number of windows w be the independent variable. _____

    b. Find the cost to install 20 windows. _____

11. A caterer charges $150 as a basic set-up fee. For the first 75 people, the charge is $2.50 per guest. For each additional guest, the charge is $2.

    a. Find the cost for the following number of guests.

    i. 30 _____   **ii.** 75 _____

    iii. 76 _____   **iv.** 100 _____

    b. What equation gives the cost for n guests, where $0 < n \leq 75$?

    c. What equation gives the cost for n guests, where $n > 75$?

    _____   _____

LESSON MASTER 3-6 A

Uses Objective J

1. The following data list pizza prices as a function of the diameter.

Diameter	Price
6″	$ 1.50
8″	$ 3.50
12″	$ 6.95
16″	$ 9.95
18″	$11.50

a. Draw a scatterplot of these data.

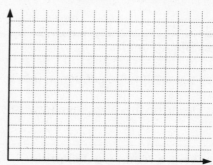

b. Write an equation for the regression line. _____

c. Interpret the strength of the linear relationship based on the correlation coefficient.

_____

_____

d. Draw the graph of the regression line on your scatterplot.

2. The following data give the number of international travelers (in thousands) to the United States from 1985 through 1992.

Year Since 1985	Number of Travelers
0	25,399
1	26,008
2	29,424
3	34,095
4	36,564
5	39,539
6	42,909
7	45,405

a. Draw a scatterplot of these data.

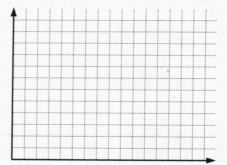

b. Write an equation for the regression line. _____

c. Draw the graph of the regression line on your scatterplot.

d. According to your regression equation, how many international travelers to the United States would be expected in the year 2000? _____

ADVANCED ALGEBRA © Scott, Foresman and Company

Name _____

A

Questions on SPUR Objectives
See pages 197-201 for objectives.

Vocabulary

1. In your own words, define *arithmetic sequence*.

_____

_____

Skills Objective D

2. Use the arithmetic sequence 0.5, 0.75, 1.00, 1.25, ...

a. Describe this sequence in words. _____

b. Write a recursive definition
for this sequence. _____

3. An arithmetic sequence has first term 6 and constant difference 4.

a. Write the first 5 terms of the sequence. _____

b. Write a recursive definition for
the sequence. _____

Properties Objective F

4. A sequence is defined recursively as $\begin{cases} a_1 = 12 \\ a_n = a_{n-1} - 3, \end{cases}$ for integers $n \geq 2$.

a. Find the first 7 terms of this sequence. _____

b. Is the sequence arithmetic? Justify your answer.

_____

5. Is the sequence 9, 27, 81, 243, . . . arithmetic? Justify your answer.

_____

Uses Objective G

6. Pak bought a pound of coffee beans. Each morning
she uses $\frac{3}{4}$ ounce to brew coffee.

a. How many ounces of coffee beans does
she have left after the first morning? _____

b. Write a recursive definition for
the amount of coffee beans left
after n mornings. _____

32

ADVANCED ALGEBRA © Scott, Foresman and Company

LESSON MASTER

3-8 A

Skills Objective D

In 1 and 2, an arithmetic sequence is given.
a. Write a formula for the nth term.   **b. Find a_{200}.**

1. 19, 25, 31, 37, . . .   a. _____   b. _____

2. -4, -6.5, -9, -11.5, . . .   a. _____   b. _____

In 3 and 4, a recursive definition for a sequence is given. Write an explicit formula for the sequence.

3. $\begin{cases} a_1 = \frac{3}{5} \\ a_n = a_{n-1} + \frac{2}{5}, \\ \text{for integers } n \geq 2. \end{cases}$ 4. $\begin{cases} d_1 = \pi \\ d_n = d_{n-1} + 2\pi, \\ \text{for integers } n \geq 2. \end{cases}$

_____   _____

5. Write a recursive definition
   for the sequence defined explicitly
   by $a_n = 9n - 7$.   _____

6. An arithmetic sequence has $a_3 = 11.1$ and $a_7 = 23.9$.

   a. Write an explicit formula for the sequence. _____

   b. Write a recursive definition
   for the sequence. _____

7. Find the 250th term of the linear sequence $5p, 8p, 11p, 14p, \ldots$ _____

Properties Objective F

In 8–10, determine whether or not the given formula describes an arithmetic sequence. Justify your answer.

8. $a_n = n^3 - 6$ _____

9. $b_n = 4n + 7$ _____

10. $c_n = \frac{2}{3}n - \frac{5}{3}$ _____

Uses Objective G

11. A TV shopping club that had 1218 gold necklaces for $125
    each sold 42 necklaces each minute the item was featured.

    a. Write an explicit formula that gives the
    number of necklaces left a_n after n minutes. _____

    b. How many minutes does this item need to be
    featured before the club would sell out? _____

LESSON MASTER 3-9 A

Skills Objective C

In 1–3, evaluate.

1. $\lfloor -8.7 \rfloor$ _____

2. $\lfloor 19.1 \rfloor$ _____

3. $\lfloor \pi \rfloor$ _____

Uses Objective K

4. *Multiple choice.* A pack of 50 sheets of construction paper is to be shared by *s* students. Which expression gives the number of sheets of paper each student may have? _____

(a) $\frac{50}{s}$ (b) $\lfloor \frac{50}{s} \rfloor$ (c) $\lfloor -\frac{50}{s} \rfloor$ (d) $\lfloor 50s \rfloor$

5. The table below gives the international air-mail rate for postcards from 1961 to 1991. The year is the first year that rate was in effect.

Year	1961	1967	1974	1976	1981	1985	1988	1991
Rate	$0.11	$0.13	$0.18	$0.21	$0.28	$0.33	$0.36	$0.40

a. Find the international air-mail rate for a postcard in each year.

    i. 1970 _____

    ii. 1987 _____

    iii. 1990 _____

b. Graph the postal rates in the table as a function of the year.

b.
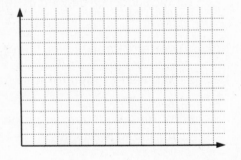

Representations Objective M

In 6 and 7, a rule for a function is given. a. Graph the function. b. Give its domain and its range.

6. $g(x) = \lfloor x \rfloor - 2$

    a.
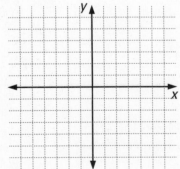

    b. _____

_____

7. $f(x) = 2\lfloor x \rfloor + 3$

    a.
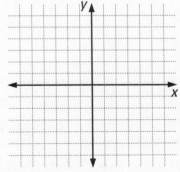

    b. _____

_____

ADVANCED ALGEBRA © Scott, Foresman and Company

LESSON MASTER

4-1
A

Questions on SPUR Objectives
See pages 266-269 for objectives.

Uses Objective G

1. According to the Census Bureau, in 1900 the median age at first marriage was 25.9 for males and 21.9 for females. In 1930, the median age at first marriage was 24.3 for males and 21.3 for females. In 1960, it was 22.8 for males and 20.3 for females. In 1990, it was 26.1 for males and 23.9 for females. Store this information in a 2 × 4 matrix. _____

2. According to the Census Bureau, in 1960 the median earnings for women was $3,257 and the median earnings for men was $5,368, with a gap of $2,111 in favor of males. (Figures are in 1990 dollars.) In 1970 the median earnings for women and men were $5,323 and $8,966, respectively, with a gap of $3,643. In 1980 the median earnings for women and men were $11,197 and $18,612, respectively, with a gap of $7,415. In 1990 the median earnings for women and men were $19,822 and $27,678, respectively, with a gap of $7,856. Store this information in a 4 × 3 matrix. _____

3. The matrix at the right gives data from the 1992 *Statistical Abstract of the United States* regarding prisoners executed under civil authority from 1930 to 1989.

$$
\begin{array}{c}
 \\
1930\text{–}1939 \\
1940\text{–}1949 \\
1950\text{–}1959 \\
1960\text{–}1969 \\
1970\text{–}1979 \\
1980\text{–}1989
\end{array}
\begin{array}{cc}
\text{White} & \text{Black} \\
\begin{bmatrix}
827 & 816 \\
490 & 781 \\
336 & 376 \\
98 & 93 \\
3 & 0 \\
68 & 49
\end{bmatrix}
\end{array}
$$

a. Give the dimensions of this matrix. _____

b. What does the entry in row 2 column 1 represent?

_____

c. How many whites were executed in the period 1970–1979? _____

► **LESSON MASTER 4-1 A** *page 2*

Representations Objective I

In 4 and 5, draw the polygon described by the matrix

4. $\begin{bmatrix} 0 & 2 & 0 \\ 0 & 5 & -3 \end{bmatrix}$

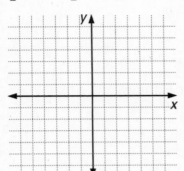

5. $\begin{bmatrix} -1 & 0 & 3 & 1 & -1 \\ -4 & -2 & -5 & 4 & 2 \end{bmatrix}$

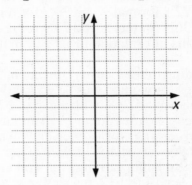

In 5 and 6, write a matrix for the given polygon.

6. *BEAR*

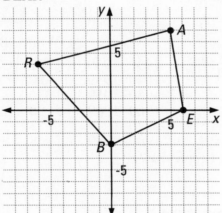

_____

7. *SHORTY*

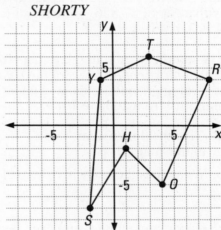

_____

LESSON MASTER

4-2
A

Skills Objective A

In 1 and 2, express as a single matrix.

1. $\begin{bmatrix} 4 & -2 & 7 \\ 3 & 6 & 0 \end{bmatrix} + \begin{bmatrix} 1 & 4 & -6 \\ 1 & 7 & -3 \end{bmatrix}$ _____

2. $\begin{bmatrix} 4 & 1 \\ 5 & -3 \\ -6 & -2 \end{bmatrix} - \begin{bmatrix} 9 & 0 \\ 5 & 2 \\ -6 & 7 \end{bmatrix}$ _____

In 3–5, let $A = \begin{bmatrix} 1 & 6 & -3 \\ -5 & 4 & -1 \\ 0 & 3 & 5 \end{bmatrix}$ and

$B = \begin{bmatrix} 1 & 3 & -2 \\ 1 & -7 & -4 \\ 0 & 8 & 2 \end{bmatrix}$. **Calculate.**

3. $A + B$ 　　　　　4. $4A - B$ 　　　　　5. $3A + 4B$

_____　　_____　　_____

In 6 and 7, solve for a and b.

6. $\begin{bmatrix} a & 3 \\ -5 & 7 \end{bmatrix} + \begin{bmatrix} 6 & -8 \\ b & 11 \end{bmatrix} = \begin{bmatrix} 10 & -5 \\ 7 & 18 \end{bmatrix}$ _____

7. $5\begin{bmatrix} 1 & -3 \\ -6 & b \end{bmatrix} - 2\begin{bmatrix} a & -7 \\ -1 & 9 \end{bmatrix} = \begin{bmatrix} 3 & -1 \\ -28 & -3 \end{bmatrix}$ _____

Properties Objective D

8. *True or false.* To be added or subtracted,
   two matrices must have the same dimensions. _____

9. *True or false.* Matrix addition is commutative. _____

Uses Objective H

10. The results of the Eastern Division of the National
    Conference of the National Football League for 1991
    and 1992 are given in the matrices below.

1991	W	L	T
Washington	14	2	0
Dallas	11	5	0
Philadelphia	10	6	0
N.Y. Giants	8	8	0
Phoenix	4	12	0

1992	W	L	T
Washington	9	7	0
Dallas	13	3	0
Philadelphia	11	5	0
N.Y. Giants	6	10	0
Phoenix	4	12	0

a. Subtract the left matrix from the
   right matrix. Call the difference M.   _____

b. What is the meaning of the second column of M?

_____

_____

c. What is the meaning of the entry in row 2 column 3 of M?

_____

_____

11. The following matrix represents the
    average daily sales of sandwiches from
    Shorty's Diner and Cutie's Deli. The
    various types of sandwiches are
    referred to as O for open-faced, G for
    grilled, and C for club.

$$\begin{array}{c} \\ \text{Shorty's} \\ \text{Cutie's} \end{array} \begin{array}{ccc} O & G & C \end{array} \begin{bmatrix} 35 & 82 & 46 \\ 49 & 88 & 21 \end{bmatrix}$$

During an upcoming festival, both
restaurants expect to triple their daily
sales. Write a matrix which represents
these anticipated sales.   _____

LESSON MASTER

4-3
A

Skills Objective B

In 1–3, calculate the product.

1. $[5 \quad 3] \begin{bmatrix} -1 \\ 0 \end{bmatrix}$

2. $\begin{bmatrix} 5 & 3 \\ -7 & -1 \\ 6 & 2 \end{bmatrix} \begin{bmatrix} 6 & 4 & 3 \\ -1 & -1 & 7 \end{bmatrix}$

_____

_____

3. $\left([-2 \quad 4] \begin{bmatrix} -1 & 0 & 1 \\ 6 & -5 & -4 \end{bmatrix} \right) \begin{bmatrix} 1 & 2 \\ -5 & 0 \\ 1 & -2 \end{bmatrix}$

_____

Properties Objective D

4. If $\begin{bmatrix} 5 & -2 & -1 \\ 2 & 4 & 7 \end{bmatrix} \cdot A = \begin{bmatrix} 7 \\ 76 \end{bmatrix}$, what are the dimensions of matrix A? _____

5. Explain how you can tell whether the matrix product $A \cdot B$ exists.

_____

6. *True or false.* Matrix multiplication is associative. _____

Uses Objective H

7. Fiona's art class painted a large mural. They used 1 can of blue paint, 3 cans of white, and 2 cans of red. A can of blue paint cost $11.50, a can of white paint cost $8.95, and a can of red paint cost $14.20.

a. Write matrices for the cost C and the number of cans used N.

$C =$ _____ $N =$ _____

b. Calculate CN to find the total cost. _____

8. Sumi and Philip have a baby-sitting service. They each charge $5 for one child and $10 for small groups. Each week, Sumi baby-sits for 3 children singly and for 4 small groups. Each week, Philip baby-sits for 2 children singly and for 5 small groups.

a. Write a matrix C for their charges and a matrix B for the numbers Sumi and Philip baby-sit.

$C =$ _____ $B =$ _____

b. Find BC and tell what it represents.

_____

$BC =$ _____ _____

LESSON MASTER

4-4
A

Vocabulary

1. Explain what is meant by a *size change*.

   _____

   _____

Properties Objective E

2. Describe a relationship between a preimage and
   its image after the application of a size change.   _____

   _____

Properties Objective F

3. The matrix $\begin{bmatrix} 7 & 0 \\ 0 & 7 \end{bmatrix}$ is associated with a ___?___ with

   center ___?___ and magnitude ___?___.

   _____   _____   _____

4. The matrix associated with a size change
   of magnitude 8 is ___?___.   _____

Representations Objective I

5. Graph the polygon $\begin{bmatrix} -1 & 0 & 3 & 0 \\ 0 & -4 & 0 & 5 \end{bmatrix}$
   and its image under S_2.

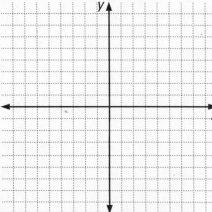

6. Graph the polygon $\begin{bmatrix} 1 & 3 & -3 \\ 3 & 6 & -6 \end{bmatrix}$
   and its image under $S_{1/3}$.

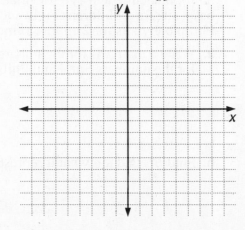

LESSON MASTER 4-5 A

Vocabulary

1. Define the *scale change* $S_{a,b}$.

_____

_____

_____

Properties Objective E

2. *True or false.* A figure and its scale-change image are similar. _____

Properties Objective F

In 3 and 4, give the matrix corresponding to the given transformation.

3. a vertical shrink of $\frac{1}{2}$ and a   **4.** $S_{2,9}$
horizontal stretch of 3

_____   _____

5. $\begin{bmatrix} 6 & 0 \\ 0 & \frac{1}{3} \end{bmatrix}$ is associated with what transformation? _____

Representations Objective I

6. a. Graph the quadrilateral $\begin{bmatrix} -2 & 6 & 2 & 0 \\ -3 & -3 & 4 & 4 \end{bmatrix}$

and its image under $\begin{bmatrix} 1 & 0 \\ 0 & 2 \end{bmatrix}$.

b. Are the image and
preimage congruent? _____

c. Are the image and
preimage similar? _____

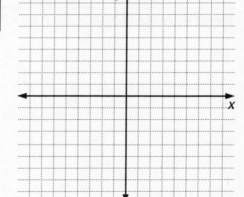

d. What type of quadrilateral is the preimage? _____

e. What type of quadrilateral is the image? _____

LESSON MASTER 4-6 A

Properties Objective E

1. *True or false.* A figure and its reflection image are congruent. _____

Properties Objective F

In 2 and 3, translate the matrix equation into English.

2. $\begin{bmatrix} 1 & 0 \\ 0 & -1 \end{bmatrix} \begin{bmatrix} -7 \\ 3 \end{bmatrix} = \begin{bmatrix} -7 \\ -3 \end{bmatrix}$. The reflection image

of the point ____?____ over the line ____?____ is the point ____?____.

_____   _____   _____

3. $\begin{bmatrix} 0 & 1 \\ 1 & 0 \end{bmatrix} \begin{bmatrix} 5 \\ 9 \end{bmatrix} = \begin{bmatrix} 9 \\ 5 \end{bmatrix}$. The reflection image of

the point ____?____ over the line ____?____ is the point ____?____.

_____   _____   _____

4. a. Multiply the matrix for $r_{y=x}$ by itself.

_____

b. Explain your result.

_____

_____

_____

_____

Representations Objective I

5. A polygon is represented by the

matrix $\begin{bmatrix} -1 & 1 & 0 & -3 \\ -4 & 4 & 6 & 2 \end{bmatrix}$. Graph

the polygon and its image under r_y.

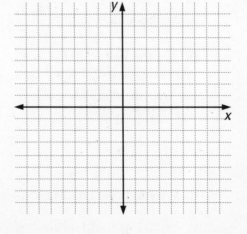

ADVANCED ALGEBRA © Scott, Foresman and Company

LESSON MASTER 4-7 A

Properties Objective D

1. *True or false.* Multiplication of 2×2 matrices is commutative. If true, prove. If false, provide a counterexample.

_____

_____

2. If *A, B,* and *C* are 2×2 matrices, what property assures that $(AB)C = A(BC)$?

_____

Properties Objective F

In 3–5, a point and its image under four composites of transformations are graphed. a. Match the composite to a graph. b. Calculate a matrix for the composite.

3. $r_y \circ r_x$

a. _____

4. $r_{y=x} \circ r_{y=x}$

a. _____

5. $r_x \circ S_{1/2}$

a. _____

b. _____

b. _____

b. _____

i. ii. iii. iv.

Representations Objective I

6. Draw the polygon $\begin{bmatrix} 4 & -1 & 1 \\ 3 & 2 & -5 \end{bmatrix}$ and its image under $r_{y=x} \circ r_y$.

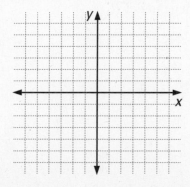

LESSON MASTER

4-8
A

Properties Objective E

1. $\triangle A'B'C'$ is the image of $\triangle ABC$ under R_{90}. Describe a relationship between $\triangle ABC$ and $\triangle A'B'C'$.

   _____

Properties Objective F

In 2 and 3, a composite of transformations is given.
a. Find a matrix for the composite. b. Describe each matrix with a single transformation.

2. $R_{180} \circ r_x$

3. $r_x \circ r_y$

   a. _____

   a. _____

   b. _____

   b. _____

4. Explain how to find the matrix for R_{270} from the matrix for R_{90}.

   _____

Representations Objective I

5. a. What rotation maps *TOM* onto *T'O'M'*?

   _____

   b. Give the matrix for the rotation in Part **a**.

   _____

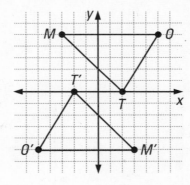

6. Draw the polygon $\begin{bmatrix} 0 & 6 & 8 & 6 & 0 & -3 \\ 0 & 0 & 3 & 6 & 6 & 3 \end{bmatrix}$ and its image under R_{90}.

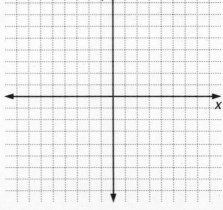

LESSON MASTER

Skills Objective A

In 1–4, write an equation for the line that goes through the given point and is perpendicular to the given line.

1. $(6, 1)$; $y = 3x - 5$ _____

2. $(-1, -7)$; $3x + 4y = 7$ _____

3. $(5, 2)$; $x = 12$ _____

4. $(5, 2)$; $y = 17$ _____

In 5 and 6, write an equation for the perpendicular bisector of the line segment with the given endpoints.

5. $(-6, 8)$, $(6, -8)$ _____

6. $(8, 16)$, $(24, -12)$ _____

Properties Objective E

7. The slope of a line is 6. What is the slope of the image of this line under R_{90}? _____

8. Let $\triangle PUT$ be represented by the matrix $\begin{bmatrix} 523 & 23 & -177 \\ -621 & 379 & 79 \end{bmatrix}$.
Let $\triangle P'U'T' = R_{90}(\triangle PUT)$.

   a. Find the slope of $\overleftrightarrow{PU}$. _____

   b. Find the slope of $\overleftrightarrow{P'U'}$. _____

**L E S S O N
M A S T E R**  **4-10**
A

Questions on SPUR Objectives
See pages 266-269 for objectives.

Properties Objective E

1. *True or false.* A triangle and its translation
   image are not necessarily congruent. _____

Properties Objective F

2. Translate the following matrix equation into English.

$$\begin{bmatrix} 1 & 1 & 1 \\ -3 & -3 & -3 \end{bmatrix} + \begin{bmatrix} 2 & 4 & -1 \\ 5 & 6 & -3 \end{bmatrix} = \begin{bmatrix} 3 & 5 & 0 \\ 2 & 3 & -6 \end{bmatrix}$$

The image of a ___?___ under a ___?___ of ___?___ units ___?___

and ___?___ units ___?___ is a ___?___ .

_____

_____   _____   _____

_____   _____

_____

3. What matrix is the identity matrix for
   translating triangles in the plane? _____

4. What matrix describes the translation
   of a quadrilateral under $T_{-2,\,6}$? _____

Representations Objective I

5. $\begin{bmatrix} -3 & 3 & 3 & -3 \\ -3 & -3 & 3 & 3 \end{bmatrix}$ represents square *SQUA*.

   a. Apply the translation $T_{1,2}$ to this square. _____

   b. Graph the preimage and the
      image on the grid at the right.

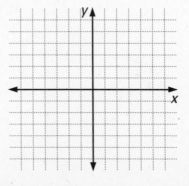

Name

LESSON MASTER **5-1** **A**

Questions on SPUR Objectives
See pages 340-343 for objectives.

Vocabulary

1. The ___?___ of two sets is the set consisting of those elements in either one set or both sets.

_____

2. The ___?___ of two sets is the set consisting of those elements common to both sets.

_____

Representations Objective H

3. Graph all solutions to $m \geq -2$ on the number line at the right.

 m

4. Write an inequality that describes the graph below.

_____

 n
-7   0

In 5 and 6, solve the inequality and graph its solution set on the number line.

5. $-3r + 11 < 20$

⟷ r

6. $4t - (2 - t) \geq 18$

⟷ t

Representations Objective K

In 7 and 8, graph on the number line.

7. $n > 3$ and $n < 12$

⟷

8. $\{s: 4 \leq s \leq 10\} \cap \{s: s \leq 6\}$

⟷

9. $v < -3$ and $v > 6$

Name _____

LESSON MASTER

Questions on SPUR Objectives
See pages 340-343 for objectives.

Properties Objective D

1. Does (-2, 5) solve the system $\begin{cases} 2x + y = 1 \\ 4x + y = 3 \end{cases}$? Justify your answer.

_____

2. Use the table at the right to solve
the system $\begin{cases} y = 9x + 1 \\ y = 3x - 2 \end{cases}$.

_____

x	y = 9x + 1	y = 3x − 2
-1.5	-12.5	-6.5
-1.0	-8	-5
-0.5	-3.5	-3.5
0	1	-2
0.5	5.5	-0.5

Representations Objective L

In 3–6, a system is given. a. Graph the system. b. Tell how many solutions the system has. c. Estimate any solutions to the nearest tenth.

3. $\begin{cases} 3x + 2y = 12 \\ x - y = 4 \end{cases}$

a.

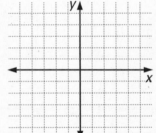

b. _____ c. _____

4. $\begin{cases} 9x - y = 12 \\ y = 9x + 6 \end{cases}$

a.

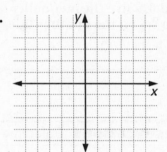

b. _____ c. _____

5. $\begin{cases} y = \dfrac{4}{x^2} \\ y = -3x + 7 \end{cases}$

a.

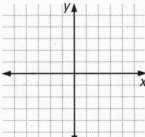

b. _____ c. _____

6. $\begin{cases} y = 3x^2 \\ y = \dfrac{10}{x} \end{cases}$

a.

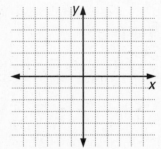

b. _____ c. _____

LESSON MASTER

5-3
A

Skills Objective A

**In 1–5, use substitution to solve the systems.
Then check.**

1. $\begin{cases} 2x + 3y = 19 \\ \quad\quad y = 3x - 1 \end{cases}$
2. $\begin{cases} xy = 100 \\ x = 4y \end{cases}$
3. $\begin{cases} .4a - .5b = 20 \\ \quad\quad .3b = .3a - 1.5 \end{cases}$

4. $\begin{cases} 2x + y + 2z = 0 \\ \quad\quad y = 3x + 1 \\ \quad\quad z = x - 4 \end{cases}$
5. $\begin{cases} x + 2y - z = 1 \\ \quad\quad y = \text{-}x \\ \quad\quad z = x + 1 \end{cases}$

Properties Objective D

6. What does it mean for a system of equations to be inconsistent?

_____

7. A system of two linear equations has no solutions. What can
you say about the graphs of the two lines?

_____

_____

Uses Objective F

8. Hotel Oakwood charges $40 a night for two people plus $5
for each additional person. Pine Valley Lodge charges $38 a
night for two people plus $6 for each additional person.

   a. Write an equation for the cost y with x additional
   people in a room for one night at each place.

   H.O. _____   P.V.L. _____

   b. For how many people will the rate for the two
   rooms be the same?   _____

9. Three-bean salad can be made by mixing green, kidney, and wax
beans. The recipe calls for the same amount of kidney beans and
wax beans, and twice as much green beans as kidney beans. Let g
be the number of cups of green beans, k the number of cups of
kidney beans, and w the number of cups of wax beans. Determine
how much of each kind of bean should be used for nine cups of salad.

   green _____   kidney _____   wax _____

LESSON MASTER 5-4 A

Skills Objective A

In 1–4, use linear combinbations to solve the systems. Then check.

1. $\begin{cases} 2x + y = 1 \\ 4x + 3y = 9 \end{cases}$

2. $\begin{cases} r + 2s - 3t = 11 \\ 2r + s + t = \text{-}1 \\ r - 3s - t = \text{-}8 \end{cases}$

3. $\begin{cases} 5w + 4z = \text{-}.7 \\ 8w + 6z = \text{-}1.2 \end{cases}$

4. $\begin{cases} f + 2g = 2 \\ 3f + 6g = 6 \end{cases}$

Properties Objective D

For 5 and 6, consider the system $\begin{cases} 12x + 6y = k \\ 2x + y = 9 \end{cases}$.

5. For what values of k will the system
   be inconsistent? _____

6. For what value of k will the system
   have infinitely many solutions? _____

Uses Objective F

7. At a restaurant, four hamburgers and two orders of fries
   cost $27.10. Three hamburgers and four orders of fries
   cost $25.20. If all hamburgers cost the same price and
   all orders of fries cost the same price, find the cost of each.

   hamburgers _____   fries _____

8. Three pounds of pears and a pound of grapes
   cost $4.36. Five pounds of pears and two
   pounds of grapes cost $7.93. Find the cost of
   six pounds of pears and four pounds of grapes.   _____

LESSON MASTER 5-5 A

Vocabulary

1. Two matrices are *inverses* of each other if and
   only if their product is ___?___.

   _____

2. Find the *determinant* of matrix $\begin{bmatrix} q & r \\ s & t \end{bmatrix}$. _____

Skills Objective B

In 3–5, a matrix is given. a. Find its determinant.
b. Find its inverse, if it exists.

3. $\begin{bmatrix} 7 & -8 \\ 3 & 4 \end{bmatrix}$

4. $\begin{bmatrix} -1 & 0 \\ 9 & -1 \end{bmatrix}$

5. $\begin{bmatrix} 14 & 2 \\ 3 & 9 \end{bmatrix}$

   a. _____ a. _____ a. _____

   b. _____ b. _____ b. _____

6. Show that $\begin{bmatrix} 5 & 4 \\ 1 & 1 \end{bmatrix}$ and $\begin{bmatrix} 1 & 4 \\ -1 & 5 \end{bmatrix}$
   are *not* inverses of each other. _____

7. Show that $\begin{bmatrix} 12 & 2 \\ 9 & 1 \end{bmatrix}$ and $\begin{bmatrix} -\frac{1}{6} & \frac{1}{3} \\ \frac{3}{2} & -2 \end{bmatrix}$

   are inverses of each other. _____

8. Consider the matrix $\begin{bmatrix} 9 & x \\ 12 & 4 \end{bmatrix}$. For what values

   of x does the matrix *not* have an inverse? _____

9. **a.** Find the inverse of
   the matrix for S_4.   **b.** Explain the result to Part a geometrically.

   _____

   _____

   _____

   _____

LESSON MASTER 5-6 A

Vocabulary

In 1 and 2, consider the system $\begin{cases} 5x - 4y = 12 \\ 2x + 3y = 7 \end{cases}$.

1. Write the *coefficient matrix*.   _____

2. $\begin{bmatrix} 12 \\ 7 \end{bmatrix}$ is called the ___?___ matrix.   _____

Skills Objective C

In 3–6, use a matrix to solve the system.

3. $\begin{cases} 4x + 2y = 0 \\ 12x + 3y = 2 \end{cases}$

4. $\begin{cases} 7m + 9n = 14 \\ -4m + 6n = 31 \end{cases}$

5. $\begin{cases} -11r + 1.5s = 46.9 \\ 10r - 3.1s = -56.18 \end{cases}$

6. $\begin{cases} 2x + 3y - 4z = 37 \\ 9x - 2y + z = -82 \\ -11x + 5y - 7z = 165 \end{cases}$

Properties Objective D

7. If the determinant of a coefficient matrix is zero,
   then the system has ___?___ solution(s).   _____

Uses Objective F

8. At the ABC MEDIA, all videotapes, all CDs,
   and all cassettes have standard prices. One
   videotape, one CD, and two cassettes cost
   $27.00. Two of each cost $47.00. Two videos
   and three CDs cost $47.75.

   a. Write a system of equations that can
      be used to find the cost of each item.

   b. Use matrices to solve the
      system.

      video _____

      CD _____

   _____   cassette _____

LESSON MASTER

5-7
A

Vocabulary

1. How do the graphs of $4x + 3y = 24$, $4x + 3y \geq 24$, and $4x + 3y > 24$ differ?

_____

_____

_____

Representations Objective J

In 2 and 3, write an inequality to describe the shaded region.

2.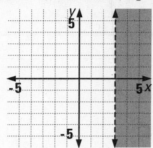

_____

3.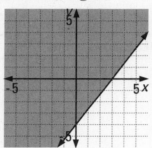

_____

In 4–7, graph the inequality on the coordinate plane.

4. $x < -2.5$

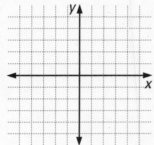

5. $y \geq 7$

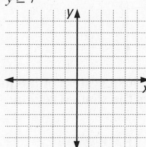

6. $y \geq \frac{2}{3}x + 1$

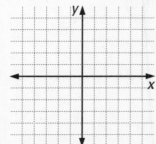

7. $5x - 4y < 40$

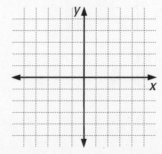

LESSON MASTER 5-8 A

Vocabulary

1. The set of solutions to a system of linear inequalities is called the ___?___ for that system. _____

Properties Objective E

2. A system of inequalities is graphed at the right. Does the given point satisfy the system?

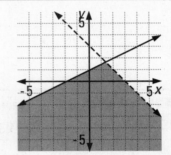

a. $(0, 0)$ _____

b. $(-4, 2)$ _____

c. $(3, 0)$ _____

Representations Objective K

In 3 and 4, graph the solution set.

3. $\begin{cases} y \le \frac{2}{3}x + 5 \\ y \ge -\frac{1}{4}x - 2 \end{cases}$

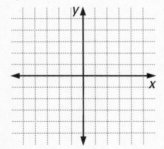

4. $\begin{cases} x \ge -2 \\ y \le 4 \\ y < -2x + 3 \end{cases}$

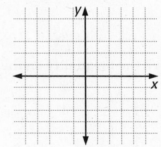

In 5 and 6, write a system of inequalities that describes the shaded region.

5.

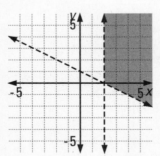

_____

6.

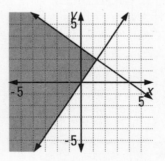

_____

ADVANCED ALGEBRA © Scott, Foresman and Company

LESSON MASTER 5-9 A

Questions on SPUR Objectives
See pages 340-343 for objectives.

Properties Objective E

1. Tell whether the shaded region could be the feasible region of a linear programming problem.

a. _____ b. _____ c. _____ d. _____

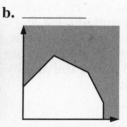   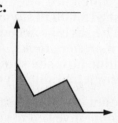

Uses Objective G

In 2–5, refer to the following situation: A batch of cookies takes 2.5 cups of flour and 48 minutes to bake. One cake takes 3.5 cups of flour and 75 minutes to bake. Brad's Bakery has 40 cups of flour and can bake for only 7 hours. Brad must make at least two batches of cookies and 3 cakes. Let k be the number of batches of cookies and let c be the number of cakes. The system of inequalities for this problem is at the right.

$$\begin{cases} 2.5k + 3.5c \leq 40 \\ 48k + 75c \leq 420 \\ k \geq 2 \\ c \geq 3 \end{cases}$$

2. Match each inequality in the system with the aspect it describes.

_____ **a.** number of batches of cookies

_____ **b.** number of cakes

_____ **c.** total number of cups of flour

_____ **d.** total cooking time.

(i) $2.5k + 3.5c \leq 40$

(ii) $k \geq 2$

(iii) $48k + 75c \leq 420$

(iv) $c \geq 3$

3. On the grid at the right, graph the feasible region. Let k be the independent variable.

4. List the vertices of the feasible region.

_____

5. Brad makes \$1.25 profit on each batch of cookies and \$1.75 profit on each cake.

a. Write an expression for Brad's total profit in terms of c and k.

_____

b. How many batches of cookies and how many cakes should Brad make to maximize the profit?

cookies _____   cakes _____

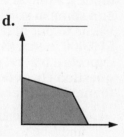

LESSON MASTER 5-10 A

Uses Objective G

In 1–5, use the following situation: **Maxine went on a TV game show and won $32,000. She wants to invest that money, some in a savings account which is relatively safe and some in stocks which are somewhat riskier. Maxine wants to put at least $15,000 in savings and at least $10,000 in stocks. The savings account pays 4% and she expects a 6% return on her stocks. Answer the following questions to determine how she should invest the money to maximize her return in a single year.**

1. Let s be the amount invested in savings and k be the amount invested in stocks. Write a system of three inequalities to describe this situation.

   _____

2. Graph the system and determine the feasible region.

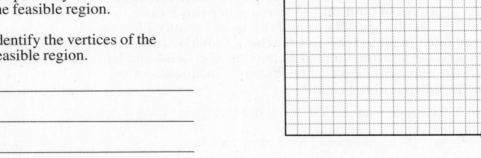

3. Identify the vertices of the feasible region.

   _____

   _____

   _____

4. Write the expression to be maximized.

   _____

5. **a.** Explain how you would use the Linear-Programming Theorem to help Maxine invest her money.

   _____

   _____

   b. What would be her yearly return?   _____

6. For his evening meal, Karl plans to eat fish sticks and mashed potatoes. Each ounce of fish sticks contains 5 grams of protein and 0.1 mg of iron. Each cup of mashed potatoes contains 4 grams of protein and .8 mg of iron. Karl wants to have at least 28 grams of protein and 2 mg of iron in his evening meal. If each ounce of fish sticks costs 30¢ and each cup of mashed potatoes costs 69¢, how much of each should Karl eat to satisfy his dietary requirements while minimizing the cost?

   fish sticks _____   potatoes _____

LESSON MASTER

6-1
A

Questions on SPUR Objectives
See pages 413-415 for objectives.

Skills Objective A

In 1–6, expand and simplify.

1. $(x + 11)^2$

2. $\frac{1}{3}(3d + 6)^2$

3. $\left(6n - \frac{1}{2}\right)^2$

4. $(5y - 8)^2$

5. $(c + 5)^2 - (c - 5)^2$

6. $-7(8z + 12)^2$

In 7 and 8, use the rectangles pictured at the right.

7. Write an expression for the area of the shaded region.

8. Determine the area of the shaded region if $x = 3$ cm.

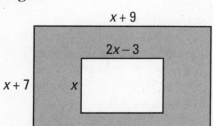

$x + 9$

$2x - 3$

$x + 7$ x

Uses Objective G

9. Cindy has an 11″ by 14″ photograph that she wishes to frame. She wants matting of width w around the edge of the photograph.

   a. Give an expression for the total area of the photograph and the matting.

   b. If $w = 2$ in., what are the inner dimensions of the frame that will hold the photograph and the matting?

   c. What is the total area of the photograph and the matting in Part b?

LESSON MASTER 6-2 A

Questions on SPUR Objectives
See pages 413-415 for objectives.

Skills Objective C

In 1–4, solve.

1. $m^2 = 20$

2. $(n - 2)^2 = 0$

3. $r^2 = 16$

4. $(2p - 4)^2 = 0$

5. $|n - 3| = 8$

4. $|2s + 7| = 10$

Properties Objective E

7. For what real numbers does $|x| = |-x|$? _____

8. Simplify $-\sqrt{(2 - 6)^2}$. _____

9. Describe how the graphs of $y = \sqrt{x^2}$ and $y = -|x|$ are related.

_____

_____

Uses Objective G

10. A rectangle measures 6 in. by 12 in. What is the radius of a circle which has the same area as the rectangle? _____

Representations Objective J

In 11 and 12, graph the equation.

11. $y = |x + 3|$

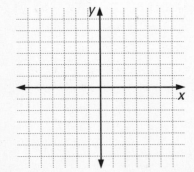

12. $y + 2 = -|x|$

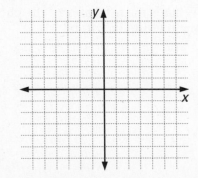

LESSON MASTER

6-3
A

Uses Objective I

1. The graph of $y = x^2$ is translated 12 units to the left and 6 units up.

   a. Write an equation for its image. _____

   b. Name the vertex of the image. _____

2. The graph of $y = -5x^2$ is translated 3 units to the right and 7 units down.

   a. Write an equation for its image. _____

   b. (1, -5) is a point on the preimage. What is
   the corresponding point on the image? _____

Representations Objective J

**In 3 and 4, assume parabola P is
a translation image of parabola Q.**

3. What translation maps parabola P
   onto parabola Q?

   _____

4. Parabola P has equation $y = -2x^2$.
   Write an equation for parabola Q.

   _____

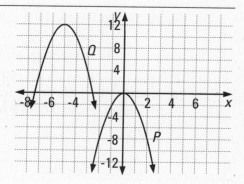

**In 6–8, an equation for a parabola is given. a. Graph the
parabola and show its axis of symmetry. b. Identify its
vertex. c. Write an equation for the axis of symmetry.**

6. $y = 3(x + 1)^2$

7. $y + 4 = -3x^2$

8. $y - 5 = (x + 3)^2$

a.

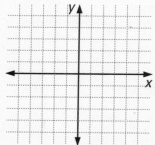

a.

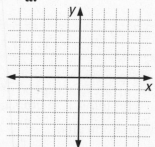

a.

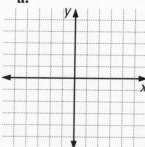

b. _____

b. _____

b. _____

c. _____

c. _____

c. _____

ADVANCED ALGEBRA © Scott, Foresman and Company

LESSON MASTER 6-4 A

Skills Objective B

In 1–3, write the equation in standard form.

1. $y = 2(x + 5)^2 - 7$

2. $y + 5 = -2(x - 6)^2$

3. $y - 3 = \frac{1}{4}(x - 2)^2$

Uses Objective G

4. Suppose a ball is thrown upward from a height of 5 feet with an initial velocity of 30 ft/sec.

   a. Write an equation relating the time t in seconds and the height h of the ball in feet. _____

   b. Find the height of the ball after 1.5 seconds. _____

5. Suppose a ball is dropped from the top of a 79-foot-tall tree.

   a. Write an equation that describes the relationship between h, the height in feet of the ball above the ground, and time t in seconds.

   _____

   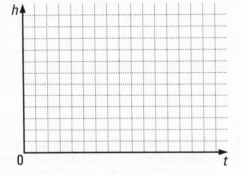

   b. On the grid at the right, graph the height h after t seconds.

   c. Estimate how long it would take the ball to reach the ground. Explain your reasoning.

   _____

   _____

6. Johanna threw a water balloon upward at a speed of 10m/sec while standing on the roof of a building 12 meters high.

   a. What was the height of the balloon after 2 seconds? _____

   b. Assume that the balloon did not land on the roof, and estimate how long it took the balloon to reach the ground. _____

ADVANCED ALGEBRA © Scott, Foresman and Company

▶ **LESSON MASTER 6-4 A** *page 2*

Representations Objective J

In 7 and 8, graph the parabola for -3 ≤ x ≤ 3.

7. $y = x^2 + x - 6$

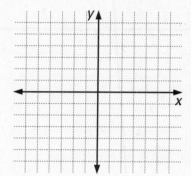

8. $y = -2x^2 + 5x + 7$

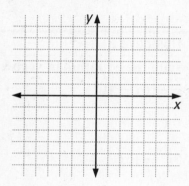

9. On the graph at the right, the height of a baseball hit upward is shown as a function of time.

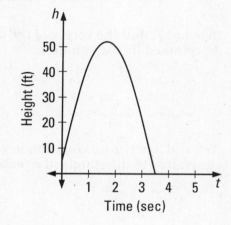

a. What was the initial height of the ball?

_____

b. When did the ball reach its maximum height?

_____

c. What was the maximum height? _____

d. When was the ball 30 ft in the air? _____

LESSON MASTER

6-5
A

Vocabulary

1. Fill in the blank to make a perfect square.

   $4d^2 - 16d +$ ___?___   _____

Skills Objective B

In 2–5, write the equation in vertex form.

2. $y = x^2 - 6x + 10$

3. $y = x^2 + 14x + 5$

   _____   _____

4. $y = 5x^2 - 15x - 4$

5. $6y = 3x^2 + 30x + 25$

   _____   _____

In 6 and 7, find the vertex of the parabola determined by the equation.

6. $y = x^2 - 12x + 24$

7. $y = -4x^2 + 6x - 7$

   _____   _____

In 8 and 9, write an equation in vertex form equivalent to the standard equation given.

8. $y = 2x^2 - 20x + 57$

9. $y = 10x^2 + 10x + 1$

   _____   _____

10. *Multiple choice.* Which equation is equivalent to
    $y = 18x^2 + 60x + 45$?   _____

    (a) $y + 3 = 2(3x + 3)^2$ (b) $y + 5 = 2(3x + 5)^2$

    (c) $y + 5 = 2(3x - 5)^2$ (d) $y - 5 = 2(3x + 5)^2$

11. *True or false.* $y = 4x^2 + 4x - 6$ and

    $y + 7 = 4(x + \frac{1}{2})^2$ have the same vertex.   _____

ADVANCED ALGEBRA © Scott, Foresman and Company

LESSON MASTER

6-6
A

Questions on SPUR Objectives
See pages 413-415 for objectives.

Uses Objective H

1. The following pictures illustrate the first five numbers in a sequence we shall call the "rectangular numbers."

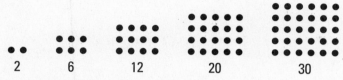

2   6   12   20   30   _____

a. Draw the next rectangular number above at the right.

b. Find the next three rectangular numbers after 30.   _____

c. Give a formula for $R(n)$, the nth rectangular number.   _____

d. Use your formula to find the 100th rectangular number.   _____

2. The following table gives the monthly salaries in 1993 for U.S. generals having various years of service.

Years of Service y	Monthly Salary s
2	$6,889.20
4	$6,889.20
8	$7,153.50
12	$7,549.80
16	$8,089.80
20	$8,631.60
26	$9,169.50

a. On the grid at the right, make a scatterplot of these data.

b. Fit a quadratic model to these data and plot it.

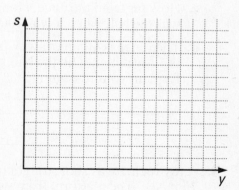

_____

c. Fit a linear model to these data and plot it.

_____

d. Use either model to estimate the monthly salary of a U.S. general with 10 years of service.   _____

LESSON MASTER 6-7 A

Questions on SPUR Objectives
See pages 413-415 for objectives.

Skills Objective C

In 1–6, use the Quadratic Formula to solve the equation.

1. $x^2 + 6x - 7 = 0$

2. $7 = 3x^2 - 4x$

3. $m(m + 6) = 36$

4. $w^2 = 5w + 3$

5. $50d^2 - 12 = -25d$

6. $(3a + 2)(5a - 1) = 2(5a - 1)$

Uses Objective G

7. Juan Torres hit a fast ball thrown by Liz Buckner. Let x be the distance on the ground in feet of the ball from home plate and $h(x)$ be the height in feet of the ball at that distance. Suppose the path of the ball is described by the function $h(x) = -.006x^2 + 2.5x + 4$.

a. How high was the ball when Juan hit it? _____

b. How far from the plate, along the ground, was the ball when it was the same height at which Juan hit it? _____

c. How far from the plate, along the ground, was the ball when it was 100 feet high? _____

d. The fence is 405 feet away from home plate, and it is 12 feet high. Did the ball go over the fence? Explain your reasoning.

_____

_____

8. A toy rocket was shot straight up with an initial velocity of 75 m/sec. The platform from which the rocket was shot is 2.3 meters high.

a. When was the rocket 100 meters above the ground? _____

b. When did the rocket hit the ground? _____

ADVANCED ALGEBRA © Scott, Foresman and Company

LESSON MASTER

6-8
A

Skills Objective C

1. Show that $i\sqrt{65}$ is a square root of -65.

_____

In 2–5, *true or false.*

2. The solution to $x^2 = -5$ are $\sqrt{5}$ and $-\sqrt{5}$.   _____

3. The solution to $g^2 = -13$ are $13i$ and $-13i$.   _____

4. $i\sqrt{31} = -i\sqrt{31}$ _____

5. $i\sqrt{17}$ is a square root of -17.   _____

In 6–7, solve.

6. $9r^2 + 13 = -12$

7. $(s + 2)(s - 2) = -8$.

Skills Objective D

In 8–18, simplify.

8. $-5i^2$ _____   9. $3i \cdot 4i$ _____

10. $\sqrt{-361}$ _____   11. $\sqrt{15} \cdot \sqrt{-15}$ _____

12. $\sqrt{-3}\,\sqrt{-3}$ _____   13. $\sqrt{-25} + \sqrt{-64}$ _____

14. $-2\sqrt{-4}$ _____   15. $12i - 18i$ _____

16. $\dfrac{\sqrt{-9}}{\sqrt{-36}}$ _____   17. $(i\sqrt{12})^2$ _____

18. $3i(4i + 5i)$ _____

LESSON MASTER **6-9 A**

Vocabulary

1. In $\sqrt{6} + \frac{3}{2}i$, name the *real* part
and the *imaginary* part.   real _____ imaginary _____

Skills Objective D

In 2 and 3, simplify.

2. $(5i - 3i)(5i + 3i)$

3. $(5i + 3i) + (5i - 3i)$

_____   _____

In 4–13, perform the operations and give the answer in $a + bi$ form.

4. $(6 - i) + (3 + 4i)$

5. $(6 - i) - (3 + 4i)$

_____   _____

6. $(1 + i)(1 - i)$

7. $\dfrac{2}{1 + i}$

_____   _____

8. $5(3 - 2i)$

9. $(4 + 2i)(-3 - i)$

_____   _____

10. $-5(3 - i)$

11. $\dfrac{2 + i}{3 - i}$

_____   _____

12. $\dfrac{8 \pm \sqrt{-36}}{2}$

13. $(\sqrt{2} + i\sqrt{2})^2$

_____   _____

**In 14–19, suppose $m = 1 + 8i$ and $n = -2 + 3i$.
Evaluate and write the answer in $a + bi$ form.**

14. mn

15. n^2

_____   _____

16. $4m + 3$

17. $4m + 3n$

_____   _____

18. $im - in$

19. $m^2 + 2m + 1$

_____   _____

LESSON MASTER 6-10 A

Questions on SPUR Objectives
See pages 413-415 for objectives.

Skills Objective C

In 1–3, solve.

1. $2x^2 - 7x + 15 = 0$ **2.** $3x = 7 + 5x^2$ **3.** $-4(2n^2 - 2n) = 3(n + 6)$

Properties Objective F

In 4 and 5, a quadratic equation is given. **a.** Evaluate its discriminant. **b.** Give the number of real solutions. **c.** Tell whether the real solutions are rational or irrational.

4. $15x^2 - 3x + 7 = 0$ **5.** $15h^2 - 11h - 14 = 0$

a. _____   a. _____

b. _____   b. _____

c. _____   c. _____

In 6–9, give the number of real solutions.

6. $5z = 12z^2 - 5$ _____   **7.** $19w^2 = 7w$ _____

8. $6c^2 - c + 15 = 0$ _____   **9.** $9 - 12t = t^2 - 3$ _____

Representations Objective K

In 10 and 11, give the number of x-intercepts of the graph of the parabola.

10. $y = 15x^2 + 7$ _____   **11.** $y + 14 = -3(x - 2)^2$ _____

12. Does the parabola with equation $y = -\frac{1}{4}x^2 + x - 3$ ever intersect the line with eqution $y = -2$? If so, how many points of intersection are there? Explain your reasoning.

_____

_____

_____

13. The graph of $y = 4x^2$ has one x-intercept. How many x-intercepts does the graph of $y = 4(x - h)^2$ have if $h \neq 0$? Explain your reasoning.

_____

_____

LESSON MASTER 7-1 A

Vocabulary

1. In the expression b^n, b is called the ___?___ . _____

2. The *identity function f* has the equation $f(x) = $ ___?___ . _____

3. If $g(x) = \dfrac{1}{x}$, is g an example of a *power function*?
   Why or why not?

   _____

   _____

Uses Objective F

4. In a game with a friend, Felipe has a $\frac{4}{7}$ chance of
   winning a round, and each round is independent.
   Suppose Felipe and his friend play six rounds. What
   is the probability that Felipe will win all six rounds? _____

Representations Objective I

5. *Multiple choice.* Which of the following could be a
   graph of an odd power function? _____

   (a) 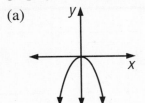   (b) 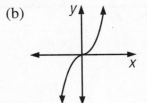   (c)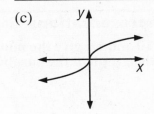

6. The point (-2, -32) is on the graph of an odd power function.

   a. What other point must be on the graph? _____

   b. Write an equation for this function. _____

7. a. On the grid at the right, sketch graphs
   of $f(x) = x^3$ and $g(x) = x^5$.

   b. For what values(s) of x is $f(x) = g(x)$?

   _____

   c. For what values of x is $f(x) > g(x)$?

   _____

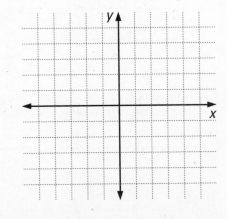

ADVANCED ALGEBRA © Scott, Foresman and Company

Name _____

LESSON MASTER 7-2 A

Questions on SPUR Objectives
See pages 473-475 for objectives.

Skills Objectives A and B

In 1–9, simplify.

1. $(x^5)^6$ _____

2. $(4w^2)^3$ _____

3. $7y^3 \cdot 8y^5$ _____

4. $-\dfrac{c^{12}}{2c^9}$ _____

5. $\dfrac{z^{18}}{(z^5)^2}$ _____

6. $\dfrac{b^4 \cdot 3b^9}{6b^5 \cdot b^6}$ _____

7. $\dfrac{(-9z^4)^3}{9^2z^{11}}$ _____

8. $\dfrac{p^6}{p^0}$ _____

9. $\left(\dfrac{v}{2}\right)^4\left(\dfrac{10}{v}\right)^3$ _____

In 10–13, evaluate.

10. $(15)^0$ _____

11. $(4^3)^2$ _____

12. $\dfrac{(12)^3}{(12)^2}$ _____

13. $2^5 \cdot 3^5$ _____

Properties Objective E

In 14–17, *true or false.* **If false, rewrite to be true.**

14. $(q^4)^6 = q^{10}$

_____

15. $(m^{10}y^7)^3 = m^{30}y^{21}$

_____

16. $r^5 \cdot r^{12} = r^{17}$

_____

17. $\dfrac{z^9}{z^3} = z^3$

_____

Properties Objective F

18. In 1985, the U.S. population was roughly $2.4 \cdot 10^8$ people, while water usage was approximately $4 \cdot 10^{11}$ gallons per day. Estimate the number of gallons of water used per person daily in the U.S. in 1985. _____

19. Jupiter's largest moon, Ganymede, is the largest moon of any planet in our solar system, with a diameter of about $5.27 \cdot 10^3$ km. Estimate Ganymede's volume. _____

LESSON MASTER 7-3 A

Skills Objectives A and B

In 1–6, write as a decimal or a simple fraction.

1. $10^{-3} \cdot 10^{-4}$ _____

2. 6^{-2} _____

3. $\left(\frac{2}{5}\right)^{-3}$ _____

4. $(-8)^{-4}$ _____

5. $\dfrac{9^{-4}}{9^{-6}}$ _____

6. $(7^{-3})^2$ _____

In 7–12, simplify the result using only positive exponents.

7. $x^{-6} \cdot x^5$ _____

8. $\dfrac{y^{-12}}{7y^5}$ _____

9. $(4m^{-3})^5$ _____

10. $(2^{-1}z^3)^4(4z^{-5}y)^3$ _____

11. $\left(\dfrac{3f}{4h}\right)^{-2}\left(\dfrac{4f^2}{3h}\right)$ _____

12. $7^{-2}g^5 \cdot 7^6g^{-9}$ _____

Properties Objective E

13. *True or false.* For any positive base b and any real exponent n, $b^{-n} = -(b^n)$. If true, prove the statement. If false, provide a counterexample.

_____

Uses Objective F

14. The Law of the Lever states that the distance d of a person from the fulcrum varies inversely as his or her weight w.

   a. Write this variation equation with positive exponents. _____

   b. Write this variation equation with negative exponents. _____

15. In Caroline's pinhole camera, the radius of the pinhole is 5.2×10^{-1} mm. Find the area of the pinhole, the region through which light can reach the film. _____

ADVANCED ALGEBRA © Scott, Foresman and Company

LESSON MASTER

7-4
A

Uses Objective G

1. Yu invested $500 in a savings account that pays
   3.2% interest compounded annually. How much
   money will be in his account after 5 years if no
   deposits or withdrawals take place during the 5 years? _____

2. Debbie invested $5,000 in a 5-year CD (certificate of
   deposit) that pays 7.8% interest compounded quarterly.
   The CD matures next February. If no deposits or
   withdrawals took place during the 5-year period, how
   much will the CD be worth when it matures? _____

3. Maria invested $6000 in an IRA (individual retirement
   account) 25 years before she planned to retire. With a 4%
   annual yield, if Maria makes no deposits or withdrawals
   during the 25 years, what will be the value of the IRA
   when it matures? _____

4. Suppose that you plan to put $1000 in a credit-union
   savings account for two years at 4% interest compounded
   daily. Shoreline Credit Union compounds 360 days a year;
   South Side Credit Union compounds 365 days a year.
   How much more money will you earn if you invest at
   South Side? _____

5. Suppose $2500 is invested for $1\frac{1}{2}$ years. Plan A pays
   3.12% interest compounded daily (365 days a year). Plan B
   pays 3.13% interest compounded quarterly. If the investment
   is untouched for the entire time, which plan will earn more
   interest? Explain your reasoning.

   _____

   _____

ADVANCED ALGEBRA © Scott, Foresman and Company

LESSON MASTER 7-5 A

Skills Objective C

In 1–5, give the first four terms of the geometric sequence described.

1. constant ratio 3, first term -1

   _____

2. constant ratio -.1, first term 12

   _____

3. first term $\sqrt{2}$, second term 2

   _____

4. $g_n = 60\left(\frac{1}{2}\right)^{n-1}$, for $n \geq 1$

   _____

5. $\begin{cases} g_1 = -2 \\ g_n = 3g_{n-1} \text{ for all integers } n \geq 2 \end{cases}$

   _____

In 6–9, a sequence is given. a. Tell if the sequence is geometric. b. If yes, give its constant ratio.

6. 12, 36, 108, 324, . . .

   a. _____ b. _____

7. 3, 6, 9, 12, 15, . . .

   a. _____ b. _____

8. .5, 5.5, 60.5, 665.5, . . .

   a. _____ b. _____

9. $\frac{9}{6}, \frac{7}{6}, \frac{5}{6}, \frac{3}{6}, \ldots$

   a. _____ b. _____

In 10 and 11, a geometic sequence is given. a. Give an explicit formula for the nth term of the sequence. b. Give a recursive formula for the sequence.

10. 10, 1, .1, .01, . . .

    a. _____ b. _____

11. 6, -1.2, .24, -.048, . . .

    a. _____ b. _____

12. Find the sixth term of the geometric sequence whose first term is 7 and whose constant ratio is 2.1. _____

Uses Objective H

13. A car was sold for $22,000. If its value decreases 12% each year, what will be its value after 5 years? _____

14. After each bounce, a ball bounces to 80% of its previous height. If it is originally dropped from a height of 6 feet, how high will it bounce after it hits the floor the 6th time? _____

LESSON MASTER 7-6 A

Skills Objectives A, B, and D

In 1–6, write as a decimal or a simple fraction.

1. $64^{\frac{1}{3}}$ _____

2. $64^{\frac{1}{6}}$ _____

3. $100^{\frac{1}{2}}$ _____

4. $(.04)^{\frac{1}{2}}$ _____

5. $-36^{\frac{1}{2}}$ _____

6. $625^{\frac{1}{4}}$ _____

7. Estimate $153^{\frac{1}{2}}$ to the nearest integer. _____

In 8–11, solve.

8. $4z^{\frac{1}{2}} = 36$

9. $-4y^{\frac{1}{5}} = 128$

10. $C^{\frac{1}{8}} + 27 = 30$

11. $2r^{\frac{1}{3}} - 5 = 6$

Properties Objective E

In 12 and 13, show that the given number is an eighth root of 65,536.

12. $4i$ _____

13. -4 _____

In 14 and 15, use the Number of Real Roots Theorem to give the number of real roots possible.

14. 6th root(s) of -41 _____

15. 7th root(s) of 68 _____

In 16–19, write <, =, or > in the blank to make the statement true.

16. $10^{\frac{1}{2}}$ _____ $10^{\frac{1}{3}}$

17. $16^{\frac{1}{4}} \cdot 81^{\frac{1}{4}}$ _____ $2 \cdot 3$

18. $34^{\frac{1}{5}}$ _____ 2

19. $\left(\frac{1}{4}\right)^{\frac{1}{2}}$ _____ $.5$

Uses Objective F

20. The equation $P_N = P_0(1 - x)^n$ describes the depreciation value of a car over n years, where P_N is the price of the car now, P_0 is the original price paid, and x is the yearly depreciation rate. If a car costs $11,453 today and cost $12,000 four months ago, find the yearly depreciation rate. _____

LESSON MASTER 7-7 A

Skills Objectives A, B, and D

In 1–9, write as a decimal or a simple fraction.
Give decimal answers to the nearest hundredth.

1. $81^{\frac{5}{4}}$ _____

2. $32^{\frac{3}{5}}$ _____

3. $4^{\frac{3}{2}}$ _____

4. $35^{1.5}$ _____

5. $3^{\frac{7}{2}}$ _____

6. $\left(\frac{27}{125}\right)^{\frac{2}{3}}$ _____

7. $21^{\frac{4}{5}}$ _____

8. $(0.09)^{\frac{5}{2}}$ _____

9. $1000^{\frac{4}{3}}$ _____

In 10–12, simplify.

10. $y^{\frac{2}{3}} \cdot y^{\frac{3}{4}}$ _____

11. $\dfrac{z^{\frac{5}{6}}}{z^{\frac{2}{3}}} \cdot z^{\frac{1}{3}}$ _____

12. $\left(a^{\frac{1}{2}}b^{\frac{2}{3}}\right)^2$ _____

In 13–16, solve.

13. $y^{\frac{2}{3}} = 25$

14. $8x^{\frac{3}{5}} = 27$

15. $32 = k^{\frac{5}{6}}$

16. $216 = 64z^{\frac{3}{4}}$

Properties Objective E

In 17 and 18, write <, =, or > in the blank
to make the statement true.

17. If $a > 1$, $a^{\frac{9}{8}}$ _____ a.

18. If $0 < b < 1$, $b^{\frac{5}{4}}$ _____ b.

19. Show that $-7i$ is *not* a fifth root of 16,807.

_____

Uses Objective F

In 20 and 21, use the following information: In 1619, Johannes Kepler
discovered that the average distance d of a planet from the sun and the
planet's period of revolution r around the sun are related by the formula
$d = kr^{\frac{2}{3}}$. When d is in millions of miles and r is in days, $k \approx 1.82$.

20. Mercury, the planet closest to the sun, orbits the sun
every 88 days. About how far is Mercury from the sun? _____

21. Neptune is about 2796 million miles from the sun.

a. Estimate Neptune's period of revolution in days. _____

b. Estimate Neptune's period of revolution in years. _____

LESSON MASTER 7-8 A

Skills Objective A

In 1–6, write as a decimal or a simple fraction.
Give decimal answers to the nearest hundredth.

1. $125^{-\frac{5}{3}}$ _____

2. $36^{-\frac{3}{2}}$ _____

3. $4 \cdot 16^{-\frac{3}{4}}$ _____

4. $\left(\frac{64}{125}\right)^{-\frac{4}{3}}$ _____

5. $8 \cdot 128^{-\frac{5}{7}}$ _____

6. $28^{-1.2}$ _____

Skills Objective B

In 7 and 8, simplify, using only positive exponents.

7. $\dfrac{-15x^7 y^{-\frac{2}{3}}}{5x^{-10}y^{\frac{1}{3}}}$ _____

8. $(m^2 n^4)^{-\frac{3}{4}}$ _____

Skills Objective D

In 9–12, solve.

9. $y^{-\frac{2}{3}} = 16$

10. $w^{-\frac{4}{9}} = 256$

11. $v^{-5} = 243$

12. $p^{-1.6} = 1024$

Properties Objective E

13. Suppose $x > 1$. Arrange the following
from least to greatest: $x^{-3}, x, x^{\frac{5}{4}}, x^{-\frac{1}{2}}$. _____

14. *True or false.* If $0 < k < 1$, then $k^{-\frac{2}{3}} > k$. _____

Uses Objective F

15. Suppose the formula $N = 150{,}000 \left(\frac{25}{9}\right)^{-\frac{t}{4}}$, where t is the time
in months and N is the number of items sold per month,
models the predicted decline in sales of a specific item
over the next 24 months. Will the company sell 54,000 items
13 months from now? Explain your reasoning.

_____

_____

LESSON MASTER 8-1 A

Skills Objective A

1. In the notation $g \circ h(x)$, which function is applied first? _____

In 2–8, consider the functions defined by $g(x) = x^2 + 2x + 1$ and $h(x) = 2x - 3$.

2. Find $g(h(4))$. _____

3. Find $h \circ g(4)$. _____

4. Find $g \circ h(-7)$. _____

5. Find $g(g(0))$. _____

6. Find $g(h(x))$. _____

7. Find $h(g(x))$. _____

8. The function $g \circ h$ maps $-\frac{1}{4}$ onto what number? _____

In 9 and 10, rules for functions f and g are given. Does $f \circ g = g \circ f$? Justify your answer.

9. $f: m \to m + 5$ and g: $m \to m - 5$

_____

_____

10. $f(t) = 4t - 3$ and $g(t) = 4t + 3$

_____

_____

11. Suppose that $r(p) = \dfrac{1}{p}$ and $s(p) = \sqrt{p}$.

   a. Find $r \circ s(p)$. _____

   b. State the restrictions on the domain of $r \circ s$. _____

12. Suppose $c(x) = x^4$ and $d(x) = x^5$. Find

   a. $c \circ d(x)$.   **b.** $d(c(x))$.   **c.** $c(x) \cdot d(x)$.

   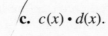

   _____   _____   _____

ADVANCED ALGEBRA © Scott, Foresman and Company

LESSON MASTER 8-2 A

Skills Objective B

In 1 and 2, a function is given. a. Give an equation for its inverse. b. Tell if the inverse is a function.

1. $f(x) = 3x + 2$ a. _____   b. _____

2. $h: x \rightarrow |2x|$ a. _____   b. _____

3. Show that $f: x \rightarrow 5x - 6$ and $g: x \rightarrow \frac{1}{5}x + 6$ are *not* inverses of each other.

_____

_____

_____

Properties Objective F

4. *True or false.* If a function has an inverse which is also a function, then the original function passes the Horizontal-Line Test.

_____

5. Let $f = \{(1, 4), (5, 8), (9, 12), (13, 16)\}$.

   a. Give the domain of f.   _____

   b. Give the domain of the inverse of f.   _____

Representations Objective I

6. *Multiple choice.* Which graph below is *not* the graph of a function which has an inverse?   _____

(a) 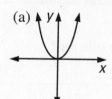   (b) 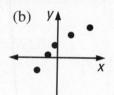   (c) 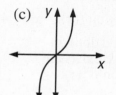   (d)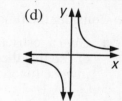

7. **a.** On the grid at the right, graph the inverse of the function with equation $y = x^4$.

   b. Is the inverse a function? Why or why not?

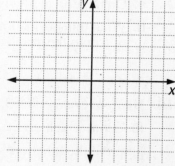

_____

_____

LESSON MASTER 8-3 A

Skills Objective B

In 1–4, write an equation for f^{-1}.

1. $f(x) = 2x - 6$

2. $f(x) = \dfrac{5}{x}$

_____

3. $f(x) = \dfrac{x - 7}{3}$

4. $f(x) = x^2$, when $x \geq 0$

_____

Properties Objective F

5. Consider the function f defined by $f(x) = -2x + 6$.

   a. Write a rule for $f^{-1}(x)$.   **b.** Find $f \circ f^{-1}(x)$.   **c.** Find $f^{-1} \circ f(x)$.

_____ _____ _____

In 6 and 7, determine whether the functions f and g as defined are inverses of each other. Justify your answer.

6. $f(m) = m^{\frac{4}{5}}$ and $g(m) = m^{\frac{5}{4}}$

_____

7. $f(m) = m^{\frac{4}{5}}$ and $h(m) = m^{-\frac{5}{4}}$

_____

Representations Objective I

8. Consider the function $f(x) = x^2 + 4$.

   a. Give a restricted domain of f so that there exists an inverse function $f^{-1}(x)$. _____

   b. Write a rule for f^{-1}.

   _____

9. Consider $f = \{(1, 6), (4, 3), (-3, 2), (-2, -1)\}$.

   a. On the grid at the right, graph f^{-1}.

   b. What transformation maps the graph of f onto the graph of f^{-1}?

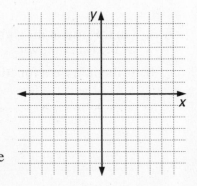

_____

10. *Multiple Choice.* If $(-3, 0)$ is on the graph of a function, which _____ point must be on the graph of the function's inverse?

   (a) $(-3, 0)$ (b) $(0, -3)$ (c) $(3, 0)$ (d) $(0, 3)$

LESSON MASTER 8-4 A

Skills Objectives C and D

In 1–6, simplify. Assume that variables are nonnegative real numbers.

1. $\sqrt[3]{.216}$ _____

2. $\sqrt[6]{64}$ _____

3. $\sqrt[4]{6561}$ _____

4. $\sqrt[3]{343}$ _____

5. $\sqrt[5]{.03125}$ _____

6. $\sqrt[5]{\dfrac{243}{32}}$ _____

In 7–9, rewrite using a single radical.

7. $\sqrt[4]{\sqrt[3]{c}}$ _____

8. $\sqrt{\sqrt{y^3}}$ _____

9. $\sqrt{\sqrt{\sqrt{256u^{16}}}}$ _____

In 10–12, estimate to the nearest hundredth.

10. $\sqrt[4]{16+81}$

11. $\sqrt[5]{28}$

12. $\sqrt[9]{100}$

_____   _____   _____

Properties Objective G

13. Give a counterexample to the statement: For all h, $\sqrt[4]{h^4} = h$.

_____

14. For the radical expression $\sqrt[m]{n}$, what are the possible values

    a. of m? _____   **b.** of n? _____

15. *Multiple choice.* When $x \geq 0$, $\sqrt[9]{x^4}$ equals which of the following?

    (a) $x^{\frac{4}{9}}$ (b) $x^{\frac{9}{4}}$ (c) $x^{-\frac{4}{9}}$ (d) $\frac{1}{9}(x^4)$ _____

Uses Objective H

16. A cone has volume $V = \frac{1}{3}\pi r^2 h$. Express the length of its radius.

    a. in radical notation.   **b.** with a rational exponent.

    _____   _____

17. Find the radius, to the nearest tenth, of a cone with volume 1063.8 cm³ and height 9.1 cm. _____

18. A sphere has volume $V = \frac{4}{3}\pi r^3$. Write an expression for r using radical notation. _____

LESSON MASTER

8-5
A

Skills Objective D

In 1 and 2, find e and f.

1. $\sqrt{600} = \sqrt{e} \cdot \sqrt{6} = f\sqrt{6}$

   $e =$ _____ $f =$ _____

2. $\sqrt[3]{1600} = \sqrt[3]{e} \cdot \sqrt[3]{25} = f\sqrt[3]{25}$

   $e =$ _____ $f =$ _____

In 3–8, simplify. Assume that the variables are nonnegative.

3. $\sqrt[3]{54x^8}$

4. $\sqrt[5]{32y^9}$

5. $\sqrt[7]{z^{21}w^{14}}$

   _____ _____ _____

6. $\sqrt[9]{2^{12}x^{14}y^{10}}$

7. $\sqrt[3]{4x^2} \cdot \sqrt[3]{2x}$

9. $\sqrt[4]{3^6w^7} \cdot \sqrt[4]{3^2w^2}$

   _____ _____ _____

9. Recall that the geometric mean of a data set is found by taking the nth root of the product of the n numbers in the data set. Calculate the geometric mean for the batting averages of the 1993 Toronto Blue Jays.

   _____

Devon White	.444
Paul Molitor	.391
John Olerud	.348
Tony Fernandez	.318
Roberto Alomar	.292
Ed Sprague	.286
Joe Carter	.259
Pat Borders	.250
Rickey Henderson	.120

Properties Objective G

In 10 and 11, *true or false*. Justify your answer.

10. $\sqrt[4]{x} \cdot \sqrt[3]{x} = \sqrt[12]{x^2}$ for $x \geq 0$

   _____

   _____

11. $\sqrt[7]{x} \cdot \sqrt[14]{x^2} = \sqrt[14]{x^4}$ for $x \geq 0$

   _____

   _____

ADVANCED ALGEBRA © Scott, Foresman and Company

LESSON MASTER **8-6 A**

Skills Objective D

In 1–6, rationalize the denominator. Assume that
all variables are positive.

1. $\dfrac{7}{\sqrt{3}}$ _____

2. $\dfrac{9x}{\sqrt{25x^5}}$ _____

3. $\dfrac{6}{y\sqrt{y}}$ _____

4. $\dfrac{4}{2+\sqrt{5}}$ _____

5. $\dfrac{x}{\sqrt{x}+3}$ _____

6. $\dfrac{5+\sqrt{7}}{5-\sqrt{7}}$ _____

In 7 and 8, write the expression in radical form with no radical
in the denominator. Assume that variables are positive.

7. $z^{\frac{3}{2}}w^{-\frac{1}{2}}$ _____

8. $r^{-\frac{5}{2}}s$ _____

9. Show that $(\sqrt{37} - 6)$ is 12 less than its reciprocal.

_____

_____

In 10–12, use the triangle at the right. Find
the ratio and rationalize the denominator.

10. $\dfrac{AC}{AB}$ _____

11. $\dfrac{AC}{BC}$ _____

12. $\dfrac{BC}{AB}$ _____

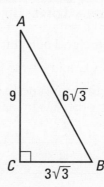

ADVANCED ALGEBRA © Scott, Foresman and Company

LESSON MASTER 8-7 A

Skills Objective C

1. Calculate $(-5)^n$ for the value given.

   a. -4 _____   b. -3 _____   c. -2 _____

   d. -1 _____   e. 0 _____   f. 1 _____

   g. 2 _____   h. 3 _____   i. 4 _____

In 2–7, write as a decimal or a simple fraction.

2. $\sqrt[5]{-243}$ _____   3. $\sqrt[7]{-128}$ _____   4. $\sqrt[3]{-27} + \sqrt[5]{-1}$ _____

5. $\sqrt[3]{-1000}$ _____   6. $\sqrt[5]{-343}$ _____   7. $\sqrt[9]{-10,077,696}$ _____

Properties Objective G

8. a. *Multiple choice.* Which of the following is *not* defined? _____

   (i) $\sqrt[5]{7776}$ (ii) $\sqrt[4]{7776}$ (iii) $\sqrt[5]{-7776}$ (iv) $\sqrt[4]{-7776}$

   b. Explain why your answer in Part a is undefined.

   _____

   _____

9. Under what conditions does $\sqrt[n]{x^n} = x$ for all values of x?

   _____

   _____

10. *True or false.* If n is an even integer, $\sqrt[n]{x^n}$ is positive. _____

Representations Objective I

11. a. On the grid at right, graph
    $y = \sqrt[3]{x}$ and $y = x^3$ for $-5 \le x \le 5$.

    b. Are the two functions inverses of
    each other? Why or why not?

    _____

    _____

    _____

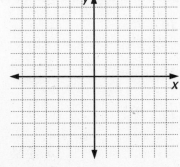

LESSON MASTER 8-8 A

Questions on SPUR Objectives
See pages 527-529 for objectives.

Skills Objective E

In 1-4, find all real solutions.

1. $\sqrt[3]{a} = 3$

2. $\sqrt[4]{c} - 8 = 3\sqrt[4]{c}$

3. $19 + \sqrt[5]{e - 3} = 18$

4. $25 - 16\sqrt[3]{f + 1} = -7$

Uses Objective H

5. Find 2 points on the line $x = -5$ that are 10 units from $(-3, 2)$. _____

6. The equation $d = 1.82 \sqrt[3]{r^2}$ gives the average distance d (in millions of miles) of a planet from the sun where r is the number of days in the planet's revolution. In our solar system, Pluto is the planet with the greatest average distance from the sun, 5899 million miles.

   a. Find the number of days in Pluto's revolution around the sun. _____

   b. Pluto was discovered by Clyde Tombaugh in 1930, based on predictions made by Percival Lowell. In what year will Pluto have completed its orbit around the sun and returned to the point where Tombaugh first found it? _____

7. A sphere with radius r has a volume of 1131 cubic millimeters. Find the length of the radius, to the nearest millimeter. _____

LESSON MASTER

9-1
A

Properties Objective D

1. Give the domain and the range of the function with equation $f(x) = 3 \cdot 7^x$.

domain _____   range _____

Uses Objective F

2. In 1991, the population of the metropolitan area of Mexico City, Mexico, was 20.899 million. This population was the second largest in the world. The estimated population for Mexico City in the near future can be modeled by $P = 20.899 \cdot 1.0269^{x-1991}$, where P is the population in millions and x is the year 1991. Estimate the population of Mexico City in the year 2000.

_____

3. In 1991, the population of the Lagos, Nigeria, metropolitan area was about 7,998,000. Use the population growth rate of about 4.06% per year to estimate the population of Lagos in the year given.

a. 1995 _____   **b.** 1980 _____

4. The population of a certain strain of bacteria grows according to the formula $N = N_0 \cdot 2^{1.31t}$, where t is the time in hours. If there are now 50 bacteria, how many bacteria will there be in 2 days?

_____

Representations Objective I

In 5 and 6, *multiple choice.*

5. Which equation has a graph which is an exponential curve?   _____

(a) $y = 2^x$ (b) $y = x^2$ (c) $y = 2x$ (d) $y = \dfrac{x}{2}$

6. Which graph could represent exponential growth?   _____

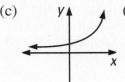
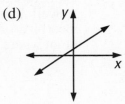

7. Locate at least 5 points on the graph of $y = 3^x$ on the grid at the right.

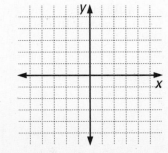

ADVANCED ALGEBRA © Scott, Foresman and Company

LESSON MASTER 9-2 A

Properties Objective D

1. Give the domain and the range of the function g
   with equation $g(x) = 3(.7)^x$.

   domain _____   range _____

2. Write equations of all asymptotes of the graph
   of the function defined by $f(x) = 5(0.9)^x$.   _____

3. *True or false.* When a and b are positive and $b \neq 1$,
   all exponential functions $y = ab^x$ have the
   same domain.   _____

Uses Objective F

**In 4 and 5, use the equation $P = 14.7(0.81)^h$, which
estimates the atmospheric pressure in pounds per square
inch as a function of the height h in miles above sea level.**

4. Estimate the atmospheric pressure at sea level.   _____

5. Estimate the atmospheric pressure at an altitude of
   6.25 miles, an approximate cruising altitude of a jet. _____

6. It is predicted that a new car costing $15,000 will
   depreciate at a rate of 11% per year. About how
   much will the car be worth in 5 years?   _____

Representations Objective I

7. *Multiple choice.* Which graph could represent
   exponential decay?   _____

   (a) 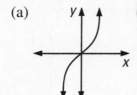   (b) 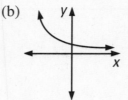   (c) 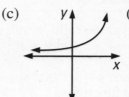   (d)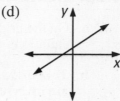

8. Locate at least 5 points on the graph
   of $y = (\frac{1}{3})^x$ on the grid at the right.

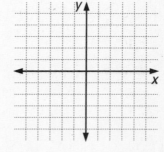

LESSON MASTER

9-3
A

Properties Objective D

1. Give the domain and the range of the function
   with equation $f(x) = 2e^{4x}$.

   domain _____   range _____

2. *Multiple choice.* Which situation does the function
   defined by $y = 5e^{2+x}$ describe?   _____

   (a) constant increase   (b) exponential growth

   (c) constant decrease   (d) exponential decay

Uses Objective F

**In 3–5, use this information: In 1992, the fastest-growing state of the Union
was Nevada. At this rate, if P is Nevada's population in thousands and t is the
number of years after 1992, then $P = 1336e^{.05t}$.**

3. What was Nevada's population in 1992?   _____

4. According to this model, what will Nevada's
   population be in the year 2000?   _____

5. According to this model, what was Nevada's
   population in 1990?   _____

6. If it is assumed that inflation remains constant at 3.44% per year,
   then the value V of a dollar n years from now can be modeled
   by the equation $V = e^{-.0344n}$. According to this model, what
   will be the value of the dollar 10 years from now? _____

Representations Objective I

7. **a.** On the grid at the right, graph the
      equations $y = e^{.5x}$ and $y = e^{-.5x}$.

   b. *True or false.* $y = e^{.5x}$ and $y = e^{-.5x}$
      are inverse functions.

      _____

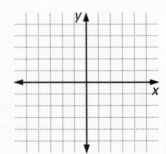

ADVANCED ALGEBRA © Scott, Foresman and Company

LESSON MASTER

9-4 A

Uses Objective G

1. Under certain conditions, algae will grow exponentially in a pond. Suppose that there are 100 algae in a pond and that 3 hours later there are 200 algae.

   a. Fit an exponential model to these data. _____

   b. Find the number of algae present after 24 hours. _____

2. A pharmaceutical company is testing a new anesthetic. They injected 14 mg of the anesthetic into the bloodstream of a laboratory rat and then monitored the level of the drug every hour. The results are in the table below.

Time (hr)	0	1	2	3	4	5	6	7	8	9
Anesthetic (mg)	14.00	9.38	6.28	4.21	2.82	1.89	1.27	.85	.57	.38

   a. Draw a scatterplot of these data on the grid at the right.

   b. Let *L* be the level of anesthetic and *t* be the time. Fit an exponential model to these data.

   _____

   c. Use your model to find the level of anesthetic after 12 hours.

   _____

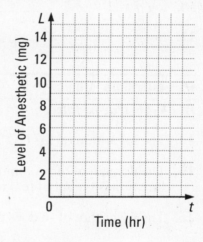

3. *Multiple choice.* For which set of data below is an exponential model most appropriate? Explain why. _____

a.

x	0	1	2	3	4	5	6
y	3	18	75	390	1800	10,000	50,000

b.

x	0	1	2	3	4	5	6
y	3	15	75	375	1875	9375	46875

c.

x	0	1	2	3	4	5	6
y	3	6	99	732	3075	9378	23331

LESSON MASTER 9-5 A

Questions on SPUR Objectives
See pages 599-601 for objectives.

Skills Objective A

In 1–6, write the number as a decimal. Do not use a calculator.

1. $\log 1000$ _____

2. $\log (0.01)$ _____

3. $\log \sqrt[9]{10}$ _____

4. $\log 10^{40}$ _____

5. $\log 10^{-17}$ _____

6. $\log (-10)$ _____

In 7–9, find the logarithm to the nearest hundredth.

7. $\log 9.63$ _____

8. $\log 14,609$ _____

9. $\log -53$ _____

Skills Objective C

In 10–13, solve.

10. $\log a = 2$ _____

11. $\log b = -3$ _____

12. $\log g = 5.1$ _____

13. $\log h = -0.19$ _____

Properties Objective E

In 14–16, *true or false.*

14. The logarithm of 1 is 0. _____

15. The domain of the common logarithm function is the set of real numbers. _____

16. The logarithm of -6 does not exist. _____

17. What is an equation of the asymptote to the graph of the function with equation $y = \log x$? _____

Representations Objective J

18. Graph $y = 10^x$ and $y = \log x$ on the grid at the right.

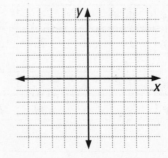

LESSON MASTER

9-6
A

Skills Objectives B and C

In 1 and 2, use the formula $D = 10 \log\left(\frac{N}{10^{-12}}\right)$, which gives

the measure in D decibels for a sound with intensity $N = \frac{w}{m^2}$.

1. The sound intensity of traffic on a busy toll road is measured at 5.87×10^{-3} w/m². How intense is this sound as measured by the decibel scale? _____

2. Find the intensity of a sound which has a relative intensity of 73 decibels. _____

In 3 and 4, use the formula pH = -log C to find the pH of a solution with concentration C of hydrogen ions, H⁺.

3. The concentration of a solution is 3.162×10^{-9} moles of H⁺ per liter.

   a. What is the pH of this solution? _____

   b. Is the solution acidic or alkaline? _____

4. A sample of blood has a pH of 7.41. What is the concentration of H⁺ ions in this sample? _____

Uses Objective H

5. Elena is speaking at a normal level of 60 decibels, while Ito is whispering at a level of 30 decibels. Elena's normal voice is how many times as intense as Ito's whisper? _____

6. While playing at a relative intensity of 115 decibels, a band was instructed to lower the output to 100 decibels. How many times as intense was the original sound as the softer sound? _____

7. What is the measure of a conversation which is twice as intense as a conversation which measures 60 decibels? _____

8. Bile can range from a concentration of pH 9 to pH 11. The stronger alkaline solution is how many times as concentrated as the weaker alkaline solution? _____

9. Hydrochloric acid has pH of 1, and gastric juices have a pH of about 2. The concentration of hydrochloric acid is about how many times that of gastric juices? _____

10. Soap A has pH 7.4 and soap B has pH 7.7. How many times as alkaline as soap A is soap B? _____

LESSON MASTER 9-7 A

Skills Objectives A and B

In 1–9, write the number as a decimal.

1. $\log_4 \frac{1}{4}$ _____

2. $\log_{26} 26$ _____

3. $\log_{16} 4$ _____

4. $\log_2 8$ _____

5. $\log_{39} 1$ _____

6. $\log_{52} 52^4$ _____

7. $\log_8 4$ _____

8. $\log_6 7776$ _____

9. $\log_5 25$ _____

In 10–13, solve. Round decimal solutions to the nearest hundredth.

10. $\log_x 4000 = \log_{17} 4000$

11. $\log_y 8 = 15.2$

12. $\log_8 z = 1.75$

13. $\log_{12} w = 2.637$

Properties Objective E

In 14 and 15, write in exponential form.

14. $\log_7 \frac{1}{343} = -3$ _____

15. $\log_9 27 = \frac{3}{2}$ _____

In 16 and 17, write in logarithmic form.

16. $6^8 = 1,679,616$

17. $x^y = z,\ x > 0$ and $x \neq 1$

_____   _____

Representations Objective J

18. Graph the equation $y = \log_5 x$ on the grid below.

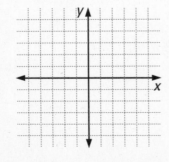

19. Graphed below is $y = \log_b x$. Find b. _____

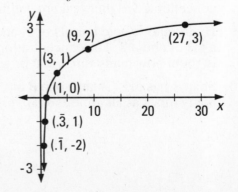

LESSON MASTER

9-8
A

Skills Objective C

In 1–4, give solutions to the nearest hundredth.

1. $\log(4z) = \log 5 + \log 4$ _____

2. $3 \log_2 4 = \log_2 m$ _____

3. $\log_5 625 - \log_5 25 = 2 \log_5 h$ _____

4. $\log_{19}(15y) = \log_{19} 3 + \log_{19} 5$ _____

Properties Objective E

In 5–12, write the number as a decimal.

5. $\log_{12} 1$ _____

6. $\log_{27} 27^{13}$ _____

7. $\log_8 4 + \log_8 2$ _____

8. $2 \log_9 27$ _____

9. $\frac{1}{3} \log_6 46{,}656$ _____

10. $\log_5 5^{-20}$ _____

11. $\log_4 3 - \log_4 48$ _____

12. $\log_{18} \sqrt[6]{18}$ _____

In 13 and 14, rewrite as a logarithm of a single quantity.

13. $\log x + 5 \log r$

14. $\log_3 4 + \log_3 x - \frac{1}{2} \log_3 d$

_____   _____

15. The following is a proof that the equation for determining a decibel measure can be written as $D = \log N^{10} + 120$. Give a reason for each step of the proof.

Proof: $D = 10 \log \left(\frac{N}{10^{-12}} \right)$ Given

$D = 10 (\log N - \log 10^{-12})$ **a.** _____

$D = 10 (\log N - -12)$ **b.** _____

$D = 10 (\log N + 12)$ Definition of Subtraction

$D = 10 \log N + 120$ Distributive Property

$D = \log N^{10} + 120$ **c.** _____

LESSON MASTER 9-9 A

Skills Objective A

In 1–3, write the number as a decimal. Do not use
a calculator.

1. $\ln e^8$ _____ **2.** $\ln e^{\frac{1}{2}}$ _____ **3.** $\ln e^{-\frac{2}{5}}$ _____

In 4–6, find the logarithm to the nearest hundredth.

4. $\ln 95$ _____ **5.** $\ln (-6.3)$ _____ **6.** $\ln 0.03$ _____

Properties Objective E

In 7 and 8, write in exponential form.

7. $\ln 15 \approx 2.708$ _____ **8.** $\ln 1.5 \approx 0.405$ _____

In 9 and 10, write in logarithmic form.

9. $e^{-1.3} \approx 0.273$ _____ **10.** $e^{15} \approx 3,269,017$ _____

In 11 and 12, give the general property of which the
statement is an instance.

11. $\ln e^5 = 5$ **12.** $\ln 50 + \ln 10 = \ln 500$

_____   _____

Uses Objective H

13. The maximum velocity v of a rocket is $v = c \cdot \ln R$, where
c is the velocity of the exhaust and R is the ratio of the mass
of the rocket with fuel to its mass without fuel. Find R
for a rocket if $c = 2000$ m/sec and $v = 2200$ m/sec. _____

Representations Objective J

14. *Multiple choice.* At the
right is the graph of
$y = \log_b x$. Point A has
coordinates $(e, 1)$. Give
the value of b. _____

(a) 2   (b) e

(b) $-e$ (d) 3

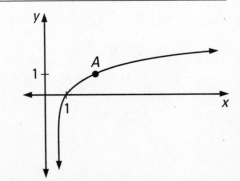

ADVANCED ALGEBRA © Scott, Foresman and Company

LESSON MASTER

9-10 A

Questions on SPUR Objectives
See pages 599-601 for objectives.

Skills Objective B

In 1–8, solve. Round solutions to the nearest hundredth.

1. $49^x = 343$

2. $13^y = 28,561$

3. $16^z = 8$

4. $19,683^w = 729$

5. $12^{m+5} = 17$

6. $4e^n = 24$

7. $(1.63)^c = e^3$

8. $17^{4d-7} = 25$

Uses Objective F

9. Sue Aimi wants to invest some money in a certificate of deposit paying interest at 5.8% compounded continuously. How long will it take the money to double? _____

10. Maria invested $3000 in an individual retirement account (IRA) which earns annual interest of 4.9%. How long will it take her to have $9000 in her IRA? _____

11. The population of a certain strain of bacteria grows according to the formula $N = N_0 \cdot 2^{1.71t}$, where t is the time in hours and N_0 is the initial population. How long will it take 50 bacteria to increase to 500,000? _____

12. In 1994, the population of the world was about 5.6 billion. The U.S. Bureau of the Census predicts that in the year 2020, the world's population will reach 7.9 billion.

    a. Write an exponential equation to model this situation. _____

    b. Use this model to estimate when the world's population will reach 10 billion. _____

ADVANCED ALGEBRA © Scott, Foresman and Company

**L E S S O N
M A S T E R**

Skills Objective A

In 1–4, use a calculator to evaluate. Round to the
nearest hundredth.

1. sin 28° _____

2. cos 62° _____

3. tan 50° _____

4. sin 62° _____

In 5 and 6, approximate the trigonometric ratio
to the nearest thousandth.

5. Refer to the triangle at the right.

   a. sin θ _____

   b. cos θ _____

   c. tan θ _____

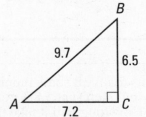

6. Refer to ΔABC at the right.

   a. sin A _____

   b. cos B _____

   c. tan B _____

Uses Objective F

7. A ship sailed 59 kilometers on a bearing of 25°.
   How far east of its original position is the ship? _____

8. Juanita used an instrument to sight the
   top of a building and got an angle
   measure of 62°. She is 5 ft tall and stood
   35 ft from the building. About how tall
   was the building?

   _____

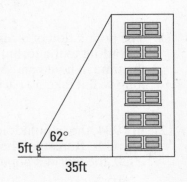

ADVANCED ALGEBRA © Scott, Foresman and Company

LESSON MASTER

10-2 A

Vocabulary

In 1–4, use the labeled angles in the picture at the right. Assume that the dashed line is parallel to the ground and that the buildings have the same height.

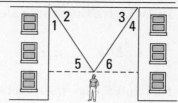

1. Name all *angles of elevation*. _____

2. *True or false.* m $\angle 2$ = m $\angle 5$ _____

3. Name all *angles of depression*. _____

4. Name two pairs of *congruent* angles. _____

Skills Objective C

In 5–8, give the measure of the acute angle θ to the nearest degree.

5. $\sin \theta = .3$ _____

6. $\tan \theta = \dfrac{\sqrt{3}}{3}$ _____

7. $\cos^{-1}(.5) = \theta$ _____

8. $\tan^{-1}(3) = \theta$ _____

Uses Objective F

9. A ramp is to be built up to a doorway. Its slope is to be $\frac{1}{13}$. What angle will the ramp make with the horizontal? _____

10. A plane flying at 31,000 feet begins its descent 125 miles from the airport. If the angle of depression is constant, find its measure.

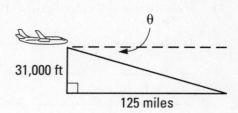

_____

11. REGULADCON is a regular decagon. If each side of the decagon measures 10, find the length of $\overline{RG}$.

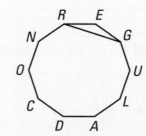

_____

LESSON MASTER 10-3 A

Questions on SPUR Objectives
See pages 669-671 for objectives.

Skills Objective B

In 1–3, give the exact value.

1. $\sin 30°$ _____

2. $\cos 30°$ _____

3. $\tan 45°$ _____

In 4 and 5, give the exact value.

4.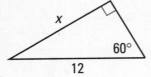

    a. $\sin 60°$ _____

    b. x _____

5.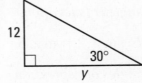

    a. $\tan 30°$ _____

    b. y _____

Properties Objective E

In 6–9, fill in the blank with the measure of an acute angle.

6. $\cos 37° = \sin$ _____

7. $\sin 25° = \cos (90° -$ _____ $)$

8. $\tan 55° = \dfrac{\sin 55°}{\cos \underline{\hspace{1cm}}}$

9. $(\sin \underline{\hspace{1cm}})^2 + (\cos 12°)^2 = 1$

10. If $\cos \theta = 0.81$ and θ is acute, then $\sin \theta \approx$ _____

11. Without using a calculator, explain why $\sin 45° = \cos 45°$.

_____

_____

_____

In 12 and 13, verify the property when $\theta = 60°$.

12. $(\sin \theta)^2 + (\cos \theta)^2 = 1$

_____

13. $\sin (90 - \theta) = \cos \theta$

_____

LESSON MASTER 10-4 A

Skills Objective B

In 1–12, give the exact value. Do not use
a calculator.

1. $\cos 90°$ _____

2. $\cos 0°$ _____

3. $\sin 270°$ _____

4. $\cos 180°$ _____

5. $\sin 180°$ _____

6. $\sin 405°$ _____

7. $\sin 630°$ _____

8. $\cos (-315°)$ _____

9. $\cos(-330°)$ _____

10. $\cos (-690°)$ _____

11. $\cos (-540°)$ _____

12. $\sin (-270°)$ _____

Representations Objective I

13. To the nearest thousandth, find the coordinates
of the image of the point $(1, 0)$ under R_{75}. _____

In 14–21, refer to the drawing at
the right of the unit circle with
the given points on it. Give
the letter that could represent
the value.

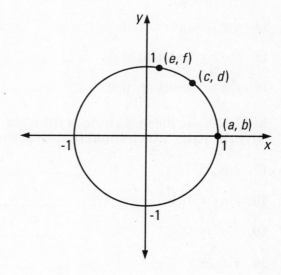

14. $\sin (-310°)$ _____

15. $\cos 0°$ _____

16. $\cos 80°$ _____

17. $\cos 50°$ _____

18. $\sin 440°$ _____

19. $\sin 1080°$ _____

20. $\cos (-670°)$ _____

21. $\sin 0°$ _____

LESSON MASTER

Questions on SPUR Objectives
See pages 669-671 for objectives.

Skills Objective A

In 1–6, use a calculator to evaluate. Round to the nearest thousandth.

1. sin 176° _____
2. cos (-1500°) _____
3. sin 1802° _____

4. cos (-397°) _____
5. sin (-255.7°) _____
6. cos 223° _____

Skills Objective B

In 7–12, give the exact value.

7. sin 660° _____
8. cos (-660°) _____
9. cos 150° _____

10. cos (-1800)° _____
11. sin 270° _____
12. sin (-405°) _____

Representations Objective I

**In 13–16, use the unit circle at the right.
Use your calculator to find**

13. the x-coordinate of A. _____

14. the y-coordinate of A. _____

15. the x-coordinate of B. _____

16. the y-coordinate of B. _____

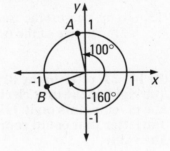

**In 17–20, use the unit circle at the right.
Give the letter which could represent the value.**

17. cos 75° _____

18. sin (-180°) _____

19. sin (-80°) _____

20. cos 280° _____

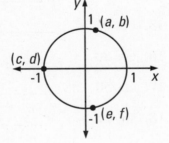

**In 21–24, use the unit circle at the right
to find the value.**

21. cos α _____

22. sin θ _____

23. α _____

24. θ _____

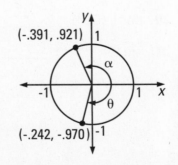

LESSON MASTER

Uses Objective G

1. A baseball infield is determined by a square with sides 90 ft long. In the diagram at the right, home plate is *H* and first base is *F*. Suppose the first baseman ran in a straight line from *F* to catch a pop-up at *B*, 120 ft. from home plate. If the measure of ∠*FHB* is 10°, how far did the first baseman run?

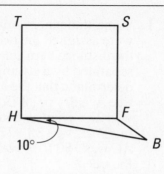

_____

2. The air distance from Chicago to Los Angeles is 1745 miles. From Los Angeles to New York the air distance is 2451 miles, and from New York to Chicago it is 714 miles. Two airplanes leave Los Angeles, one heading straight for Chicago and the other straight for New York. Use the Law of Cosines to estimate the measure of the angle they will form.

_____

Representations Objective H

3. Find *BC*. _____

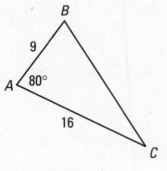

4. Find *TA*. _____

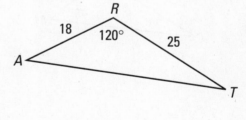

5. Find m∠*K*. _____

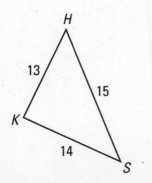

6. Find the measure of the smallest angle. _____

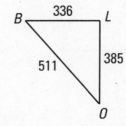

LESSON MASTER

10-7 A

Questions on SPUR Objectives
See pages 669-671 for objectives.

Uses Objective G

1. Some students in Advanced Algebra were assigned the task of measuring the distance between two trees separated by a swamp. They determined that the angle formed by tree A, a dry point C, and tree B was 27°. They also knew that m∠ABC was 85°. They found that AC was 150 ft. How far apart are the trees?

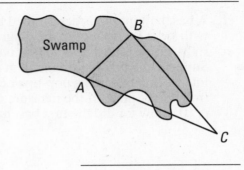

_____

2. Two lookout towers, L and M, are 50 kilometers apart. The ranger in Tower L, Mary Eagle Wing, saw a fire at point C such that m∠CLM = 40°. The ranger in Tower M, Raul Sonoma, saw the fire such that m∠CML = 65°. How far was the fire from Mary?

_____

Representations Objective H

3. Find JM. _____

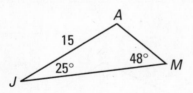

4. Find DF. _____

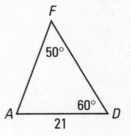

5. Find PA. _____

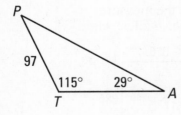

6. Find the length of the shortest side. _____

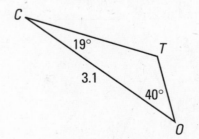

Name _____

LESSON MASTER **10-8 A**

Questions on SPUR Objectives
See pages 669-671 for objectives.

Representations Objective J

In 1–3, *true or false*. **If false, rewrite the statement to make it true.**

1. The range of the sine function is the set of all real numbers.

_____

_____

2. The graph of the sine function has *x*-intercepts at the even-numbered multiples of 90°.

_____

_____

3. The graphs of $f(\theta) = \cos \theta$ and $g(\theta) = \sin \theta$ are congruent.

_____

_____

4. a. At the right, graph $f: x \rightarrow \sin x$ for $-360° \leq x \leq 360°$.

b. Give the *y*-intercept of the sine function.

_____

c. Give the period of the sine function.

_____

d. What are the *x*-intercepts of the sine function on this domain?

_____

5. a. At the right, graph the cosine function $g(x) = \cos x$ for $-360° \leq x \leq 360°$.

b. Give the *y*-intercept of the cosine function.

_____

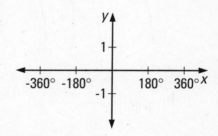

c. Give the period of the cosine function.

_____

d. What are the *x*-intercepts of the cosine function on this domain?

_____

6. $y = \sin x$ is the image of $y = \cos x$
   under what translation?   _____

In 7 and 8, fill in the blanks.

7. As x increases from 90° to 180°, $\sin x$ decreases from _____ to _____.

8. As x increases from 180° to 270°, $\cos x$ increases from _____ to _____.

In 9 and 10, use the graph of $y = f(x)$ below.

9. Does this function seem
   to be periodic? If
   so, what is its period?

   _____

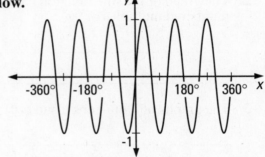

10. Is this function sinusoidal?
    Explain your reasoning.

    _____

    _____

    _____

**In 11 and 12, a function is graphed. a. Does
the function seem to be periodic?
b. If so, what is its period?**

11.

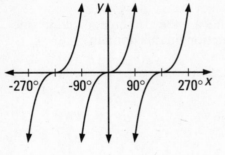

a. _____

b. _____

12.

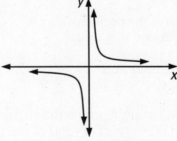

a. _____

b. _____

LESSON MASTER

10-9
A

Skills Objective C

In 1 and 2, solve for all θ between 0° and 180°.
Give θ to the nearest degree.

1. $\sin \theta = .163$ _____

2. $\sin \theta = -.707$ _____

In 3 and 4, solve for all θ between 0° and 180°.
Give exact values.

3. $\sin \theta = \dfrac{\sqrt{3}}{2}$ _____

4. $\sin \theta = \dfrac{\sqrt{2}}{2}$ _____

Properties Objective E

In 5–7, fill in the blank.

5. Give the measure of an acute angle. $\sin 68° = \sin (180° -$ _____ $)$

6. If $\sin \theta = .6$ and $0° < \theta < 180°$, then $\cos \theta =$ _____ or $\cos \theta =$ _____.

7. If $\sin \theta = .7$ and θ is obtuse, to the nearest thousandth, $\cos \theta =$ _____.

8. *True or false.* $\cos (180° - \theta) = \sin \theta$.   _____

Uses Objective G

9. Elinor, Juan, and Machiko are playing catch. Elinor and Juan are
   59 feet apart, and Machiko and Juan are 46 feet apart. The line from
   Elinor to Machiko is at a 51° angle with the line from Elinor to Juan.

   a. Find the measure of the angle where Machiko
   stands. (Hint: There are two answers.)   _____

   b. Use your answers to Part a to find the distance
   from Machiko to Elinor.   _____

Representations Objective H

10. Given $\triangle YES$, with m $\angle Y = 30°$, $YE = 6$, and $ES = 4$, solve the triangle and
    sketch each possibility.

LESSON MASTER 10-10 A

Skills Objective A

In 1–6, evaluate to the nearest thousandth.

1. $\sin\left(\frac{11\pi}{6}\right)$ _____

2. $\tan\left(\frac{3\pi}{10}\right)$ _____

3. $\cos\left(-\frac{7\pi}{24}\right)$ _____

4. $\tan(-10)$ _____

5. $\sin(16\pi)$ _____

6. $\cos(-2.46)$ _____

Skills Objective B

In 7–12, give the exact value.

7. $\sin\left(\frac{\pi}{2}\right)$ _____

8. $\cos\left(-\frac{\pi}{4}\right)$ _____

9. $\tan\left(\frac{13\pi}{6}\right)$ _____

10. $\cos\left(-\frac{3\pi}{4}\right)$ _____

11. $\tan\left(-\frac{3\pi}{4}\right)$ _____

12. $\sin\left(\frac{5\pi}{6}\right)$ _____

Skills Objective D

In 13–18, convert to radians.

13. $-45°$ _____

14. $90°$ _____

15. $720°$ _____

16. $27°$ _____

17. $1°$ _____

18. $-18°$ _____

In 19–24, convert to degrees.

19. -2π _____

20. $-\frac{3}{5}\pi$ _____

21. $\frac{3\pi}{8}$ _____

22. $\frac{7\pi}{12}$ _____

23. 1 _____

24. $\frac{29\pi}{3}$ _____

Representations Objective J

In 25–28, use the unit circle at the right. Give the letter which could represent the given function.

25. $\sin\left(\frac{\pi}{6}\right)$ _____

26. $\cos\left(\frac{13\pi}{6}\right)$ _____

27. $\sin\left(\frac{2\pi}{3}\right)$ _____

28. $\cos\left(-\frac{2\pi}{3}\right)$ _____

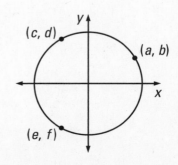

Name _____

LESSON MASTER 11-1 A

Questions on SPUR Objectives
See pages 741-745 for objectives.

Properties Objective E

1. *True or false.* $9x^2 + 4x - 1 + 3x^{-1}$ is a polynomial. _____

In 2–4, a polynomial is given. a. Give its degree.
b. Name its leading coefficient.

2. $m^3 - 3m^7$ **3.** $4n - 15 - 3n^2$ **4.** $8p^2 - 1$

a. _____   a. _____   a. _____

b. _____   b. _____   b. _____

Uses Objective H

5. Diane Chang invested her savings in an account paying $r\%$
interest compounded annually. Suppose she invests $90 at the beginning of
each year for six years. No additional money is added or withdrawn.

    a. Write a polynomial expression for the total amount
in Diane's account at the end of the sixth year.

_____

_____

    b. Evaluate how much Diane will have if the
account earns 3.9% interest each year. _____

Representations Objective J

In 6 and 7, graph the function given.

6. $p(x) = x^4 - .2x^3 - 8x^2 - 1.5x + 5$ **7.** $k(x) = 5x^5 - 3x - 3$

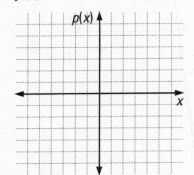
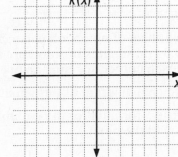

ADVANCED ALGEBRA © Scott, Foresman and Company

105

LESSON MASTER 11-2 A

Skills Objective A

In 1–4, expand and write in standard form.

1. $(a - 3)(2a^3 - 3a^2)$

2. $(b + 7)(b - 1)(b + 4)$

3. $(7 - c)^2 (2 - c)$

4. $(-d + 1)(5d^2 - 2d - 3)$

In 5 and 6, multiply and simplify.

5. $(10e + 2f)(6f - 3g + 1)$

6. $(2h + j - k)(h - j - k)$

Properties Objective E

In 7–9, an expression is given. a. Classify it as a
monomial, **a** *binomial*, **or a** *trinomial*. **b. Give its degree.**

7. $13t^2 + 4t^3$

8. $384m^6n^2 - m^6n^2$

9. $r^5t^5u^2 - u - 1$

a. _____

a. _____

a. _____

b. _____

b. _____

b. _____

Uses Objective I

10. The largest figure at the right is a rectangle.

    a. What are its dimensions?

    _____

    b. What is its area?

    _____

11. From a sheet of notebook paper 26.7 cm by 20.3 cm, squares of side x are removed from each corner, forming an open box.

    a. Sketch a diagram of this situation.

    b. Write a formula for the volume $V(x)$ of the box.

    _____

    c. Write a formula for its surface area $S(x)$.

    _____

ADVANCED ALGEBRA © Scott, Foresman and Company

LESSON MASTER 11-3 A

Vocabulary

1. Is $a^2 - 39$ prime

   a. over the set of polynomials with rational coefficients? _____

   b. over the set of polynomials with real coefficients? _____

   c. Explain your answers to Parts **a** and **b**.

   _____

   _____

   _____

2. The Discriminant Theorem for Factoring Quadratics applies to quadratics with ___?___ coefficients. _____

Skills Objective B

In 3–6, fill in the blanks.

3. $19m^2n - 114mn^2 = 19mn \,($ _____ $-$ _____ $)$

4. $24p^3t + 60p^3 =$ _____ $(2t + 5)$

5. $5wz + 25w^2z - 35w^3z = 5wz \,($ _____ $+$ _____ $-$ _____ $)$

6. $(3 - 2h)^3 + (3 - 2h)^4 = (3 - 2h)^3 ($ _____ $+$ _____ $)$

In 7–12, factor.

7. $a^2 - 12a + 36$ 8. $9c^2 + 6c + 1$ 9. $30e^3 - 60e^2 + 30e$

_____   _____   _____

10. $g^2 - 64h^6$ 11. $k^4 - 25k^2$ 12. $5r^2 + 9r - 18$

_____   _____   _____

13. **a.** Write $t^4 - 16$ as the product of two binomials. _____

    b. Write $t^4 - 16$ as the product of three binomials. _____

14. *True or false.* $3x^2 - y^2 = (x\sqrt{3} + y)(x\sqrt{3} - y)$ _____

15. *True or false.* $9a^2 + b^2 = (3a + bi)(3a - bi)$ _____

LESSON MASTER 11-4 A

Questions on SPUR Objectives
See pages 741-745 for objectives.

Representations Objective K

In 1 and 2, estimate the real zeros of the described function to the nearest tenth.

1. $f(x) = 2x^4 - 10x^2 + 3$

_____

2. $y = 2x^5 - 5x^3 - 2x^2 + 3x + 1$

_____

In 3 and 4, use the graph of the function to determine its integer zeros.

3. $y = x^3 - 9x^2 + 23x - 15$

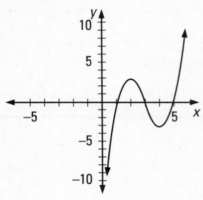

_____

4. $h(x) = 4 - 3x^2 - x^3$

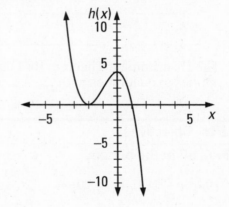

_____

5. a. Complete the table of values for the function Q with equation $Q(x) = .09x^3 - 2x + 16$.

x	-10	-8	-6	-4	-2	0	2	4	6
Q(x)									

b. Use the table to tell how many zeros the function has. _____

c. For each zero, indicate the two consecutive even integers between which the zero must lie. _____

d. Describe how you could use a graph to justify your response to Part **b**.

_____

_____

e. Use technology to find each zero to the nearest hundredth. _____

LESSON MASTER 11-5 A

Skills Objective C

In 1–3, give the exact zeros of the function described.

1. $A(x) = x(x - 3)(x + 4)(2x - 1)$ _____

2. $B(x) = x^2 - 100$ _____

3. $C(x) = x^3 - x$ _____

Skills Objective D

4. Give equations for 3 different polynomial functions with zeros at -8, $\frac{2}{3}$, and $\frac{5}{2}$.

_____ _____

_____

Properties Objective F

In 5 and 6, consider the functions with equations.

$M(x) = x(x - 1)(x - 2)$ and $N(x) = x^2(x - 1)(x - 2)$.

5. *True or false.* M and N have the same graphs. _____

6. *True or false.* M and N have the same zeros. _____

7. *True or false.* 3 is *not* a solution to $(g - 3)(g + 4) = 7$. _____

8. Consider the polynomial $R(x) = 2x^3 - 19x^2 + 35x$.

   a. List its factors. _____

   b. List its zeros. _____

   c. Which theorem allows you to proceed from Part **a** to Part **b** without graphing? _____

Representations Objectives J and K

9. At the right, graph the function P with $P(x) = x^5 - 13x^3 + 36x$. Give the real zeros of the function.

   _____

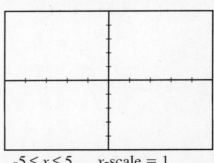

$-5 \le x \le 5$ x-scale $= 1$
$-50 \le y \le 50$ y-scale $= 10$

LESSON MASTER

11-6 A

Skills Objective B and C

In 1–4, a polynomial is given. **a. Factor over the set of *complex* numbers. b. Identify all *real* zeros. c. Check by graphing.**

1. $A(r) = 6r^2 + 5r - 4$

a. _____

b. _____

c.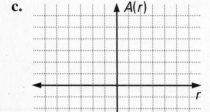

2. $B(t) = 6t^3 + 33t^2 - 18t$

a. _____

b. _____

c.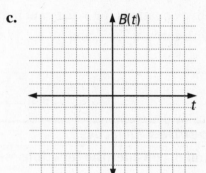

3. $A(x) = x^2 + 5x - 7$

a. _____

b. _____

c.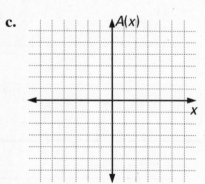

4. $T(y) = y - 3y^2 - 4$

a. _____

b. _____

c.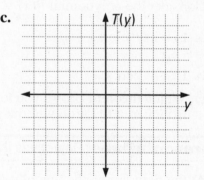

LESSON MASTER 11-7 A

Properties Objective G

**In 1 and 2, use the Rational Zero Theorem
to factor the polynomial.**

1. $L(x) = 30x^3 - 31x^2 + 10x - 1$

_____

2. $M(x) = x^4 + 2x^3 + x^2$

_____

**In 3–7, a polynomial is given. a. Use the Rational
Zero theorem to list all possible rational zeros.
b. Find all rational zeros.**

3. $P(x) = 7x^5 - 3x^4 - 2$

a. _____

b. _____

4. $Q(m) = 64m^3 - 1$

a. _____

b. _____

5. $R(n) = 3n^2 - 15n - 18$

a. _____

b. _____

6. $S(x) = 2x^4 - 7x^3 + 5x^2 - 7x + 3$

a. _____

b. _____

7. $T(x) = x^5 + 2x^3 - x^2 - 2$

a. _____

b. _____

Representations Objective J

8. Consider $U(x) = 5x^6 + 6x^4 + x^2 + 12$.

a. Use the Rational Zero Theorem to list
all possible rational zeros.

_____

_____

b. Graph this polynomial on the
grid at the right.

c. Use Parts **a** and **b** to find all rational
zeros of this polynomial.

_____

_____

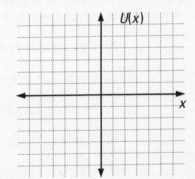

LESSON MASTER

11-8
A

Vocabulary

1. *Multiple choice.* Consider the equation
   $(x + 1)^6(x - 2)(x - 1) = 0$. Which is true? _____
   (a) 1 is a double root.   (b) -1 is a double root.
   (c) 1 is a root with multiplicity 6.   (d) -1 is a root with multiplicity 6.

Properties Objective F

In 2 and 3, use the equation $\sqrt{6}\,x^3 - 5ix + .4x^2 - 2 = 0$.

2. *True or false.* This equation has at least one complex solution. _____

3. This equation has exactly ___?___ roots. _____

4. Consider the equation $(x - 3)^6(x^2 - 3)(x^2 + 9) = 0$.

   a. This equation has exactly ___?___ roots if
      multiplicities of multiple roots are counted. _____

   b. _____ is a rational root with multiplicity _____.

      _____ is an irrational root with multiplicity _____.

      _____ is an irrational root with multiplicity _____.

      _____ is a complex root with multiplicity _____.

      _____ is a complex root with multiplicity _____.

Culture Objective L

**In 5–10, match each mathematician with his contribution
toward solving all polynomial equations.**

_____ 5. Omar Khayyam, 1100s

_____ 6. Ludovico Ferrari, 1500s

_____ 7. Niccolo Tartaglia, 1500s

_____ 8. Karl Friedrich Gauss, 1700s

_____ 9. Évariste Galois, 1800s

_____ 10. Niels Abel, 1800s

a. discovered how to solve quartic
   equations using complex numbers

b. proved the Fundamental Theorem
   of Algebra

c. discovered how to solve all cubic
   equations

d. first showed how to solve many
   cubic equations

e. proved the general quartic equation
   cannot be solved using a formula

f. described method for determining
   which polynomials of degree 5 or
   more can be solved with a formula

Name _____

LESSON MASTER 11-9 A

Skills Objective D

In 1 and 2, a function is described. a. Determine whether the function is a polynomial function of degree ≤ 5. b. If so, give the degree of the function.

1. the function (n, a_n) where $a_1 = 2$ and $a_n = a_{n-1} + 3$

   a. _____   b. _____

2.

x	10	20	30	40	50	60	70	80	90
y	-200	-209	-280	-443	-584	-325	1096	4945	13,112

   a. _____   b. _____

3. Suppose the sequence 3, 4, 11, 24, 43, 68, 99, . . . has a formula with degree ≤ 4. Use the method of finite differences to predict the next term. _____

4. Can the method of finite differences be used with this set of data? Explain why or why not.

x	1	3	6	10	15	21	28	36	45
y	24	49	74	99	124	149	174	199	224

_____

_____

Uses Objective H

In 5 and 6, use the results of an experiment involving rolling a marble down an inclined plane.

Time Passed (seconds)	0	1	2	3	4	5	6
Distance of Marble from Given Point (cm)	10	12.4	14.8	17.2	19.6	22	24.4

5. What degree polynomial would you use to best model these data? Explain your answer.

_____

6. Use your polynomial to predict how far the marble would be from the given point after 10 seconds. _____

LESSON MASTER

11-10
A

Questions on SPUR Objectives
See pages 741-745 for objectives.

Skills Objective D

1. Consider the values in the table below.

x	1	2	3	4	5	6	7	8
y	2	20	50	92	146	212	290	380

    a. This data can be modeled by a polynomial equation
of the form $y = ax^2 + bx + c$. List three equations
which can be used to solve for a, b, and c.

_____   _____   _____

    b. Solve the system to find a formula
which models the data above.   _____

**In 2–4, write a formula of degree $n \leq 5$ which
models the data.**

2.

x	1	2	3	4	5	6	7	8
y	-22.5	-24	-15.5	12	67.5	160	298.5	492

_____

3.

x	1	2	3	4	5	6	7	8
y	-3	-16	-27	0	125	432	1029	2048

_____

4.

x	1	2	3	4	5	6	7	8
y	-2	3	4	-5	-30	-77	-152	-261

_____

Uses Objective H

5. Suppose that Sylvia stacks soccer balls in a triangular
pyramid display. That is, one ball is in the top row, three
are in the second row, six are in the third row, and so on.

    a. Complete the table.

Number of rows (n)	1	2	3	4	5	6
Total Number of Balls (T)	1	4	10			

    b. How many soccer balls are needed for n rows?   _____

ADVANCED ALGEBRA © Scott, Foresman and Company

LESSON MASTER 12-1 A

Skills Objective B

In 1 and 2, write an equation for the parabola satisfying the given conditions.

1. focus (0, 3) and directrix $y = -3$. _____

2. focus (-5, 0) and directrix $x = 5$. _____

3. Given $F = (0, -2)$ and line ℓ with equation $y = 2$, write an equation for the set of points equidistant from F and ℓ. _____

Properties Objectives E, F, and G

4. In the diagram at the right, locate five points on the parabola with directrix m and focus F, including the vertex of the parabola.

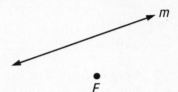

In 5 and 6, an equation for a parabola is given. a. Tell whether the parabola opens up or down. b. Name the focus. c. Name its vertex. d. Name the directrix.

5. $y = 0.6x^2$

6. $y = -7(x + 3)^2$

a. _____ b. _____   a. _____ b. _____

c. _____ d. _____   c. _____ d. _____

Representations Objective J

7. a. Graph the parabola with equation $y = -\frac{1}{4}x^2$.

   b. Plot and label the focus.

   c. Plot and label the directrix.

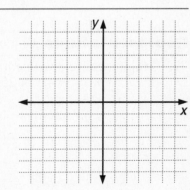

LESSON MASTER 12-2 A

Skills Objective B

In 1 and 2, write an equation for the circle satisfying the given conditions.

1. center at origin, radius 5

   _____

2. center at (-3, 7), radius 8

   _____

Properties Objectives F and G

In 3 and 4, identify the center and radius of the circle.

3. $(x + 3)^2 + y^2 = 26$

   center _____

   radius _____

4. $(x - 7.5)^2 + (y + 2.5)^2 = \dfrac{1}{25}$

   center _____

   radius _____

5. *True or false.* The distance between any two points on a circle is a constant.

   _____

Uses Objective H

6. A seismograph located 10 miles due north of a recording station detects an earthquake with epicenter 15 miles away.

   a. Write an equation that could be used to describe possible locations of the epicenter.

   _____

   b. A worker was 8 miles due east of the station when the quake occurred. Use your answer to Part **a** to determine whether the epicenter could have been right below her.

   _____

Representations Objective J

7. Graph the circle with equation $(x - 3)^2 + (y - 4)^2 = 25$.

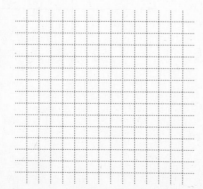

8. Write an equation for the circle graphed below.

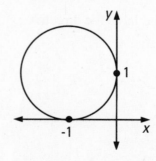

   _____

ADVANCED ALGEBRA © Scott, Foresman and Company

LESSON MASTER 12-3 A

Skills Objective B

1. What equation describes the lower
   semicircle of the circle $x^2 + y^2 = 10$? _____

2. **a.** Write a sentence describing all
       points in the interior of the circle
       $(x - 3)^2 + (y + 5)^2 = 13$. _____

   b. Use your answer to Part **a** to show that the
       point (1, -3) is inside the circle.

   _____

   _____

Uses Objective H

3. A truck 7 feet high and 4 feet wide approaches a semicircular
   tunnel which has a diameter of 16 feet.

   a. Will the truck fit through the tunnel? Justify your answer.

   _____

   _____

   b. Find the radius of the smallest
       tunnel the truck could enter. _____

4. The pilot of a small plane tells an air-traffic controller
   that he is within a 14-mile radius of a town that is
   22 miles north of the airport. Write a sentence that
   describes his possible locations (x, y) from the
   point of view of the controller. _____

Representations Objective J

In 5 and 6, graph the inequality.

5. $(x + 1)^2 + (y + 6)^2 \geq 4$

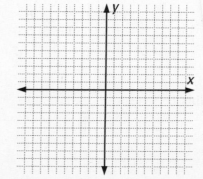

6. $1 \leq (x + 2)^2 + (y - 3)^2 \leq 4$

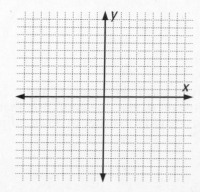

ADVANCED ALGEBRA © Scott, Foresman and Company

LESSON MASTER 12-4 A

Skills Objective B

In 1–5, write an equation for an ellipse satisfying the given conditions.

1. foci at (-4, 0) and (4, 0); focal constant 12   _____

2. foci at (8, 0) and (-8, 0); focal constant 18   _____

3. foci at (0, 3) and (0, -3); major axis length 10   _____

4. foci at (-1, 0) and (1, 0); minor axis length $\sqrt{5}$ _____

5. center at origin, horizontal major axis 8,
   vertical minor axis 6   _____

Properties Objectives E, F, and G

6. Use the conic grid below with centers 10 units apart to draw
   the set of points P satisfying the condition $PF_1 + PF_2 = 12$.

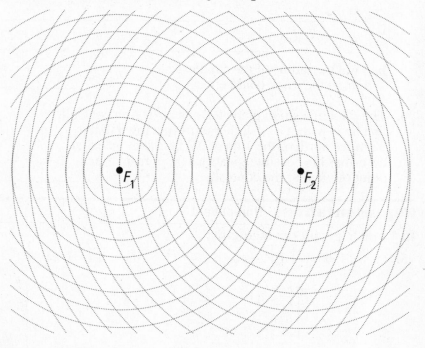

7. Given two fixed points F_1 and F_2 and a focal
   constant d, give the condition that a set of points P
   must satisfy in order to be an ellipse.   _____

▶ **LESSON MASTER 12-4 A** *page 2*

8. Consider the ellipse with equation $\frac{x^2}{15} + \frac{y^2}{26} = 1$.

    a. Give the length of its major axis. _____

    b. Name its vertices. _____

    c. Which axis contains the foci of this ellipse? _____

    d. Find the foci F_1 and F_2. _____

    e. If P is on this ellipse, find $PF_1 + PF_2$. _____

Uses Objective H

9. The orbit of Mars around the sun approximates an ellipse with the sun at one focus. The closest and farthest distances of Mars from the center of the sun are 128.5 and 155.0 million miles, respectively.

    a. How far is F_2 from the center of the sun? _____

    b. What is the length of the orbit's minor axis? _____

Representations Objective J

10. Sketch the graph of $\frac{x^2}{4} + \frac{y^2}{9} = 1$ on the grid at the right.

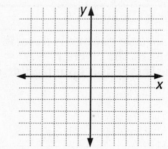

11. **a.** The ellipse shown at the right has integer intercepts. Write an equation for it.

       _____

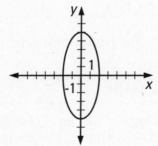

    b. Verify that the point $(1, \frac{5\sqrt{3}}{2})$ is on the ellipse.

       _____

    c. Write a sentence describing the interior of the ellipse. _____

    d. Use your answer to Part **c** to verify that the point (-1, 4) is in the interior of the ellipse.

       _____

ADVANCED ALGEBRA © Scott, Foresman and Company

LESSON MASTER 12-5 A

Skills Objective C

In 1 and 2, find the area of an ellipse satisfying the given conditions.

1. Its equation is $\dfrac{x^2}{169} + \dfrac{y^2}{324} = 1$.   _____

2. The endpoints of its major and minor axes are (0, 3) and (0, -3), and (1.5, 0) and (-1.5, 0).   _____

3. Which has a greater area, a circle with diameter 10 or an ellipse with major and minor axes of lengths 12 and 8?   _____

4. Find the area of the shaded region at the right between a circle with radius 4 and an ellipse with major axis of length 16 and minor axis of length 10.

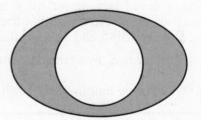

_____

Properties Objective G

In 5 and 6, a scale change is described. a. Write an equation for the image of the circle $x^2 + y^2 = 1$ under the scale change. b. Tell if the image is a noncircular ellipse.

5. $S: (x, y) \rightarrow (8x, 8y)$

6. $S(x, y) = (3x, 6y)$

   a. _____

   a. _____

   b. _____

   b. _____

7. *True or false.* Not every circle is an ellipse.   _____

Uses Objective H

8. A jewel shaped like an ellipse is placed on a background that is also an ellipse. The jewel has major axis 4 mm and minor axis 3 mm. The background has major axis 6 mm and minor axis 4 mm. What percent of the background is covered by the jewel?   _____

LESSON MASTER

12-6 A

Skills Objective B

In 1–2, write an equation for the hyperbola satisfying the given conditions.

1. foci at (5, 0) and (-5, 0); focal constant 8 _____

2. vertices at $(-\sqrt{6}, 0)$ and $(\sqrt{6}, 0)$; containing the point (6, 4) _____

Properties Objectives E, F, and G

3. Use the conic grid below with centers 10 units apart to draw the set of points P satisfying the condition $|PF_1 - PF_2| = 6$.

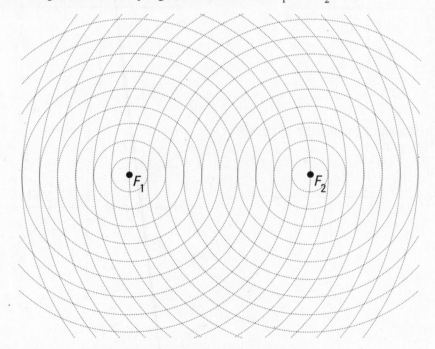

**In 4 and 5, the equation for a hyperbola is given.
a. Name its vertices. b. Write equations of
its asymptotes.**

4. $\dfrac{x^2}{36} - \dfrac{y^2}{16} = 1$

5. $x^2 - \dfrac{y^2}{4} = 1$

a. _____

a. _____

b. _____

b. _____

▶ **LESSON MASTER 12-6 A** *page 2*

6. Given two fixed points F_1 and F_2 and a focal
   constant d, give the condition that a set of
   points P must satisfy in order to be a hyperbola. _____

Representations Objective J

In 7 and 8, sketch the graph of the equation.

7. $\dfrac{x^2}{36} - \dfrac{y^2}{16} = 1$

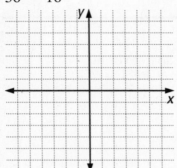

8. $x^2 - \dfrac{y^2}{4} = 1$

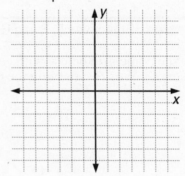

9. Write an equation for the hyperbola
   at the right.

   _____

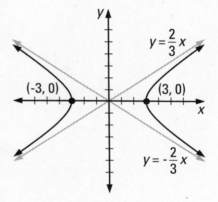

LESSON MASTER 12-7 A

Skills Objective A

In 1–4, rewrite the equation in the form
$Ax^2 + Bxy + Cy^2 + Dx + Ey + F = 0.$

1. $(x + 5)^2 + (y - 2)^2 = 16$ _____

2. $\dfrac{x^2}{36} + \dfrac{y^2}{49} = 1$ _____

3. $y = 2(x - 3)^2 + 5$ _____

4. $3y = \pm\sqrt{2x^2 - 16}$ _____

Skills Objective B

5. **a.** Write an equation for the hyperbola with foci
at (3, -3) and (-3, 3), and focal constant 6. _____

   b. Verify that the point (-0.5, 9) is on the hyperbola.

   _____

   c. Verify that the point (3, -3) is *not* on the hyperbola.

   _____

Properties Objectives F and G

6. Identify the asymptotes of the hyperbola with
equation $xy = 6$. _____

7. *True or false.* Every hyperbola has an equation of
the form $xy = k$, where $k \neq 0$. _____

8. Consider the hyperbola with equation $xy = -18$. Name its

   a. foci   **b.** asymptotes   **c.** focal constant.

   _____ _____ _____

▶ **LESSON MASTER 12-7 A** *page 2*

Uses Objective H

9. The total cost of *n* pencils at a price of *m* each
   was $15. Write an equation for the conic section
   which describes all possible combinations (*n, m*). _____

Representations Objective J

**In 10 and 11, *multiple choice*. Select the equation
that best describes the graph.**

(a) $\dfrac{x^2}{a^2} + \dfrac{y^2}{b^2} = 1$ (b) $\dfrac{x^2}{a^2} - \dfrac{y^2}{b^2} = 1$ (c) $y = ax^2$ (d) $y = \dfrac{a}{x}$

10. _____

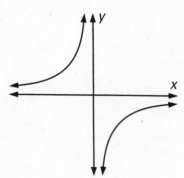

11. _____

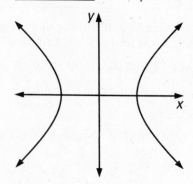

**In 12 and 13, write an equation for the
rectangular hyperbola.**

12. _____

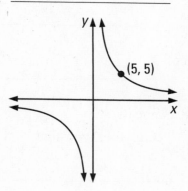

13. _____

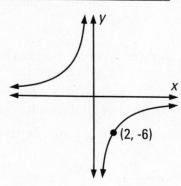

LESSON MASTER 12-8 A

Skills Objective D

In 1–3, solve the system.

1. $\begin{cases} y = 2x^2 - 1 \\ \frac{2}{3}x + y - \frac{1}{3} = 0 \end{cases}$

2. $\begin{cases} (x - 1)^2 + (y + 6)^2 = 8 \\ 2x - y - 6 = 0 \end{cases}$

3. $\begin{cases} ab = -12 \\ 3a - b = 0 \end{cases}$

Uses Objective I

4. A rectangular picture has an area of 300 in^2 and perimeter of 80 in. Find its dimensions. _____

Representations Objective K

In 5 and 6, give two equations whose graphs illustrate the situation.

5. a line intersecting an ellipse in exactly 1 point

6. a line intersecting a parabola in exactly two points

_____

_____

_____

_____

In 7 and 8, graph and estimate the solutions.

7. $\begin{cases} y = x^2 + 3 \\ 3x - y + 4 = 0 \end{cases}$

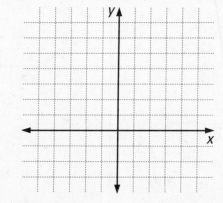

8. $\begin{cases} x^2 + y^2 = 25 \\ x + y = 4 \end{cases}$

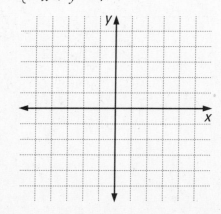

LESSON MASTER 12-9 A

Skills Objective D

In 1 and 2, solve the system using substitution or linear combinations.

1. $\begin{cases} x^2 + y^2 = 4 \\ 3x^2 + 2y^2 = 10 \end{cases}$

2. $\begin{cases} a^2 + (b - 2)^2 = 7 \\ a^2 - b + 1 = 0 \end{cases}$

3. $\begin{cases} m^2 + 9n^2 = 36 \\ m^2 - 2n^2 = 3 \end{cases}$

Uses Objective I

4. Temp-O, which manufactures thermometers, made $876,960 in sales last year. This year Temp-O made $888,096 by raising the price for each thermometer by $.04 and selling the same number of thermometers.

  a. Write a system of equations to describe this situation. _____

  b. What was the price of a Temp-O thermometer last year? _____

  c. How many thermometers were sold this year? _____

Representations Objective K

5. Give equations for a parabola and an ellipse that intersect in exactly 3 points.

  _____

  _____

6. Graph $\begin{cases} x^2 + y^2 = 16 \\ xy = -8 \end{cases}$ and estimate the solutions.

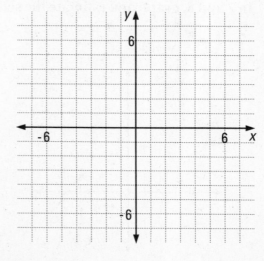

LESSON MASTER

13-1
A

Questions on SPUR Objectives
See pages 880-883 for objectives.

Skills Objective A

In 1–6, evaluate the given arithmetic series.

1. $3 + 6 + 9 + \ldots + 99$

_____

2. the sum of the first 25 terms of the sequence defined by

$$\begin{cases} a_1 = 44 \\ a_n = a_{n-1} - 5, \text{ for integers } n \geq 2. \end{cases}$$

_____

3. the sum of the first 40 positive integers

_____

4. $-16 - 14 - 12 + \ldots + 16 + 18 + 20$

_____

5. the sum of the first 20 odd positive integers

_____

6. the sum of the first 20 even positive integers

_____

7. The sum of the integers $1 + 2 + 3 + \ldots + k$ is 2145. Find k.

_____

Uses Objective G

8. Mary began each workout with sit-ups, and increased the number of sit-ups she did each week. The first week she did 50; the second week she did 60; the following week she did 70. Each week thereafter, she did 10 more sit-ups than she had done the previous week.

a. How many sit-ups did Mary do in the 19th week?

_____

b. In which week did Mary first do 500 sit-ups?

_____

9. A house of cards is built with 54 cards on the first level, 50 cards on the second level, and 4 fewer cards on each successive level. If the house of cards has 8 levels, how many cards are used in all?

_____

LESSON MASTER 13-2 A

Skills Objective B

In 1–6, evaluate the geometric series.

1. $1 + 2 + 4 + 8 + \ldots + 256$

_____

2. the sum of the first 10 terms of the sequence defined by
$$\begin{cases} g_1 = 50 \\ g_n = .5g_{n-1}, \text{ for integers } n \geq 2. \end{cases}$$

_____

3. $1 - 3 + 9 - 27 + 81 - 243$

_____

4. $.003 + .006 + .012 + \ldots + .003(2)^{10}$

_____

5. the sum of the first 13 terms of the sequence defined by
$$\begin{cases} g_1 = 2000 \\ g_n = -\frac{1}{4}g_{n-1}, n \geq 2. \end{cases}$$

_____

6. $7 - 21 + 63 + \ldots + 7(-3)^8$

_____

Uses Objective G

7. A ball is dropped from a height of 6 feet and bounces up to 80% of its previous height on each bounce. When it hits the ground for the 11th time, how far has it traveled in the vertical direction? _____

8. On the third of January for eight consecutive years, Ben deposited $2000 in a retirement fund which earns an annual yield of 3.5%.

a. Write a geometric series that represents the value of this investment on January 3rd of the eighth year.

_____

b. Evaluate the series in Part **a**. _____

LESSON MASTER

13-3
A

Skills Objectives C and D

**In 1 and 2, a series is given. a. Write the terms
of the series. b. Evaluate the series.**

1. $\sum_{n=-3}^{2} (.1)^n$

a. _____

_____

b. _____

2. $\sum_{i=0}^{5} (3i - 4)$

a. _____

_____

b. _____

In 3 and 4, rewrite the series using Σ-notation.

3. $1 - 4 + 9 - 16 + 25 - 36 + 49$

4. $-8 - 6 - 4 - 2 - 0 + 2 + 4 + 6 + 8$

_____

_____

In 5 and 6, evaluate the expression.

5. $8!$ _____

6. $\dfrac{12!}{9!}$ _____

In 7 and 8, consider the four digits 1, 2, 3, and 4.

7. **a.** List all permutations of these digits.

b. How many permutations of four
different digits are possible? _____

8. How many four-digit numbers can be
created with a 3 as the first digit? _____

Uses Objective H

9. How many different baseball line-ups can
be made with a 9-person baseball team? _____

10. How many different ways can 7 books
be placed on a shelf? _____

LESSON MASTER **13-4**
A

Skills Objective I

In 1 and 2, a set of grades is given. a. Find the mean.
b. Find the median c. Find the mode.

1. 71, 72, 74, 85, 85, 93

2. 91, 85, 87, 82, 94, 86, 87, 85

a. _____

a. _____

b. _____

b. _____

c. _____

c. _____

3. Data set $A = \{10, 20, 30, 30, 40, 50\}$ and data set
$B = \{28, 29, 30, 30, 31, 32\}$. Both sets have the same
mean, median, and mode.

   a. Calculate the standard deviation of set A.   _____

   b. Calculate the standard deviation of set B.   _____

   c. *Multiple choice.* Set $C = \{29, 29, 30, 30, 30, 32\}$.
   This set has the same mean, median, and mode as
   sets A and B. Which phrase best describes the
   standard deviation of set C?   _____

   (a) greater than the standard deviation of set A and set B

   (b) less than the standard deviation of set A and set B

   (c) greater than the standard deviation of set A and less
        than the standard deviation of set B

   (d) greater than the standard deviation of set B and less
        than the standard deviation of set A

4. The 1994 Statistical Abstract of the United States lists the
following data regarding cigarette-smoking habits of people
in the U.S. who are 18 years of age or older.

Year	1965	1974	1979	1983	1985	1988	1991
% of population that smokes	42.4	37.1	33.5	32.1	30.1	28.1	25.6

   a. Find the mean, median, and standard deviation of the smoking
   habits of adults in the United States for these data.

   mean _____   med. _____   st. dev. _____

   b. Which of these measures *best* describes the data? Why?

   _____

   _____

LESSON MASTER

13-5 A

Skills Objective D

In 1–8, evaluate.

1. $\binom{7}{2}$ _____

2. $\binom{6}{4}$ _____

3. $\binom{11}{1}$ _____

4. $\binom{35}{0}$ _____

5. $\binom{12}{11}$ _____

6. $\binom{8}{5}$ _____

7. $\binom{10}{10}$ _____

8. $\binom{3}{n}$ _____

Properties Objective F

9. Rows 0 to 2 of Pascal's triangle are given below. Write the next 6 rows.

$$1$$ row 0

$$1 \quad 1$$ row 1

$$1 \quad 2 \quad 1$$ row 2

_____ row 3

_____ row 4

_____ row 5

_____ row 6

_____ row 7

_____ row 8

In 10–12, use your work above to evaluate the expressions.

10. $\binom{6}{1}$ _____

11. $\binom{8}{0}$ _____

12. $\binom{5}{2}$ _____

13. $\binom{16}{3}$ represents the _____ element in the _____ row.

14. Verify that for $n = 6$, $\binom{n}{3} + \binom{n}{4} = \binom{n+1}{4}$.

_____

15. Row 10 of Pascal's Triangle is: 1, 10, 45, 120, 210, 252, 210, 120, 45, 10, 1. Write 45 two different ways using $\binom{n}{r}$ notation. _____

In 16–18, true or false.

16. $8 \cdot 7! = 8!$

17. $\binom{65}{10} = \binom{65}{55}$

18. $\binom{n}{n} = 1$ for all positive integers n

_____   _____   _____

LESSON MASTER **13-6 A**

Skills Objective E

1. Fill in the blanks to expand the binomial $(3m + 2n^2)^5$.
   Let $a = 3m$ and $b = 2n^2$.

   a. First, fill in the coefficients.

   $(a + b)^5 = ($ $)a^5 + ($ $)a^4b + ($ $)a^3b^2 + ($ $)a^2b^3 + ($ $)ab^4 + ($ $)b^5$

   b. Now substitute the values for a and b. $(3m + 2n^2)^5 =$

   _____

   c. Simplify.

   _____

In 2–5, expand the binomial.

2. $(x^2 + 1)^8$ _____

   _____

3. $(3c - 5)^3$ _____

4. $(x^3 - y)^4$ _____

5. $(\frac{1}{2} + 2d)^4$ _____

6. **a.** Use the first three terms of the binomial
   expansion of $(1 + .03)^8$ to estimate $(1.03)^8$. _____

   b. Find $(1.03)^8$ using a calculator. Do you think the answer in
   Part **a** is an acceptable estimate? Why or why not?

   _____

   _____

In 7–9, convert to an expression in the form $(a + b)^n$.

7. $\sum_{r=0}^{n} \binom{n}{r}x^{n-r}4^r$ 8. $\sum_{r=0}^{n} \binom{n}{r}(2t)^{n-r}(-u)^r$ 9. $\sum_{t=0}^{n} \binom{n}{t}z^{n-t}\left(\frac{w}{2}\right)^n$

_____   _____   _____

Uses Objective F

10. Which entry in Pascal's triangle is the coefficient
    of a^4b^2 in the binomial expansion of $(a + b)^6$? _____

LESSON MASTER

13-7
A

Questions on SPUR Objectives
See pages 880-883 for objectives.

Skills Objective D

1. *Multiple choice.* Which is *not* a subset of {P, E, A, R}? _____

   (a) {A, E, R}   (b) {   }

   (c) {P, E, T, R}   (d) {R, E, A, P}

2. **a.** How many subsets of {P, E, A, R}
   have 3 elements? _____

   b. List the subsets with 3 elements.

   _____

3. Suppose a set has 9 elements. What does $\binom{9}{3}$ represent?

   _____

   _____

Properties Objective F

In 4–6, *true or false.* **If true, verify the statement.**
If false, rewrite so that the statement is true.

4. $\binom{6}{0} + \binom{6}{1} + \binom{6}{2} + \binom{6}{3} + \binom{6}{4} + \binom{6}{5} + \binom{6}{6}$ equals the
   total number of subsets of a set with 7 elements.

   _____

5. $\binom{6}{0} + \binom{6}{1} + \binom{6}{2} + \binom{6}{3} + \binom{6}{4} + \binom{6}{5} + \binom{6}{6} = 2^6$

   _____

6. $\binom{6}{0} + \binom{6}{1} + \binom{6}{2} + \binom{6}{3} + \binom{6}{4} + \binom{6}{5} + \binom{6}{6}$ equals the
   sum of row 7 of Pascal's triangle.

   _____

7. What does the symbol $_8C_4$ represent?

   _____

   _____

► **LESSON MASTER 13-7 A** *page 2*

8. *Multiple choice.* Which equation is correct?   _____

   (a) $_9C_7 = \binom{9}{7}$ (b) $_7C_9 = \binom{9}{7}$ (c) $_9C_7 = 7^9$ (d) $_7C_9 = 7^9$

9. **a.** Evaluate $_5C_0 + {_5C_1} + {_5C_2} + {_5C_3} + {_5C_4} + {_5C_5}$.   _____

   b. What does this have to do with Pascal's triangle?

   _____

Uses Objective H

In 10 and 11, use this information: Sam has a collection of 16 compact discs, five of which are by the group *MATH-MANIA*.

10. How many different ways can Sam choose 6 CDs from all the discs in his collection?   _____

11. How many mini-collections of 3 CDs could be formed from the *MATH-MANIA* CDs?   _____

In 12–14, use this information: Julie has an extensive stamp collection with 10 particulary valuable stamps from Mexico and 8 from Spain.

12. Write an expression to show how many ways she can choose 10 of these stamps.   _____

13. **a.** How many possible displays of at least one stamp can be made up entirely of Spanish stamps?   _____

   b. How many possible displays of at least one stamp can be made up entirely of Mexican stamps?   _____

14. How many possible displays of five stamps can be made with 2 Spanish and 3 Mexican stamps?   _____

LESSON MASTER 13-8 A

Vocabulary

1. Define *independent events.*

   _____

   _____

2. Define *mutually-exclusive events.*

   _____

   _____

3. Explain the difference between a *trial* and an *experiment.*

   _____

   _____

Uses Objective J

In 4–7, a coin with $P(H) = .8$ is tossed four times.

4. **a.** Calculate the probability of 0 tails.   _____

   b. Calculate the probability of exactly 1 tail.   _____

   c. Calculate the probability of exactly 2 tails.   _____

   d. Calculate the probability of exactly 3 tails.   _____

   e. Calculate the probability of exactly 4 tails.   _____

5. In Question 4, which events are mutually exclusive? Explain.

   _____

   _____

6. **a.** What is the probability of getting at least 2 tails? _____

   b. What is the probability of getting at most 2 tails? _____

7. Are the events in 6a and 6b mutually exclusive?
   Why or why not?

   _____

   _____

▶ **LESSON MASTER 13-8 A** *page 2*

In 8–10, consider this situation: You answer each item on a true-false test by guessing. The probability of correctly answering each question is 0.6.

a. Write the expression to calculate the probability of the given event. b. Calculate the probability of the event.

8. 8 questions, 5 correct.

   a. _____

   b. _____

9. 8 questions, at least 5 correct.

   a. _____

   b. _____

10. Suppose you answer 2 questions correctly on an 8-item test. What is the probability you will now get at least 5 correct?

   a. _____

   b. _____

11. Suppose a fair coin is tossed 9 times. Give the probability of each event.

   a. exactly 3 heads   b. exactly 4 tails.

   _____   _____

12. Suppose a fair coin is tossed *n* times.

   a. How many different ways can *r* heads occur? _____

   b. How many different combinations of heads and tails are possible? _____

   c. What is the probability that *r* of *n* times a head will occur? _____

ADVANCED ALGEBRA © Scott, Foresman and Company

LESSON MASTER

13-9
A

Uses Objective J

1. In Washington State's Daily Game, players select a
3-digit number using any combinations of 0 through 9.

   a. What is the probability of winning the
   jackpot by matching all three digits? _____

   b. What are the odds against winning the jackpot? _____

   c. If the Daily game costs $1 to play, and the jackpot is worth
   $500, does the State of Washington gain money, lose money,
   or break even in the long run? Explain your reasoning.

   _____

   _____

2. In Minnesota's GOPHER 5 game, 5 balls are chosen from
balls numbered 1–39. You can win prizes for matching 3 of
the 5 balls and 4 of the 5 balls.

   a. What is the probability of picking exactly
   3 of the 5 winning numbers? _____

   b. What are the odds against picking exactly
   4 of the 5 winning numbers? _____

   c. Minnesota clains that the *odds on* picking 4 of the 5 wining
   numbers are 1:3386.8. Do *odds on* and *odds against* have
   the same meaning? Explain your reasoning.

   _____

   _____

3. Suppose you wanted to create a Lotto game called *Easy-Does-It*.
The entrant would choose 10 numbers from 1–75.

   a. What is the probability of matching 5 out
   of 10 numbers? _____

   b. What is the probability of matching 8 out
   of 10 numbers? _____

   c. How much would you pay out for someone who matched
   9 out of 10 numbers? Explain how you arrived at this amount.

   _____

   _____

   _____

ADVANCED ALGEBRA © Scott, Foresman and Company

LESSON MASTER

Uses Objective I

**In 1–3, ACT scores range from 1–36 with a mean
near 21 and a standard deviation near 5. Assume
the scores are normally distributed.**

1. About what percent of students have a score

   a. below 21?   **b.** above 26?   **c.** below 11?

   _____   _____   _____

2. Within what interval of scores would you expect the
   top 16% of the students to be?   _____

3. What percent of students should have scores between
   16 and 31?   _____

Representations Objective L

In 4 and 5, consider the function P with $P(n) = \dfrac{\binom{8}{n}}{2^8}$.

4. Graph P.

5. What name is given to P?

   _____

   _____

   _____

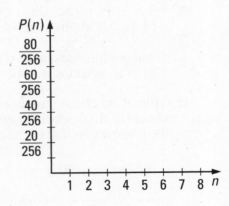

**In 6–8, consider normally distributed
data with mean 20 and standard
deviation 4 as pictured at the right.**

6. About what percent of the
   data are greater than 16?

   _____

7. About what percent of the data are between 12 and 24?

   _____

8. **a.** Shade the portions of the graph representing data
      more than two standard deviations away from 20.

   b. About what percent of the graph should be shaded? _____

LESSON MASTER

13-11
A

Uses Objective K

In 1 and 2, suppose a company manufactures
thermometers in lots of 2500. To ensure the
quality of each lot, the company randomly
selects 5% of the thermometers from each lot
and tests them for accuracy.

1. What is the population size in this situation? _____

2. What is the sample size in this situation? _____

3. The Marketing Director at a local TV station wants to
   conduct a viewing-audience poll in order to convince
   a video-game manufacturer to buy advertising time
   during certain programs. What type of sampling should
   be used? Explain your answer.

   _____

   _____

   _____

In 4 and 5, suppose in an experiment a six-sided
die thought to be fair is thrown 720 times and that
this experiment is repeated many times.

4. The mean number of times a 3 should appear in such samples is

   _____ and the standard deviation is _____ .

5. This implies that 95% of the time, from _____ to

   _____ 3s should appear.

6. Suppose a particular TV show has a rating of 10, and
   a random sample of 2000 households with televisions
   is polled.

   a. What should be the mean number of people
      tuned to this particular show for a sample
      of this size? _____

   b. 68% of the time the number of people tuned
      in to this show should be within what interval? _____

LESSON MASTER 1-1 A

Questions on SPUR Objectives
See pages 66–69 for objectives.

Vocabulary

1. Name all the *variables* in $\pi r^2 h$. — r, h

2. Give an example of a sentence that is an *equation* but not a *formula*. — Sample: $3x + 5y = 8$

Skills Objective A

3. The formula for the surface area of a sphere is $A = 4\pi r^2$. Find the surface area if $r = 5$m. — 100π m²

4. In the formula $E = \frac{1}{2}mv^2$, find E if $m = 4$ kg and $v = 9\frac{m}{s}$. — $162\ \frac{kg \cdot m^2}{s^2}$

In 5–7, evaluate the expression $4n^3 + 3n - \frac{1}{2}$ for the given value.

5. $n = 3$ — $116\frac{1}{2}$ 6. $n = -4$ — $-268\frac{1}{2}$ 7. $n = \frac{1}{2}$ — $1\frac{1}{2}$

8. To evaluate $30 \div 2 \cdot 5$, Martina stated that the first step was $2 \cdot 5$. Do you agree with Martina? Why or why not?
Sample: No; multiplication and division should be done in order from left to right.

9. Evaluate $5 \cdot 8 - 3^4 + 24 \div 4$. — -35

Uses Objective I

10. Ruby drove M miles in h hours. Write an expression for her average speed. — $\frac{M}{h}$ mph

11. An airplane is traveling at P miles per hour. Write an expression for the distance the airplane travels in t hours. — Pt miles

12. In the downtown area of a city are G parking garages, each accommodating c cars, and S street parking spots, each accommodating one car. How many cars can be parked in the downtown area? — $cG + S$ cars

13. R ounces of juice sell for c cents. What is the price of one ounce of juice? — $\frac{c}{R}$ cents

ADVANCED ALGEBRA © Scott, Foresman and Company

LESSON MASTER 1-2 A

Questions on SPUR Objectives
See pages 66–69 for objectives.

Vocabulary

1. The equation $h = 2t$ gives the number of inches h of new snow after t hours if snow falls during a storm at the rate of 2 inches per hour. Identify the *independent* and *dependent* variables.
independent: t; dependent: h

In 2–4, give an example of a number satisfying the given conditions.

2. an integer that is *not* a natural number — Sample: -2

3. a real number that is *not* an integer — Sample: 0.9

4. an integer that is *not* a real number — not possible

Skills Objective A

5. Evaluate the function $p = \frac{4y}{y^2 - 3}$ if the independent variable has a value of 5. — $\frac{10}{11}$

6. Evaluate $t = 450(3)^n$ when $n = 4$. — 36,450

Properties Objective G

7. Determine whether or not the table below describes r as a function of s. Justify your answer.

s	1	1	2	2	3	3
r	3	-3	6	-6	9	-9

Sample: No; each s-value is not paired with exactly one r-value.

ADVANCED ALGEBRA © Scott, Foresman and Company

▶ **LESSON MASTER 1-2 A** *page 2*

8. The table at the right gives the high school enrollment, in millions, in the United States from 1985 to 1991. Is the female enrollment a function of the year? Explain your answer.

Year	Male	Female
1985	7.2	6.9
1986	7.2	7.0
1987	7.0	6.8
1988	6.7	6.4
1989	6.6	6.3
1990	6.5	6.4
1991	6.8	6.4

Sample: yes; each year is paired with exactly one female enrollment figure.

Properties Objective H

9. If y is a function of x, what real numbers are *not* in the domain of $y = \frac{1}{x^2 - 64}$? — 8, -8

In 10 and 11, identify the domain and the range for the function.

10. $\{(2, 4), (7, 11), (9, 13), (8, -4)\}$
Domain $\{2, 7, 8, 9\}$ Range $\{-4, 4, 11, 13\}$

11. $y = x^4 - 3$
Domain all real numbers   Range $\{y: y \geq -3\}$

Uses Objective J

12. The volume of a sphere is given by $V = \frac{4}{3}\pi r^3$. How much air does it take to blow up a beach ball to a radius of 8 inches? — ≈ 2145 in³

13. Near the surface of Jupiter, the distance d that an object falls in t seconds is given by $d = \frac{1}{2}gt^2$, where $g = 84.48\ \frac{ft}{sec^2}$. Find the distance an object falls in 3 seconds. — 380.16 ft

14. Sara recently bought a house. She made a down payment of $10,600 and will make payments of $369.35 each month.
   a. Write a formula that gives the total amount p she has paid as a function of the number of months n she has been making her payments. — $p = 10,600 + 369.35n$
   b. Find the total amount she will pay if she pays the house off in 15 years. — $77,083

ADVANCED ALGEBRA © Scott, Foresman and Company

LESSON MASTER 1-3 A

Questions on SPUR Objectives
See pages 66–69 for objectives.

Vocabulary

In 1 and 2, use the function g defined by $g(p) = p^4 + 1$.

1. Identify the *argument* of the function. — p

2. Rewrite the function in *mapping notation*. — $g: p \to p^4 + 1$

Skills Objective B

In 3–5, let function r be defined by $r(x) = 3x^2 - 5$.

3. Find $r(7)$. — 142   4. Find $r(\pi)$. — $3\pi^2 - 5$ 5. Find $r(c)$. — $3c^2 - 5$

6. Consider the function d defined by $dn \to \frac{1}{2}n^3 + \frac{1}{3}n^2$. Then $d: -4 \to \underline{\ ?\ }$. — $-26\frac{2}{3}$

7. Let the table define function s.

a	0	1	2	3	4
$s(a)$	3	7	14	15	19

Evaluate $s(4) - s(1)$. — 12

Uses Objective J

In 8–10, $C(x)$ is the number of cellular-phone subscribers, in thousands, in the United States in year x.

x	1984	1985	1986	1987	1988	1989	1990	1991
$C(x)$	92	340	682	1231	2069	3509	5283	7557

8. a. Find $C(1986)$. — 682
   b. Tell in words what $C(1986)$ means. — Number of cellular-phone subscribers in 1986

9. Calculate $C(1991) - C(1984)$. — 7465

10. a. Calculate $\frac{C(1990) - C(1985)}{1990 - 1985}$. — 988.6
    b. Tell in words what the calculation in Part a represents. — Average increase in cellular-phone subscribers per year from 1985 to 1990.

11. Marlene makes $4.75 an hour. The function P, defined by $P(h) = 4.75h$, gives her gross pay as a function of the number of hours worked, h. Find Marlene's gross pay when she works 15 hours in one week. — $71.25

ADVANCED ALGEBRA © Scott, Foresman and Company

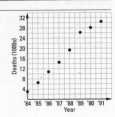

LESSON MASTER 1-4 A

Questions on SPUR Objectives
See pages 66–69 for objectives.

Uses Objective J

1. The graph at the right gives the number of deaths due to AIDS from 1984 to 1991 in the U.S.

   a. If $D(x)$ represents the number of deaths in year x, estimate $D(1988)$.

   ≈ 20,000

   b. Estimate $D(1991) - D(1990)$ and write a sentence that describes what this result means.

   Sample: ≈ 3,000; the number of AIDS deaths increased by about 3,000 from 1990 to 1991.

Representations Objective L

In 2 and 3, a function is graphed.

2.

   a. Give the range. $\{y: 0 \leq y \leq 3\}$

   b. Give the domain. $\{x: -2 \leq x \leq 2\}$

   c. For what values of x is $f(x) = 0$?   -2, 2

3.

   a. Give the range. $\{2\}$

   b. Give the domain.   all reals

   c. Find $g(-3)$.   2

5 ▶

▶ **LESSON MASTER 1-4 A** *page 2*

Representations Objective M

In 4–7, determine whether or not the graph represents a function. How can you tell?

4.

No; each x-value is not paired with exactly one y-value.

5.

Yes; each x-value is paired with exactly one y-value.

6.

Yes; each x-value is paired with exactly one y-value.

7.

No; each x-value is not paired with exactly one y-value.

8. Explain why a horizontal line can be the graph of a function, but a vertical line cannot.

Sample: Each x-value on a horizontal line is paired with exactly one y-value; each x-value on a vertical line is paired with an infinite number of y-values.

6

LESSON MASTER 1-5 A

Questions on SPUR Objectives
See pages 66–69 for objectives.

Skills Objective C

In 1–4, solve and check the equation. **Checks are not shown.**

1. $\frac{3}{5}x = 12$

   $x = 20$

2. $\frac{3}{4} = \frac{2}{3}(z - 15)$

   $z = \frac{129}{8}$, or $16\frac{1}{8}$

3. $\frac{1}{2}x + \frac{1}{4}x + \frac{1}{8}x = 84$

   $x = 96$

4. $.03(2000 - y) + .05y = 90$

   $y = 1500$

5. Suppose $h(x) = \frac{4}{3}x + 9$. For what value of x is $h(x) = 65$?

   $x = 42$

Uses Objective K

6. Devin plans to drive from Tampa to Chicago, roughly 1240 miles. At 60 miles an hour, $d(h) = 1240 - 60h$ gives his distance from Chicago after h hours of driving.

   a. How far is Devin from Chicago after 10 hours of driving?   **640 miles**

   b. About how long has Devin driven when he is 490 miles from Chicago?   **12$\frac{1}{2}$ hours**

7. When Ms. Jones's students asked her age, she gave them the following problem to solve: "I spent $\frac{1}{8}$ of my life before entering school, $\frac{3}{10}$ of my life in elementary and secondary schools, and $\frac{1}{5}$ of my life in college and graduate school. Since completing my degrees, I have been teaching 15 years." How old is Ms. Jones?   **40 years**

8. For electrical service, Lynne pays a fixed cost of $8.12 a month plus a charge for electricity used. If $k =$ the number of kilowatts of electricity used, then $C(k) = 8.12 + .07k$ represents the amount of her bill.

   a. Find the amount of Lynne's bill if she used 1000 kilowatts during the month.   **$78.12**

   b. If her November bill was $200.62, how much electricity was used during the month?   **2750 kw**

7

LESSON MASTER 1-6 A

Questions on SPUR Objectives
See pages 66–69 for objectives.

Skills Objective D

In 1 and 2, use the formula $w = \frac{v}{r}$, which gives the angular velocity w for an object traveling at a velocity v along a circle with radius r.

1. Solve this formula for r. $r = \frac{v}{w}$

2. Solve this formula for v. $v = rw$

3. The formula $F = ma$ describes the force on an object with mass m and acceleration a. Solve this equation for m. $m = \frac{F}{a}$

4. a. Solve $r = a + (n - 1)d$ for d. $d = \frac{r - a}{n - 1}$

   b. Use your result in Part a to find the value of d when $r = 15$, $a = -6$, and $n = 4$. $d = 7$

5. Solve the formula $r = 2p + ps$ for p. $p = \frac{r}{2 + s}$

6. The current I, in amps, needed to operate an electrical appliance is given by the formula $I = \frac{P}{V}$, where P is the power in watts and V is the voltage in volts.

   a. Solve this formula for the power. $P = IV$

   b. How many watts of power are needed by a slow cooker that uses 1.5 amps of current and runs on 115 volts?   **172.5 watts**

7. The volume V of a pyramid is given by $V = \frac{1}{3}Bh$, where B is the area of the base and h is the altitude. Solve this formula for Bh. $Bh = 3V$

Uses Objective K

8. When engineers design and build roads, they must allow for expansion so that the road does not buckle and crack. The formula $I = k\ell(T - t)$ gives the expansion I (in feet) that should be allowed for a road of length ℓ (in feet), at a temperature T (in Fahrenheit) if the road were built at temperature t. (k is a constant.)

   a. Solve this formula for T. $T = \frac{I}{k\ell} + t$

   b. Find the temperature on a day when a 1 mile (5280 ft) stretch of road built at 65° expands 0.5 feet. Use $k = .000012$.   **≈ 73°F**

8

Name _____

Vocabulary

1. Write the notation for "s sub 4 equals 81." $s_4 = 81$

2. Write the notation for the eighteenth term of a sequence p. p_{18}

3. Tell how the equation "$r_3 = -7$" should be read.
r sub three equals negative seven.

Skills Objective E

4. Give the first 6 terms of the sequence defined by the formula $b_n = 3n^2 + 1$. **4, 13, 28, 49, 76, 109**

5. If $p_n = 4^{n-1}$, find p_7. $p_7 = 4096$

6. a. Draw the next term in the sequence.

   b. Give a formula for T_n, the number of dots in the nth term. $T_n = n(n + 2)$

7. Write the third, fourth and fifth terms of the sequence whose explicit formula is $a_n = \frac{n+1}{n+2}$. $\frac{4}{5}$ $\frac{5}{6}$ $\frac{6}{7}$

8. *Multiple choice.* Which is an explicit formula for the nth term of the sequence 3, 6, 11, 18, 27, … ? **c**

   (a) $t_n = 3n$ (b) $t_n = 2n + 2$ (c) $t_n = n^2 + 2$

Uses Objective J

9. At the end of each week at a discount store, the price of all remaining items is reduced 10%. So after week n, the price of a $60 jacket is given by $p_n = 60(.9)^n$. Find the price of the jacket after 3 weeks if it remains unsold. **$43.74**

10. A group of students took a bike trip across the country, averaging 60 miles of riding each day. The sequence $d_n = 60n$ gives the distance they have biked after n days. How far has the group biked after 7 days? **420 miles**

Name _____

Skills Objective E

In 1–3, write the first six terms of the sequence defined by the recursive formula.

1. The first term is -3; each term after the first is 7 less than the previous term.
-3, -10, -17, -24, -31, -38

2. $\begin{cases} a_1 = 9 \\ a_n = (3 \cdot \text{previous term}) + 11, \text{ for integers } n \geq 2. \end{cases}$
9, 38, 125, 386, 1169, 3518

3. $\begin{cases} s_1 = 1 \\ s_n = \boxed{\text{ANS}}^2 + 1, \text{ for integers } n \geq 2. \end{cases}$
1, 2, 5, 26, 677, 458,330

Skills Objective F

4. Consider the sequence 9, 7, 5, 3, … .
   a. Use words to describe this sequence recursively.
   The first term is 9; each succeeding term is 2 less than the previous term.

   b. Use symbols to write a recursive formula for the sequence. $\begin{cases} a_1 = 9 \\ a_n = \boxed{\text{ANS}} -2, \text{ for } n \geq 2. \end{cases}$

5. Consider the sequence defined explicitly as $t_n = 3n + 18$.
   a. Give the first six terms of the sequence.
   21, 24, 27, 30, 33, 36

   b. Write a recursive definition for the sequence. $\begin{cases} a_1 = 21 \\ a_n = \boxed{\text{ANS}} +3, \text{ for } n \geq 2. \end{cases}$

Uses Objective A

6. Debbie has 520 books in her library. Each year she buys an average of 50 new books.
   a. Write a recursive formula that gives the number of books b_n in Debbie's library in year n. $\begin{cases} b_1 = 520 \\ b_n = \text{previous term} + 50, \text{ for } n \geq 2. \end{cases}$

   b. How many books will Debbie have in her library ten years from now? **1020 books**

Name _____

Vocabulary

1. a. If t_n represents the nth term of a sequence, what notation is used to denote the previous term? t_{n-1}

   b. What notation denotes the term following t_n? t_{n+1}

2. With a sequence a, would you use an *explicit* formula or a *recursive* formula if you wanted to find a_{200}? Explain your choice.
Sample: Explicit formula; with a recursive formula, the first 199 terms would need to be determined; with an explicit formula, determining the 200th term would take one step.

Skills Objective A

3. Write the first four terms of the sequence defined by the following recursive formula.
$\begin{cases} w_1 = 81 \\ w_n = \frac{1}{3} w_{n-1} + 9, \text{ for integers } n \geq 2. \end{cases}$ **81, 36, 21, 16**

4. Find p_6 if $\begin{cases} p_1 = 3 \\ p_n = 5p_{n-1}, \text{ for integers } n \geq 2. \end{cases}$ $P_6 = 9375$

5. The formula $\begin{cases} a_1 = 1 \\ a_2 = 3 \\ a_n = 2a_{n-1} + a_{n-2}, \text{ for integers } n \geq 3 \end{cases}$ describes a sequence recursively. Find the first seven terms of this sequence.
1, 3, 7, 17, 41, 99, 239

Name _____

▶ **LESSON MASTER 1-9 A** *page 2*

Skills Objective F

6. Consider the sequence 7, 35, 175, 875, … .
   a. Describe this sequence recursively using words.
   The first term is 7; each succeeding term is 5 times the previous term.

   b. Write a recursive formula for this sequence. $\begin{cases} s_1 = 7 \\ s_n = 5 \cdot s_{n-1}, \text{ for } n \geq 2. \end{cases}$

7. Consider the sequence 1, 16, 81, 256, 625, … . Write an appropriate formula for the sequence. $a_n = n^4$

8. a. Write a recursive formula for the sequence -2, 6, 14, 22, … . $\begin{cases} e_1 = -2 \\ e_n = e_{n-1} + 8, \text{ for } n \geq 2. \end{cases}$

   b. *Multiple choice.* Which explicit formula also describes the sequence in Part a? **ii**

   (i) $t_n = (-2)^n$ (ii) $t_n = 8n - 10$ (iii) $t_n = -4n + 2$

Skills Objective A

9. A new company projects that its annual revenue will grow by roughly 10% each year. The company's projected annual revenue for the first year is $100,000.
   a. Let r_n be the company's projected annual revenue in year n. Find $r_1, r_2, r_3, r_4,$ and r_5.
$100,000; $110,000; $121,000; $133,100; $146,410

   b. Write a recursive formula for the sequence. $\begin{cases} r_1 = 100,000 \\ r_n = 1.1r_{n-1}, \text{ for } n \geq 2. \end{cases}$

   c. *Multiple choice.* Which of the following is an explicit formula for the sequence? **iii**

   (i) $t_n = 100,000(.1)^n$ (ii) $t_n = 100,000(1.1)^n$ (iii) $t_n = 100,000(1.1)^{n-1}$

   d. If you wanted to find the projected annual revenue in the company's fifteenth year, which formula, explicit or recursive, would you use? Explain your choice.
Sample: Explicit formula; 100,000 (1.1)^{14} is easily determined with a calculator.

LESSON MASTER 2-1 A

Skills Objective A

In 1–5, translate into a variation equation.
Let k be the constant of variation.

1. m varies directly as the fourth power of n.

$$m = kn^4$$

2. y is directly proportional to the fifth power of x.

$$y = kx^5$$

3. The height h of a cottonwood tree varies directly as the square of its circumference C.

$$h = kC^2$$

4. The distance d a star is from the earth is directly proportional to the length of time t it takes for its light to get here.

$$d = kt$$

5. The volume V of a cylinder with constant height varies directly as the square of the diameter d of its base.

$$V = kd^2$$

Skills Objective B

6. y varies directly as x. If $y = 8$ when $x = -3$, find y when $x = 16$.

$$y = -\frac{128}{3}, \text{ or } -42\frac{2}{3}$$

7. c is directly proportional to d^4. If $c = -13,824$ when $d = 12$, find c when $d = 6$.

$$c = -864$$

Uses Objective F

In 8 and 9, *true or false.*

8. The cost of filling a car's gas tank with gas varies directly as the volume of the tank.

true

9. The outdoor temperature varies directly as the time of day.

false

Uses Objective G

10. The number of volts across an electrical circuit with constant resistance varies directly as the strength of the current in amps. There are 500 volts across a circuit of 25 amps. What would be the voltage across a circuit of 60 amps?

1200 volts

11. The surface of a sphere is directly proportional to the square of its radius. The surface area of a sphere with radius 3 cm is 36π cm². What is the surface area of a sphere with radius 12 cm?

$$576\pi \text{ cm}^2$$

LESSON MASTER 2-2 A

Vocabulary

1. Explain how *direct* and *inverse variation* differ.

Sample: In direct variation, the constant is multiplied by a positive power of the independent variable; in inverse variation the constant is divided by a positive power of the independent variable.

Skills Objective A

In 2–6, translate into a variation equation.
Let k be the constant of variation.

2. y is inversely proportional to x.

$$y = k/x$$

3. F varies inversely with the square of r.

$$F = k/r^2$$

4. The gravitational pull F of the earth on a spaceship varies inversely as the square of the distance d of the spaceship from the earth.

$$F = k/d^2$$

5. In a spherical balloon with a constant mass of air, the pressure varies inversely as the cube of the radius.

$$p = k/r^3$$

6. In photography, the exposure E is inversely proportional to the square of the f-stop f.

$$E = k/f^2$$

7. Write the variation equation $y = \frac{k}{x^5}$ in words.

y varies inversely as the fifth power of x.

Skills Objective B

8. y varies inversely as the cube of x. If $y = 5$ when $x = 2$, find y when $x = 6$.

$$y = \frac{5}{27}$$

9. y varies inversely as the fourth power of x. If $y = 5$ when $x = \frac{1}{2}$, find y when $x = \frac{1}{3}$.

$$y = \frac{405}{16}, \text{ or } 25\frac{5}{16}$$

▶ **LESSON MASTER 2-2** A *page 2*

Uses Objective F

In 10–14, complete with "directly," "inversely," or "neither directly nor inversely."

10. The perimeter of a square varies ___?___ as the length of the side.

directly

11. A telephone bill varies ___?___ as the number of telephone calls made.

neither

12. The temperature in a house varies ___?___ as the setting on the thermostat.

neither

13. The intensity of light from a lamp varies ___?___ as the square of the distance one sits from it.

inversely

14. The time required to fly from Charlotte to San Antonio varies ___?___ with the speed at which the airplane flies.

inversely

Uses Objective G

15. The length of an organ pipe varies inversely as its pitch. If the pipe is $5\frac{1}{3}$ ft long, its frequency is 96 cycles per second. What is the frequency of a pipe which is 8 ft long?

64 cycles/sec

16. The number of spans of steel needed to construct a bridge over a river varies inversely as the length of each span. If 10 spans are used, each span is 18 ft long. How long would each span be if 12 spans were used?

15 ft

17. The resistance in a certain electrical circuit varies inversely as the square of the current through it. The resistance of the circuit is 10 ohms when the current is 15 amps. What is the resistance in the circuit when the circuit is 20 amps?

5.625 ohms

18. The force needed to keep a car on the road varies inversely as the radius of the curve. It requires 1286 N of force to keep a 1000-kg car traveling at 50 km/hr from skidding on a curve of radius 150 m. How much force is necessary to keep the same car traveling at the same speed from skidding on a curve of radius 750 m?

$\approx$ 257 N

LESSON MASTER 2-3 A

Properties Objective D

In 1–4, suppose that in a variation problem the value of x is tripled. How is the value of y changed if

1. y varies directly as x?

y is tripled.

2. y varies inversely as x?

y is divided by 3.

3. y varies directly as x^2?

y is multiplied by 9.

4. y varies inversely as x^3?

y is divided by 27.

In 5–8, suppose that m varies directly as the fourth power of q. How does the value of m change if

5. q is doubled?

m is multiplied by 16.

6. q is quadrupled?

m is multiplied by 256.

7. q is multiplied by 6?

m is multiplied by 1296.

8. q is multiplied by $\frac{1}{3}$?

m is multiplied by $\frac{1}{81}$.

In 9–12, suppose that p varies inversely as the fifth power of n. How does the value of p change if

9. n is doubled?

p is divided by 32.

10. n is quadrupled?

p is divided by 1024.

11. n is multiplied by 6?

p is divided by 7776.

12. n is multiplied by $\frac{1}{3}$?

p is divided by $\frac{1}{243}$.

13. If $w = kz^n$ and z is multiplied by a constant c, what happens to w?

w is multiplied by c^n.

14. If $w = \frac{k}{z^n}$ and z is multiplied by a constant c, what happens to w?

w is divided by c^n.

LESSON MASTER 2-4 A

Skills Objective C

In 1–3, find the slope of the line through the two points.

1. (9, 12), (15, 21) $\dfrac{3}{2}$

2. (-3, 8), (-5, -7) $\dfrac{15}{2}$

3. (6.3, -7.1), (-7.1, 6.3) -1

Properties Objective E

4. The graph of the equation $y = 0.13x$ is a line with slope 0.13.

5. The graph of the equation $y = -17x$ is a line with slope -17.

Representations Objective I

In 6 and 7, graph the equation.

6. $y = \dfrac{2}{5}x$

7. $y = 4x$

Representations Objective J

8. Match each graph with its equation. The x- and y-axes have the same scale.

i. $y = 1.5x$
ii. $y = -1.5x$
iii. $y = \dfrac{2}{3}x$
iv. $y = -\dfrac{2}{3}x$

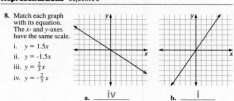

a. iv

b. i

LESSON MASTER 2-5 A

Skills Objective C

In 1 and 2, $y = 3x^2$.

1. Find the rate of change between $x = -2$ and $x = -1$. -9

2. Find the rate of change between $x = 1$ and $x = 2$. 9

In 3 and 4, $y = -8x^2$.

3. Find the rate of change between $x = 2$ and $x = 4$. -48

4. Find the rate of change between $x = 4$ and $x = 6$. -80

Properties Objective E

In 5 and 6, refer to the graphs of these equations.

(a) $y = 5x$ (b) $y = -5x$ (c) $y = 3x^2$ (d) $y = -7x^2$

5. Which graphs are parabolas? c, d

6. Which graphs are symmetric to the y-axis? c, d

Representations Objective I

In 7–10, graph the equation.

7. $y = 4x^2$

8. $y = -4x^2$

▶ **LESSON MASTER 2-5A** *page 2*

9. $y = \dfrac{1}{4}x^2$

10. $y = -\dfrac{1}{4}x^2$

Representations Objective J

Multiple choice. In 11 and 12, select the equation whose graph looks most like the one shown. Assume the scales on both axes are the same.

11.
(a) $y = 3.5x$
(b) $y = 3.5x^2$
(c) $y = -3.5x$
(d) $y = -3.5x^2$

d

12.
(a) $y = 5x$
(b) $y = -5x$
(c) $y = 5x^2$
(d) $y = -5x^2$

c

Representations Objective K

14. *Multiple choice.* Which of the following graphs could be the graph of the equation $y = -4x^2$? Explain why.

c; R is negative, so the graph opens down.

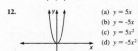

(a) $-1 \le x \le 1$, x-scale = 1
$-2 \le x \le 10$, y-scale = 5

(b) $-2 \le x \le 2$, x-scale = 1
$-1 \le y \le 4$, y-scale = 1

(c) $-2 \le x \le 2$, x-scale = 1
$-4 \le x \le 1$, y-scale = 1

LESSON MASTER 2-6 A

Skills Objective C

In 1–4, find the rate of change between $x = 3$ and $x = 4$.

1. $y = \dfrac{16}{x}$ $-\dfrac{4}{3}$

2. $y = \dfrac{16}{x^2}$ $-\dfrac{7}{9}$

3. $y = -\dfrac{16}{x}$ $\dfrac{4}{3}$

4. $y = -\dfrac{16}{x^2}$ $\dfrac{7}{9}$

Properties Objective E

In 5–8, refer to the graphs of these equations.

(a) $y = kx$ (b) $y = kx^2$ (c) $y = \dfrac{k}{x}$ (d) $y = \dfrac{k}{x^2}$

5. Which graphs have two symmetry lines? c

6. Which graphs have asymptotes? c, d

7. When $k < 0$, which graphs have some points in the first quadrant?   none

8. Which graphs are hyperbolas? c

Representations Objective I

In 9–12, graph the equation.

9. $y = \dfrac{24}{x}$

10. $y = -\dfrac{24}{x}$

11. $y = \dfrac{24}{x^2}$

12. $y = -\dfrac{24}{x^2}$

Representations Objective J

In 13–16, *multiple choice.* Select the equation whose graph is most like that shown.

13.

(a) $y = \dfrac{5}{x^2}$ (b) $y = 5x$

(c) $y = \dfrac{5}{x}$ (d) $y = 5x^2$

b

14.

(a) $y = -\dfrac{2}{x}$ (b) $y = 2x^2$

(c) $y = -\dfrac{2}{x^2}$ (d) $y = \dfrac{2}{x}$

d

15.

(a) $y = \dfrac{12}{x^2}$ (b) $y = -12x^2$

(c) $y = -\dfrac{12}{x^2}$ (d) $y = 12x^2$

c

16.

(a) $y = x^2$ (b) $y = -x^2$

(c) $y = \dfrac{1}{x^2}$ (d) $y = \dfrac{1}{x}$

b

17. In the graph of $y = \dfrac{k}{x^2}$ below, what type of number is k?

positive

18. In the graph of $y = \dfrac{k}{x}$ below, what type of number is k?

positive

Name _____

LESSON MASTER **2-7 A**

Questions on SPUR Objectives
See pages 134–137 for objectives.

Uses Objective H

In 1 and 2, do Steps a through d.
a. Draw a graph to represent the situation.
b. Write a general variation equation to represent the situation.
c. Find the value of the constant of variation and rewrite the variation equation.
d. Answer the question stated in the problem.

1. A science class investigated the relationship between the horizontal range an object would travel and the initial velocity at which it was shot. The object was shot at a constant angle of 40° to the ground. The class collected these data.

Velocity (m/s)	10	20	30	40	50	60
Range (m)	10	40	90	161	251	362

How far would the object travel if it were shot at 100 m/s?

a.
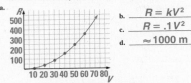

b. $R = kV^2$

c. $R = .1V^2$

d. ≈ 1000 m

2. A group studied the relationship between the resistance and the strength of the current in an electrical circuit. The power of the circuit remained constant. The group obtained these data.

Current (amps)	10	20	30	40	50
Resistance (ohms)	.150	.0375	.0167	.00938	.00600

What would the resistance be if the current were 75 amps?

a.
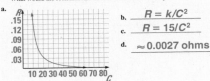

b. $R = k/C^2$

c. $R = 15/C^2$

d. ≈ 0.0027 ohms

Name _____

LESSON MASTER **2-8 A**

Questions on SPUR Objectives
See pages 134–137 for objectives.

Uses Objective H

1. An automotive engineer performed tests on a new tire to find the relationship between the air pressure P in pounds per square inch, the volume V in cubic inches, and the temperature T in degrees Kelvin. The engineer obtained the graph on the left by measuring pressure and volume when the temperature was 280°K. The graph on the right was obtained by measuring the pressure and the temperature when the volume was 2200 in³.

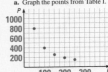

Write an equation relating P, V, and T. Do *not* find the constant of variation.

$P = \dfrac{kT}{V}$

2. Jeremy and Jenny performed an experiment to discover the relationship between the power of an electric light and the resistance in the circuit and the voltage supplied. They first collected the following data relating the power P and the resistance R on circuits with 2 volts.

I.
Resistance (ohms)	50	100	150	200	250
Power (watts)	800	400	267	200	160

Then they collected data when the resistance in the circuit was 200 ohms. These data relate the power P and the voltage V.

II.
Voltage (volts)	1	2	3	4	5
Power (watts)	50	200	450	800	1250

a. Graph the points from Table I.
b. Graph the points from Table II.

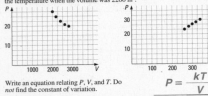

c. How does P vary with R? **inversely**

d. How does P vary with V? **directly**

e. Use the Converse of the Fundamental Theorem of Variation to write an equation relating P, R, and V. Do *not* find the constant of variation.

$P = \dfrac{kV^2}{R}$

Name _____

LESSON MASTER **2-9 A**

Questions on SPUR Objectives
See pages 134–137 for objectives.

Skills Objective A

In 1 and 2, translate into a variation equation.

1. The volume V of a rectangular prism varies jointly as its length L, its width W, and its height H.

$V = kLWH$

2. R varies directly as the square of P, directly as L, and inversely as the square root of A.

$R = \dfrac{kP^2L}{\sqrt{A}}$

In 3 and 4, write each variation equation in words.

3. $P = kIRT$

P varies jointly as *I*, *R*, and *T*.

4. $E = \dfrac{2(V_1 - V_0)}{X}$

E varies directly as $(V_1 - V_0)$ and inversely as *X*.

Skills Objective B

5. w varies directly as the square of x and inversely as y. When $x = 5$ and $y = 2$, $w = 23.75$. Find w when $x = -3$ and $y = -6$.

$w = -2.85$

6. z varies jointly as the square root of x and the cube of y. When $x = 9$ and $y = 2$, $z = 4$. Find z when $x = 25$ and $y = -5$.

$z = -\dfrac{625}{6}$, or $-104\frac{1}{6}$

Uses Objective G

7. The amount that a piece of copper wire 50 ft long stretches varies directly as the force applied to it and inversely as the cross-sectional area of the wire. When a 250-lb force is applied to a wire with cross-sectional area 0.0032 in², the wire stretches 1.08 in. How far would the wire stretch if a force of 300 lb were applied to a wire of cross-sectional area 0.005 in²?

$\approx .8294$ in.

8. The kinetic energy of an object varies jointly as its mass and the square of its velocity. The kinetic energy of an object with mass 12 kg moving at 8 m/s is 384 joules. Find the kinetic energy of an object with mass 8 kg moving at 12 m/s.

576 joules

LESSON MASTER 3-1 A

Vocabulary

1. Write the *slope-intercept* form of an equation of a line.

$y = mx + b$

Skills Objective A

In 2–4, complete the table.

Equation	Slope	*y*-intercept
2. $y = 5x + 2$	5	2
3. $y = -\frac{7}{3}x$	$-\frac{7}{3}$	0
4. $y = \frac{2}{3}x + \frac{1}{4}$	$\frac{2}{3}$	$\frac{1}{4}$

Properties Objective E

5. *True or false.* If $m > 0$, the equation $y = mx + b$ models a constant-decrease situation.

False

6. In the equation $y = mx + b$, the initial value of the dependent variable occurs when ___?___ .

$x = 0$

Uses Objective G

7. Dolores bought a box of 200 plastic garbage bags. She uses an average of 3 bags a week.

   a. Write an equation relating the number of bags b left after w weeks.

   $b = 200 - 3w$

   b. How many bags are left after 15 weeks?

   155 bags

   c. Will the box of bags last Dolores for an entire year? Justify your answer.

   Sample: Yes, since there are 52 weeks in a year, Dolores needs only 52·3, or 156 bags.

8. A postal container weighing 29 oz when empty is filled with letters averaging 4 oz each.

   a. Write an equation relating the total weight of the container w when it is filled with r letters.

   $w = 29 + 4r$

   b. Will 200 letters fit in the postal container without exceeding a 50-pound weight limit? Justify your answer.

   Sample; no; 50 pounds = 800 ounces, and 200 letters would give a weight of 829 ounces.

Uses Objective K

9. Graph this situation. The temperature in a freezer is initially 0.8°C. It rises at a rate of 0.2°C an hour over a period of 6 hours, after which it holds constant for 2 hours. It then falls at a rate of 0.5°C over a period of 6 hours.

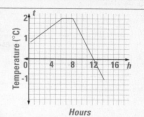

Hours

Representations Objective M

10. Refer to the graph below. Anita drove from school to her dentist's office, where she stayed 35 minutes, and then she drove home.

   a. How far is the dentist's office from Anita's school?

   12 miles

   b. How fast was Anita traveling on the last 4 miles of the trip to the dentist?

   24 mph

   c. How fast was Anita traveling on her trip from the dentist's office to her home?

   $\approx$ 27 mph

   d. What was the total distance Anita traveled? ____ 28 miles

---

LESSON MASTER 3-2 A

Skills Objective A

In 1–4, give the slope and the *y*-intercept of the line with the given equation.

1. $y = 7x - 2$

   7   -2

2. $4x + 5y = 11$

   $-\frac{4}{5}$ $\frac{11}{5}$

3. $y = -9$

   0   -9

4. $2x - y = 15$

   2   -15

Skills Objective B

In 5–7, write an equation for the line described.

5. line with slope $\frac{2}{5}$ and *y*-intercept 7

   $y = \frac{2}{5}x + 7$

6. horizontal line through (-8, 17)

   $y = 17$

7. line with *y*-intercept 6 and parallel to $y = -\frac{1}{2}x + \frac{3}{8}$

   $y = -\frac{1}{2}x + 6$

Properties Objective E

8. A line has a slope of $-\frac{4}{3}$. Fill in the blanks.

   a. As you move one unit to the right, it ___?___ $\frac{4}{3}$ units.

   drops

   b. As you move ___?___ units to the right, it drops ___?___ units.

   3   4

9. Give the domain and the range of the function f when $f(x) = 10$.

   all reals   {10}

Representations Objective L

In 10–13, on the grid at the right, graph the line described. Label each graph.

10. $y = \frac{2}{3}x + 3$

11. slope = -3 and *y*-intercept = 4

12. *y*-intercept = -3 and parallel to $y = \frac{1}{2}x + 16$

LESSON MASTER 3-3 A

Vocabulary

1. Write an expression that is a *linear combination* of R and S.

Sample: $2R + 5S$

Uses Objective H

2. In football, touchdowns are worth 6 points, extra points are worth 1 point, and field goals are worth 3 points. Suppose the Manatee Cougars earn T touchdowns, P extra points, and F field goals.

   a. Write an expression that gives the total number of points earned.

   $6T + P + 3F$

   b. Suppose the Cougars scored 44 points and had 3 field goals. If they made an extra point on each touchdown, how many touchdowns did they make?

   5 touchdowns

3. Ivan bought P pounds of peaches at 79¢ a pound and G pounds of grapes at $1.99 a pound.

   a. Write an expression that gives the amount Ivan paid for the peaches and the grapes.

   $0.79P + 1.99G$

   b. If he paid $7.55 and bought 3 pounds of grapes, how many pounds of peaches did he buy?

   2 pounds

4. A chemist mixed A ounces of a 30% chlorine solution with B ounces of 40% chlorine solution. The final mixture contained 18 ounces of chlorine.

   a. Write an equation to model this situation.

   $.3A + .4B = 18$

   b. Graph the solutions to the equation.

   c. Give three pairs of integer values for A and B that satisfy this equation.

   $A = 0$, $B = 45$ Samples
   $A = 20$, $B = 30$ are
   $A = 40$, $B = 15$ given.

   d. If 18.6 ounces of the 40% chlorine solution were used, how much of the 30% chlorine was used?

   35.2 ounces

5. Make up a problem leading to the expression $12.99P + 8.99T$.

   Sample: Alex bought P pairs of pants at $12.99 each and T shirts at $8.99 each.

LESSON MASTER 3-4 A

Questions on SPUR Objectives
See pages 197-201 for objectives.

Skills Objective A

In 1–4, complete the table. All equations should be in standard form with integers for A, B, and C.

	Equation	Slope	y-intercept	x-intercept
1.	$2x + 5y = 20$	$-\frac{2}{5}$	4	10
2.	$4x + 3y = 21$	$-\frac{4}{3}$	7	$\frac{21}{4}$
3.	$y = 12$	0	12	none

Properties Objective E

In 4–6, determine whether each line is *oblique*, *horizontal*, or *vertical*.

4. $12y = 18$ __horizontal__

5. $4x + 9y = 27$ __oblique__

6. $-7x = 21$ __vertical__

7. Identify the domain and the range of $y = 3x + 2$. __all reals__ __all reals__

8. For what values of A, B, and C is $Ax + By = C$ a horizontal line? __$A = 0$, $B \neq 0$, $C =$ a real number__

Representations Objective L

9. Graph $5x = 30$.

10. Use intercepts to graph $3x + 5y = 30$.

In 11–13, tell whether the slope of the line graphed is *positive, negative, zero,* or *undefined*.

11.

__zero__

12.

__negative__

13.
__undefined__

29

LESSON MASTER 3-5 A

Questions on SPUR Objectives
See pages 197-201 for objectives.

Skills Objective B

In 1–7, write an equation for the given line in standard form with integers for A, B, and C.

1. slope $\frac{7}{3}$, through (-2, 9) __$7x - 5y = -59$__

2. slope -4, through (8, 11) __$4x + y = 43$__

3. through (12, 7) and (-4, 5) __$x - 8y = -44$__

4. through (6, 8), parallel to $3x + y = 9$ __$3x + y = 26$__

5. through (5, 6), y-intercept -2 __$8x - 5y = 10$__

6. x-intercept 10, parallel to $3x - 2y = 5$ __$3x - 2y = 30$__

7. through (15, 20) with undefined slope __$x = 15$__

Properties Objective E

In 8 and 9, *true* or *false*. Justify your answer.

8. The point (7, 2) lies on the line with equation $y - 7 = 3(x - 2)$. __false; the point does not satisfy the equation.__

9. A line parallel to $8x = 9$ has a slope of 0. __false; a line parallel to $8x = 9$ is vertical with slope undefined.__

Uses Objectives I and K

10. The cost of installation for 10 windows is $800 and for 12 windows is $1000. Assume the relationship between the cost of installation and the number of windows is linear.

a. Write an equation for the relationship. Let the number of windows w be the independent variable. __$cost = 100w - 200$__

b. Find the cost to install 20 windows. __$1800__

11. A caterer charges $150 as a basic set-up fee. For the first 75 people, the charge is $2.50 per guest. For each additional guest, the charge is $2.

a. Find the cost for the following number of guests.

i. 30 __$225__　　ii. 75 __$337.50__

iii. 76 __$339.50__　　iv. 100 __$387.50__

b. What equation gives the cost for n guests, where $0 < n \leq 75$? __$c = 150 + 2.5n$__

c. What equation gives the cost for n guests, where $n > 75$? __$c = 187.50 + 2n$__

30

LESSON MASTER 3-6 A

Questions on SPUR Objectives
See pages 197-201 for objectives.

Uses Objective J

1. The following data list pizza prices as a function of the diameter.

Diameter	Price
6"	$ 1.50
8"	$ 3.50
12"	$ 6.95
16"	$ 9.95
18"	$11.50

__Sample equations are given for 1b and 2b.__

a. Draw a scatterplot of these data.

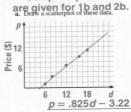

b. Write an equation for the regression line. __$p = .825d - 3.22$__

c. Interpret the strength of the linear relationship based on the correlation coefficient. __Sample: $r = .9989$, so the relationship is nearly perfect.__

d. Draw the graph of the regression line on your scatterplot.

2. The following data give the number of international travelers (in thousands) to the United States from 1985 through 1992.

Year Since 1985	Number of Travelers
0	25,399
1	26,008
2	29,424
3	34,095
4	36,564
5	39,539
6	42,909
7	45,405

a. Draw a scatterplot of these data.

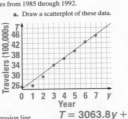

b. Write an equation for the regression line. __$T = 3063.8y + 24,194.5$__

c. Draw the graph of the regression line on your scatterplot.

d. According to your regression equation, how many international travelers to the United States would be expected in the year 2000? __$\approx 70,151,000$ trav.__

31

LESSON MASTER 3-7 A

Questions on SPUR Objectives
See pages 197-201 for objectives.

Vocabulary

1. In your own words, define *arithmetic sequence*. __Sample: A sequence with a constant difference between consecutive terms__

Skills Objective D

2. Use the arithmetic sequence 0.5, 0.75, 1.00, 1.25, ...

a. Describe this sequence in words. __Arithmetic sequence with first term 0.5, constant difference 0.25__

b. Write a recursive definition for this sequence. $\begin{cases} a_1 = 0.5 \\ a_n = a_{n-1} + 0.25, \text{ for } n \geq 2 \end{cases}$

3. An arithmetic sequence has first term 6 and constant difference 4.

a. Write the first 5 terms of the sequence. __6, 10, 14, 18, 22__

b. Write a recursive definition for the sequence. $\begin{cases} a_1 = 6 \\ a_n = a_{n-1} + 4, \text{ for } n \geq 2 \end{cases}$

Properties Objective F

4. A sequence is defined recursively as $\begin{cases} a_1 = 12 \\ a_n = a_{n-1} - 3, \end{cases}$ for integers $n \geq 2$.

a. Find the first 7 terms of this sequence. __12, 9, 6, 3, 0, -3, -6__

b. Is the sequence arithmetic? Justify your answer. __Sample: Yes; it has a constant difference of -3.__

5. Is the sequence 9, 27, 81, 243, . . . arithmetic? Justify your answer. __Sample: No; there is no constant difference.__

Uses Objective G

6. Pak bought a pound of coffee beans. Each morning she uses $\frac{3}{4}$ ounce to brew coffee.

a. How many ounces of coffee beans does she have left after the first morning? __$15\frac{1}{4}$ ounces__

b. Write a recursive definition for the amount of coffee beans left after n mornings. $\begin{cases} a_1 = 15\frac{1}{4} \\ a_n = a_{n-1} - \frac{3}{4}, \text{ for } n \geq 2. \end{cases}$

32

LESSON MASTER 3-8 A

Questions on SPUR Objectives
See pages 197-201 for objectives.

Skills Objective D

In 1 and 2, an arithmetic sequence is given.
a. Write a formula for the *n*th term. b. Find a_{200}.

1. 19, 25, 31, 37, ... a. $a_n = 6n + 13$ b. __1213__

2. -4, -6.5, -9, -11.5, ... a. $a_n = -2.5n - 1.5$ b. __-501.5__

In 3 and 4, a recursive definition for a sequence is given. Write an explicit formula for the sequence.

3. $\begin{cases} a_1 = \frac{3}{5} \\ a_n = a_{n-1} + \frac{2}{5}, \end{cases}$ 4. $\begin{cases} d_1 = \pi \\ d_n = d_{n-1} + 2\pi, \end{cases}$

$a_n = \frac{2}{5}n + \frac{1}{5}$ $d_n = 2n\pi - \pi$

5. Write a recursive definition for the sequence defined explicitly by $a_n = 9n - 7$. $\begin{cases} a_1 = 2 \\ a_n = a_{n-1} + 9, \text{ for } n \geq 2. \end{cases}$

6. An arithmetic sequence has $a_3 = 11.1$ and $a_7 = 23.9$.

a. Write an explicit formula for the sequence. $a_n = 3.2n + 1.5$

b. Write a recursive definition for the sequence. $\begin{cases} a_1 = 4.7 \\ a_n = a_{n-1} + 3.2, \text{ for } n \geq 2. \end{cases}$

7. Find the 250th term of the linear sequence 5*p*, 8*p*, 11*p*, 14*p*, ... __752*p*__

Properties Objective F

In 8–10, determine whether or not the given formula describes an arithmetic sequence. Justify your answer. Samples

8. $a_n = n^3 - 6$ No; there is no constant difference.

9. $b_n = 4n + 7$ Yes; there is a constant difference, 4.

10. $c_n = \frac{2}{3}n - \frac{5}{3}$ Yes; there is a constant difference, $\frac{2}{3}$.

Uses Objective G

11. A TV shopping club that had 1218 gold necklaces for $125 each sold 42 necklaces each minute the item was featured.

a. Write an explicit formula that gives the number of necklaces left a_n after *n* minutes. $a_n = 1218 - 42n$

b. How many minutes does this item need to be featured before the club would sell out? __29 minutes__

33

LESSON MASTER 3-9 A

Questions on SPUR Objectives
See pages 197-201 for objectives.

Skills Objective C

In 1–3, evaluate.

1. $\lfloor -8.7 \rfloor$ __-9__ 2. $\lfloor 19.1 \rfloor$ __19__ 3. $\lfloor \pi \rfloor$ __3__

Uses Objective K

4. *Multiple choice.* A pack of 50 sheets of construction paper is to be shared by *s* students. Which expression gives the number of sheets of paper each student may have? __b__

(a) $\frac{50}{s}$ (b) $\lfloor \frac{50}{s} \rfloor$ (c) $\lceil -\frac{50}{s} \rceil$ (d) $\lfloor 50s \rfloor$

5. The table below gives the international air-mail rate for postcards from 1961 to 1991. The year is the first year that rate was in effect.

Year	1961	1967	1974	1976	1981	1985	1988	1991
Rate	$0.11	$0.13	$0.18	$0.21	$0.28	$0.33	$0.36	$0.40

a. Find the international air-mail rate for a postcard in each year.

i. 1970 __$.13__

ii. 1987 __$.33__

iii. 1990 __$.36__

b. Graph the postal rates in the table as a function of the year.

Representations Objective M

In 6 and 7, a rule for a function is given. a. Graph the function. b. Give its domain and its range.

6. $g(x) = \lfloor x \rfloor - 2$ 7. $f(x) = 2\lfloor x \rfloor + 3$

a.   a.

b. all real numbers b. all real numbers
   all integers all odd integers

34

LESSON MASTER 4-1 A

Questions on SPUR Objectives
See pages 266-269 for objectives.

Uses Objective G

1. According to the Census Bureau, in 1900 the median age at first marriage was 25.9 for males and 21.9 for females. In 1930, the median age at first marriage was 24.3 for males and 21.3 for females. In 1960, it was 22.8 for males and 20.3 for females. In 1990, it was 26.1 for males and 23.9 for females. Store this information in a 2 × 4 matrix. **(See below.)**

2. According to the Census Bureau, in 1960 the median earnings for women was $3,257 and the median earnings for men was $5,368, with a gap of $2,111 in favor of males. (Figures are in 1990 dollars.) In 1970 the median earnings for women and men were $5,323 and $8,966, respectively, with a gap of $3,643. In 1980 the median earnings for women and men were $11,197 and $18,612, respectively, with a gap of $7,415. In 1990 the median earnings for women and men were $19,822 and $27,678, respectively, with a gap of $7,856. Store this information in a 4 × 3 matrix. **(See below.)**

3. The matrix at the right gives data from the 1992 *Statistical Abstract of the United States* regarding prisoners executed under civil authority from 1930 to 1989.

	White	Black
1930–1939	827	816
1940–1949	490	781
1950–1959	336	376
1960–1969	98	93
1970–1979	3	0
1980–1989	68	49

a. Give the dimensions of this matrix. __6 × 2__

b. What does the entry in row 2 column 1 represent?

the number of whites executed 1940–1949

c. How many whites were executed in the period 1970–1979? __3 whites__

	1900	1930	1960	1990
(#1) Male	25.9	24.3	22.8	26.1
Female	21.9	21.3	20.3	23.9

	Women	Men	Gap
(#2) 1960	3,257	5,368	2,111
1970	5,323	8,966	3,643
1980	11,197	18,612	7,415
1990	19,822	27,678	7,856

35

▶ **LESSON MASTER 4-1 A** *page 2*

Representations Objective I

In 4 and 5, draw the polygon described by the matrix

4. $\begin{bmatrix} 0 & 2 & 0 \\ 0 & 5 & -3 \end{bmatrix}$ 5. $\begin{bmatrix} -1 & 0 & 3 & 1 & -1 \\ -4 & -2 & -5 & 4 & 2 \end{bmatrix}$

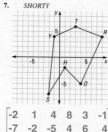

In 5 and 6, write a matrix for the given polygon.

6. *BEAR* 7. *SHORTY*

$\begin{bmatrix} 0 & 6 & 5 & -6 \\ -3 & 0 & 7 & 4 \end{bmatrix}$ $\begin{bmatrix} -2 & 1 & 4 & 8 & 3 & -1 \\ -7 & -2 & -5 & 4 & 6 & 4 \end{bmatrix}$

36

LESSON MASTER 4-2 A

Skills Objective A

In 1 and 2, express as a single matrix.

1. $\begin{bmatrix} 4 & -2 & 7 \\ 3 & 6 & 0 \end{bmatrix} + \begin{bmatrix} 1 & 4 & -6 \\ 1 & 7 & -3 \end{bmatrix}$ $\begin{bmatrix} 5 & 2 & 1 \\ 4 & 13 & -3 \end{bmatrix}$

2. $\begin{bmatrix} 4 & 1 \\ 5 & -3 \\ -6 & -2 \end{bmatrix} - \begin{bmatrix} 9 & 0 \\ 5 & 2 \\ -6 & 7 \end{bmatrix}$ $\begin{bmatrix} -5 & 1 \\ 0 & -5 \\ 0 & -9 \end{bmatrix}$

In 3–5, let $A = \begin{bmatrix} 1 & 6 & -3 \\ -5 & 4 & -1 \\ 0 & 3 & 5 \end{bmatrix}$ and

$B = \begin{bmatrix} 1 & 3 & -2 \\ 1 & -7 & -4 \\ 0 & 8 & 2 \end{bmatrix}$. Calculate.

3. $A + B$ $\begin{bmatrix} 2 & 9 & -5 \\ -4 & -3 & -5 \\ 0 & 11 & 7 \end{bmatrix}$

4. $4A - B$ $\begin{bmatrix} 3 & 21 & -10 \\ -21 & 23 & 0 \\ 0 & 4 & 18 \end{bmatrix}$

5. $3A + 4B$ $\begin{bmatrix} 7 & 30 & -17 \\ -11 & -16 & -19 \\ 0 & 41 & 23 \end{bmatrix}$

In 6 and 7, solve for a and b.

6. $\begin{bmatrix} a & 3 \\ -5 & 7 \end{bmatrix} + \begin{bmatrix} 6 & -8 \\ b & 11 \end{bmatrix} = \begin{bmatrix} 10 & -5 \\ 7 & 18 \end{bmatrix}$ $a = 4, b = 12$

7. $5\begin{bmatrix} 1 & -3 \\ -6 & b \end{bmatrix} - 2\begin{bmatrix} a & -7 \\ -1 & 9 \end{bmatrix} = \begin{bmatrix} 3 & -1 \\ -28 & -3 \end{bmatrix}$ $a = 1, b = 3$

Properties Objective D

8. *True or false*: To be added or subtracted, two matrices must have the same dimensions. **true**

9. *True or false*. Matrix addition is commutative. **true**

Uses Objective H

10. The results of the Eastern Division of the National Conference of the National Football League for 1991 and 1992 are given in the matrices below.

1991
	W	L	T
Washington	14	2	0
Dallas	11	5	0
Philadelphia	10	6	0
N.Y. Giants	8	8	0
Phoenix	4	12	0

1992
	W	L	T
Washington	9	7	0
Dallas	13	3	0
Philadelphia	11	5	0
N.Y. Giants	6	10	0
Phoenix	4	12	0

a. Subtract the left matrix from the right matrix. Call the difference M. (See below.)

b. What is the meaning of the second column of M? **the teams' difference in losses between 1992 and 1991**

c. What is the meaning of the entry in row 2 column 3 of M? **Dallas had the same number of ties in 1991 as in 1992.**

11. The following matrix represents the average daily sales of sandwiches from Shorty's Diner and Cutie's Deli. The various types of sandwiches are referred to as O for open-faced, G for grilled, and C for club.

$\begin{array}{c} \\ \text{Shorty's} \\ \text{Cutie's} \end{array} \begin{array}{ccc} O & G & C \\ \end{array} \begin{bmatrix} 35 & 82 & 46 \\ 49 & 88 & 21 \end{bmatrix}$

During an upcoming festival, both restaurants expect to triple their daily sales. Write a matrix which represents these anticipated sales. (See below.)

(#10a) $M = \begin{bmatrix} -5 & 5 & 0 \\ 2 & -2 & 0 \\ 1 & -1 & 0 \\ -2 & 2 & 0 \\ 0 & 0 & 0 \end{bmatrix}$

(#11) $\begin{array}{c} \\ S \\ C \end{array} \begin{array}{ccc} O & G & C \\ \end{array} \begin{bmatrix} 105 & 246 & 138 \\ 147 & 264 & 63 \end{bmatrix}$

LESSON MASTER 4-3 A

Skills Objective B

In 1–3, calculate the product.

1. $\begin{bmatrix} 5 & 3 \end{bmatrix} \begin{bmatrix} -1 \\ 0 \end{bmatrix}$ $[-5]$

2. $\begin{bmatrix} 5 & 3 \\ -7 & -1 \\ 6 & 2 \end{bmatrix} \begin{bmatrix} 6 & 4 & 3 \\ -1 & -1 & 7 \end{bmatrix}$ $\begin{bmatrix} 27 & 17 & 36 \\ -41 & -27 & -28 \\ 34 & 22 & 32 \end{bmatrix}$

3. $\left(\begin{bmatrix} -2 & 4 \end{bmatrix} \begin{bmatrix} -1 & 0 & 1 \\ 6 & -5 & -4 \end{bmatrix} \right) \begin{bmatrix} 1 & 2 \\ -5 & 1 \\ 0 & -2 \end{bmatrix}$ $[108 \ \ 88]$

Properties Objective D

4. If $\begin{bmatrix} 5 & -2 & -1 \\ 2 & 4 & 7 \end{bmatrix} \cdot A = \begin{bmatrix} 7 \\ 76 \end{bmatrix}$, what are the dimensions of matrix A? 3×1

5. Explain how you can tell whether the matrix product $A \cdot B$ exists. **No. of columns in A = number of rows in B.**

6. *True or false*. Matrix multiplication is associative. **true**

Uses Objective H

7. Fiona's art class painted a large mural. They used 1 can of blue paint, 3 cans of white, and 2 cans of red. A can of blue paint cost $11.50, a can of white paint cost $8.95, and a can of red paint cost $14.20.

a. Write matrices for the cost C and the number of cans used N.

$C = \begin{bmatrix} 11.50 & 8.95 & 14.20 \end{bmatrix}$ $N = \begin{bmatrix} 1 \\ 3 \\ 2 \end{bmatrix}$

b. Calculate CN to find the total cost. $\$66.75$

8. Sumi and Philip have a baby-sitting service. They each charge $5 for one child and $10 for small groups. Each week, Sumi baby-sits for 3 children singly and for 4 small groups. Each week, Philip baby-sits for 2 children singly and for 5 small groups.

a. Write a matrix C for their charges and a matrix B for the numbers Sumi and Philip baby-sit.

$C = \begin{bmatrix} 5 \\ 10 \end{bmatrix}$ $B = \begin{bmatrix} 3 & 4 \\ 2 & 5 \end{bmatrix}$

b. Find BC and tell what it represents.

$BC = \begin{bmatrix} 55 \\ 60 \end{bmatrix}$ **the amounts earned by Sumi and Philip**

LESSON MASTER 4-4 A

Vocabulary

1. Explain what is meant by a *size change*. **A size change of magnitude k maps (x, y) onto (kx, ky).**

Properties Objective E

2. Describe a relationship between a preimage and its image after the application of a size change. **Sample: The preimage and its image are similar.**

Properties Objective F

3. The matrix $\begin{bmatrix} 7 & 0 \\ 0 & 7 \end{bmatrix}$ is associated with a ___?___ with center ___?___ and magnitude ___?___. **size change** **(0, 0)** **7**

4. The matrix associated with a size change of magnitude 8 is ___?___. $\begin{bmatrix} 8 & 0 \\ 0 & 8 \end{bmatrix}$

Representations Objective I

5. Graph the polygon $\begin{bmatrix} -1 & 0 & 3 & 0 \\ 0 & -4 & 0 & 5 \end{bmatrix}$ and its image under $S_{1/3}$.

6. Graph the polygon $\begin{bmatrix} 1 & 3 & -3 \\ 3 & 6 & -6 \end{bmatrix}$ and its image under S_2, and its

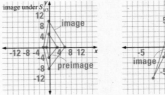

Lesson Master 4-5 A

Name _____

LESSON MASTER **4-5 A**

Questions on SPUR Objectives
See pages 266-269 for objectives.

Vocabulary

1. Define the *scale change* $S_{a,b}$.

Sample: $S_{a,b}$ maps (x, y) onto (ax, by), where a is the horizontal magnitude and b is the vertical magnitude.

Properties Objective E

2. *True or false.* A figure and its scale-change image are similar.   **false**

Properties Objective F

In 3 and 4, give the matrix corresponding to the given transformation.

3. a vertical shrink of $\frac{1}{2}$ and a horizontal stretch of 3

$$\begin{bmatrix} 3 & 0 \\ 0 & \frac{1}{2} \end{bmatrix}$$

4. $S_{2,9}$

$$\begin{bmatrix} 2 & 0 \\ 0 & 9 \end{bmatrix}$$

5. $\begin{bmatrix} 6 & 0 \\ 0 & \frac{1}{3} \end{bmatrix}$ is associated with what transformation? $S_{6,\,1/3}$

Representations Objective I

6. a. Graph the quadrilateral $\begin{bmatrix} -2 & 6 & 2 & 0 \\ -3 & -3 & 4 & 4 \end{bmatrix}$

and its image under $\begin{bmatrix} 1 & 0 \\ 0 & 2 \end{bmatrix}$.

b. Are the image and preimage congruent?   **no**

c. Are the image and preimage similar?   **no**

d. What type of quadrilateral is the preimage?   **trapezoid**

e. What type of quadrilateral is the image?   **trapezoid**

ADVANCED ALGEBRA © Scott, Foresman and Company

41

Lesson Master 4-6 A

Name _____

LESSON MASTER **4-6 A**

Questions on SPUR Objectives
See pages 266-269 for objectives.

Properties Objective E

1. *True or false.* A figure and its reflection image are congruent.   **true**

Properties Objective F

In 2 and 3, translate the matrix equation into English.

2. $\begin{bmatrix} 1 & 0 \\ 0 & -1 \end{bmatrix} \begin{bmatrix} -7 \\ 3 \end{bmatrix} = \begin{bmatrix} -7 \\ -3 \end{bmatrix}$. The reflection image

of the point __?__ over the line __?__ is the point __?__.

(-7, 3)   **$y = 0$**   **(-7, -3)**

3. $\begin{bmatrix} 0 & 1 \\ 1 & 0 \end{bmatrix} \begin{bmatrix} 5 \\ 9 \end{bmatrix} = \begin{bmatrix} 9 \\ 5 \end{bmatrix}$. The reflection image of

the point __?__ over the line __?__ is the point __?__.

(5, 9)   **$y = x$**   **(9, 5)**

4. a. Multiply the matrix for $r_{y=x}$ by itself.

$$\begin{bmatrix} 0 & 1 \\ 1 & 0 \end{bmatrix} \begin{bmatrix} 0 & 1 \\ 1 & 0 \end{bmatrix} = \begin{bmatrix} 1 & 0 \\ 0 & 1 \end{bmatrix}$$

b. Explain your result.

Sample: If a figure is reflected over the line $y = x$ and the image is then reflected over $y = x$, the image of the image coincides with the original figure.

Representations Objective I

5. A polygon is represented by the matrix $\begin{bmatrix} -1 & 1 & -3 \\ -4 & 4 & 6 & 2 \end{bmatrix}$. Graph the polygon and its image under r_y.

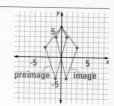

ADVANCED ALGEBRA © Scott, Foresman and Company

42

Lesson Master 4-7 A

Name _____

LESSON MASTER **4-7 A**

Questions on SPUR Objectives
See pages 266-269 for objectives.

Properties Objective D

1. *True or false.* Multiplication of 2×2 matrices is commutative. If true, prove. If false, provide a counterexample.   **false**

Sample: $\begin{bmatrix} 1 & 0 \\ 6 & 2 \end{bmatrix} \begin{bmatrix} 2 & 1 \\ 0 & 3 \end{bmatrix} = \begin{bmatrix} 2 & 1 \\ 12 & 12 \end{bmatrix}$;

$\begin{bmatrix} 2 & 1 \\ 0 & 3 \end{bmatrix} \begin{bmatrix} 1 & 0 \\ 6 & 2 \end{bmatrix} = \begin{bmatrix} 8 & 2 \\ 18 & 6 \end{bmatrix}$

2. If A, B, and C are 2×2 matrices, what property assures that $(AB)C = A(BC)$?
Associative Property of Matrix Multiplication

Properties Objective F

In 3–5, a point and its image under four composites of transformations are graphed. a. Match the composite to a graph. b. Calculate a matrix for the composite.

3. $r_y \circ r_x$
a. **ii**

4. $r_{y=x} \circ r_{y=x}$
a. **iii**

5. $r_x \circ S_{1/2}$
a. **i**

b. $\begin{bmatrix} -1 & 0 \\ 0 & -1 \end{bmatrix}$

b. $\begin{bmatrix} 1 & 0 \\ 0 & 1 \end{bmatrix}$

b. $\begin{bmatrix} \frac{1}{2} & 0 \\ 0 & -\frac{1}{2} \end{bmatrix}$

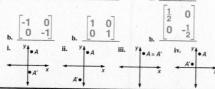

Representations Objective I

6. Draw the polygon $\begin{bmatrix} 4 & -1 & 1 \\ 3 & 2 & -5 \end{bmatrix}$ and its image under $r_{y=x} \circ r_y$.

ADVANCED ALGEBRA © Scott, Foresman and Company

43

Lesson Master 4-8 A

Name _____

LESSON MASTER **4-8 A**

Questions on SPUR Objectives
See pages 266-269 for objectives.

Properties Objective E

1. $\triangle A'B'C'$ is the image of $\triangle ABC$ under R_{90}. Describe a relationship between $\triangle ABC$ and $\triangle A'B'C'$.
Sample: $\triangle ABC \cong \triangle A'B'C'$

Properties Objective F

In 2 and 3, a composite of transformations is given. a. Find a matrix for the composite. b. Describe each matrix with a single transformation.

2. $R_{180} \circ r_x$

a. $\begin{bmatrix} -1 & 0 \\ 0 & -1 \end{bmatrix}$

b. r_y

3. $r_x \circ r_y$

a. $\begin{bmatrix} -1 & 0 \\ 0 & -1 \end{bmatrix}$

b. R_{180}

4. Explain how to find the matrix for R_{270} from the matrix for R_{90}.
Sample: Apply the matrix R_{90} three times.

Representations Objective I

5. a. What rotation maps *TOM* onto *T'O'M'*?
R_{180}

b. Give the matrix for the rotation in Part a.

$\begin{bmatrix} -1 & 0 \\ 0 & -1 \end{bmatrix}$

6. Draw the polygon $\begin{bmatrix} 0 & 6 & 8 & 6 & 0 & -3 \\ 0 & 0 & 3 & 6 & 6 & 3 \end{bmatrix}$ and its image under R_{90}.

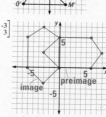

ADVANCED ALGEBRA © Scott, Foresman and Company

44

151

LESSON MASTER 4-9 A

Skills Objective A

In 1–4, write an equation for the line that goes through
the given point and is perpendicular to the given line.

1. $(6, 1)$; $y = 3x - 5$ $y - 1 = -\frac{1}{3}(x - 6)$

2. $(-1, -7)$; $3x + 4y = 7$ $y + 7 = \frac{4}{3}(x + 1)$

3. $(5, 2)$; $x = 12$ $y = 2$

4. $(5, 2)$; $y = 17$ $x = 5$

In 5 and 6, write an equation for the perpendicular
bisector of the line segment with the given endpoints.

5. $(-6, 8)$, $(6, -8)$ $y = \frac{3}{4}x$

6. $(8, 16)$, $(24, -12)$ $y - 2 = \frac{4}{7}(x - 16)$

Properties Objective E

7. The slope of a line is 6. What is the slope of the
image of this line under R_{90}? $-\frac{1}{6}$

8. Let $\triangle PUT$ be represented by the matrix $\begin{bmatrix} 523 & 23 & -177 \\ -621 & 379 & 79 \end{bmatrix}$.
Let $\triangle P'U'T' = R_{90}(\triangle PUT)$.

   a. Find the slope of $\overleftrightarrow{PU}$. -2

   b. Find the slope of $\overleftrightarrow{P'U'}$. $\frac{1}{2}$

LESSON MASTER 4-10 A

Properties Objective E

1. *True or false.* A triangle and its translation
image are not necessarily congruent.   false

Properties Objective F

2. Translate the following matrix equation into English.
$$\begin{bmatrix} 1 & 1 & 1 \\ -3 & -3 & -3 \end{bmatrix} + \begin{bmatrix} 2 & 4 & -1 \\ 5 & 6 & -3 \end{bmatrix} = \begin{bmatrix} 3 & 5 & 0 \\ 2 & 3 & -6 \end{bmatrix}$$

The image of a _?_ under a _?_ of _?_ units _?_
and _?_ units _?_ is a _?_ .

    triangle with vertices (2, 5), (4, 6), (-1, -3)

    translation   1   right

    3   down

    triangle with vertices (3, 2), (5, 3), (0, -6)

3. What matrix is the identity matrix for
translating triangles in the plane? $\begin{bmatrix} 0 & 0 & 0 \\ 0 & 0 & 0 \end{bmatrix}$

4. What matrix describes the translation
of a quadrilateral under $T_{-2, 6}$? $\begin{bmatrix} -2 & -2 & -2 & -2 \\ 6 & 6 & 6 & 6 \end{bmatrix}$

Representations Objective I

5. $\begin{bmatrix} -3 & 3 & 3 & -3 \\ -3 & -3 & 3 & 3 \end{bmatrix}$ represents square $SQUA$.

   a. Apply the translation $T_{1,2}$ to this square. $\begin{bmatrix} -2 & 4 & 4 & -2 \\ -1 & -1 & 5 & 5 \end{bmatrix}$

   b. Graph the preimage and the
   image on the grid at the right.

LESSON MASTER 5-1 A

Vocabulary

1. The _?_ of two sets is the set consisting of
those elements in either one set or both sets.   union

2. The _?_ of two sets is the set consisting
of those elements common to both sets.   intersection

Representations Objective H

3. Graph all solutions to $m \geq -2$
on the number line at the right.

4. Write an inequality that describes the
graph below. $n > -7$

In 5 and 6, solve the inequality and graph its
solution set on the number line.

5. $-3r + 11 < 20$ $r > -3$

6. $4t - (2 - t) \geq 18$ $t \geq 4$

Representations Objective K

In 7 and 8, graph on the number line.

7. $n > 3$ and $n < 12$

8. $\{s: 4 \leq s \leq 10\} \cap \{s: s \leq 6\}$

9. $v < -3$ and $v > 6$

LESSON MASTER 5-2 A

Properties Objective D

1. Does $(-2, 5)$ solve the system $\begin{cases} 2x + y = 1 \\ 4x + y = 3 \end{cases}$? Justify your answer.
   No; $2(-2) + 5 = 1$, $4(-2) + 5 = -3 \neq 3$

2. Use the table at the right to solve
the system $\begin{cases} y = 9x + 1 \\ y = 3x - 2 \end{cases}$.
    $(-0.5, -3.5)$

x	y = 9x + 1	y = 3x − 2
-1.5	-12.5	-6.5
-1.0	-8	-5
-0.5	-3.5	-3.5
0	1	-2
0.5	5.5	-0.5

Representations Objective L

In 3–6, a system is given. a. Graph the system. b. Tell how many solutions the
system has. c. Estimate any solutions to the nearest tenth.

3. $\begin{cases} 3x + 2y = 12 \\ x - y = 4 \end{cases}$

   a.

   b. 1   c. $(4, 0)$

4. $\begin{cases} 9x - y = 12 \\ y = 9x + 6 \end{cases}$

   a.

   b. none   c.

5. $\begin{cases} y = \frac{4}{x} \\ y = -3x + 7 \end{cases}$

   a.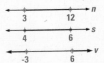

   b. 3   c. $(1, 4), (2, 1)$ $(-.7, 9)$,

6. $\begin{cases} y = 3x^2 \\ y = \frac{10}{x} \end{cases}$

   a.

   b. 1   c. $(1.5, 6.7)$

Lesson Master 5-3 (page 49)

LESSON MASTER 5-3 **A**

Questions on SPUR Objectives
See pages 340-343 for objectives.

Skills Objective A

In 1–5, use substitution to solve the systems. Then check.   **Checks are not shown.**

1. $\begin{cases} 2x + 3y = 19 \\ y = 3x - 1 \end{cases}$ 2. $\begin{cases} xy = 100 \\ x = 4y \end{cases}$ 3. $\begin{cases} .4a - .5b = 20 \\ .3b = .3a - 1.5 \end{cases}$

(2, 5)   (20, 5) (-20, -5)   (-175, -180)

4. $\begin{cases} 2x + y + 2z = 0 \\ y = 3x + 1 \\ z = x - 4 \end{cases}$ 5. $\begin{cases} x + 2y - z = 1 \\ y = -x \\ z = x + 1 \end{cases}$

(1, 4, -3)   (-1, 1, 0)

Properties Objective D

6. What does it mean for a system of equations to be inconsistent?
Sample: The system has no solutions.

7. A system of two linear equations has no solutions. What can you say about the graphs of the two lines?
Sample: The graphs of the equations are parallel.

Uses Objective F

8. Hotel Oakwood charges $40 a night for two people plus $5 for each additional person. Pine Valley Lodge charges $38 a night for two people plus $6 for each additional person.
   a. Write an equation for the cost y with x additional people in a room for one night at each place.
   H.O. $y = 40 + 5x$ P.V.L. $y = 38 + 6x$
   b. For how many people will the rate for the two rooms be the same?   **4 people**

9. Three-bean salad can be made by mixing green, kidney, and wax beans. The recipe calls for the same amount of kidney beans and wax beans, and twice as much green beans as kidney beans. Let g be the number of cups of green beans, k the number of cups of kidney beans, and w the number of cups of wax beans. Determine how much of each kind of bean should be used for nine cups of salad.
   green $4\frac{1}{2}$ C   kidney $2\frac{1}{4}$ C   wax $2\frac{1}{4}$ C

ADVANCED ALGEBRA © Scott, Foresman and Company

Lesson Master 5-4 (page 50)

LESSON MASTER 5-4 **A**

Questions on SPUR Objectives
See pages 340-343 for objectives.

Skills Objective A

In 1–4, use linear combinations to solve the systems. Then check.   **Checks are not shown.**

1. $\begin{cases} 2x + y = 1 \\ 4x + 3y = 9 \end{cases}$ 2. $\begin{cases} r + 2s - 3t = 11 \\ 2r + s + t = -1 \\ r - 3s - t = -8 \end{cases}$

   (-3, 7)   (-1, 3, -2)

3. $\begin{cases} 5w + 4z = -.7 \\ 8w + 6z = -1.2 \end{cases}$ 4. $\begin{cases} f + 2g = 2 \\ 3f + 6g = 6 \end{cases}$

   (-.3, .2)   **infinitely many solutions**

Properties Objective D

For 5 and 6, consider the system $\begin{cases} 12x + 6y = k \\ 2x + y = 9 \end{cases}$.

5. For what values of k will the system be inconsistent? $k \neq 54$

6. For what value of k will the system have infinitely many solutions? $k = 54$

Uses Objective F

7. At a restaurant, four hamburgers and two orders of fries cost $27.10. Three hamburgers and four orders of fries cost $25.20. If all hamburgers cost the same price and all orders of fries cost the same price, find the cost of each.
   hamburgers $5.80   fries $1.95

8. Three pounds of pears and a pound of grapes cost $4.36. Five pounds of pears and two pounds of grapes cost $7.93. Find the cost of six pounds of pears and four pounds of grapes. $12.70

ADVANCED ALGEBRA © Scott, Foresman and Company

Lesson Master 5-5 (page 51)

LESSON MASTER 5-5 **A**

Questions on SPUR Objectives
See pages 340-343 for objectives.

Vocabulary

1. Two matrices are *inverses* of each other if and only if their product is ___?___. $\begin{bmatrix} 1 & 0 \\ 0 & 1 \end{bmatrix}$

2. Find the *determinant* of matrix $\begin{bmatrix} q & r \\ s & t \end{bmatrix}$. $qt - rs$

Skills Objective B

In 3–5, a matrix is given. a. Find its determinant.
b. Find its inverse, if it exists.

3. $\begin{bmatrix} 7 & -8 \\ 3 & 4 \end{bmatrix}$ 4. $\begin{bmatrix} -1 & 0 \\ 9 & -1 \end{bmatrix}$ 5. $\begin{bmatrix} 14 & 2 \\ 3 & 9 \end{bmatrix}$

   a. 52   a. 1   a. 120

   b. $\begin{bmatrix} \frac{4}{52} & \frac{8}{52} \\ -\frac{3}{52} & \frac{7}{52} \end{bmatrix}$ b. $\begin{bmatrix} -1 & 0 \\ -9 & -1 \end{bmatrix}$ b. $\begin{bmatrix} \frac{9}{120} & -\frac{2}{120} \\ -\frac{3}{120} & \frac{14}{120} \end{bmatrix}$

6. Show that $\begin{bmatrix} 5 & 4 \\ 1 & 1 \end{bmatrix}$ and $\begin{bmatrix} 1 & 4 \\ -1 & 5 \end{bmatrix}$ are *not* inverses of each other.
$\begin{bmatrix} 5 & 4 \\ 1 & 1 \end{bmatrix}\begin{bmatrix} 1 & 4 \\ -1 & 5 \end{bmatrix} = \begin{bmatrix} 1 & 40 \\ 0 & 9 \end{bmatrix} \neq \begin{bmatrix} 1 & 0 \\ 0 & 1 \end{bmatrix}$

7. Show that $\begin{bmatrix} 12 & 2 \\ 9 & 1 \end{bmatrix}$ and $\begin{bmatrix} -\frac{1}{6} & \frac{1}{3} \\ \frac{3}{2} & -2 \end{bmatrix}$ are inverses of each other.
$\begin{bmatrix} 12 & 2 \\ 9 & 1 \end{bmatrix}\begin{bmatrix} -1/6 & 1/3 \\ 3/2 & -2 \end{bmatrix} = \begin{bmatrix} 1 & 0 \\ 0 & 1 \end{bmatrix}$

8. Consider the matrix $\begin{bmatrix} 9 & x \\ 12 & 4 \end{bmatrix}$. For what values of x does the matrix *not* have an inverse? $x = 3$

9. a. Find the inverse of the matrix for S_4.
   $\begin{bmatrix} 1/4 & 0 \\ 0 & 1/4 \end{bmatrix}$
   b. Explain the result to Part a geometrically.
   S_4 is size change magnitude 4. Its inverse is size change magnitude $\frac{1}{4}$.

ADVANCED ALGEBRA © Scott, Foresman and Company

Lesson Master 5-6 (page 52)

LESSON MASTER 5-6 **A**

Questions on SPUR Objectives
See pages 340-343 for objectives.

Vocabulary

In 1 and 2, consider the system $\begin{cases} 5x - 4y = 12 \\ 2x + 3y = 7 \end{cases}$.

1. Write the *coefficient matrix*. $\begin{bmatrix} 5 & -4 \\ 2 & 3 \end{bmatrix}$

2. $\begin{bmatrix} 12 \\ 7 \end{bmatrix}$ is called the ___?___ matrix.   **constant**

Skills Objective C

In 3–6, use a matrix to solve the system.

3. $\begin{cases} 4x + 2y = 0 \\ 12x + 3y = 2 \end{cases}$ 4. $\begin{cases} 7m + 9n = 14 \\ -4m + 6n = 31 \end{cases}$

   $\left(\frac{1}{3}, -\frac{2}{3}\right)$ (-2.5, 3.5)

5. $\begin{cases} -11r + 1.5s = 46.9 \\ 10r - 3.1s = -56.18 \end{cases}$ 6. $\begin{cases} 2x + 3y - 4z = 37 \\ 9x - 2y + z = -82 \\ -11x + 5y - 7z = 165 \end{cases}$

   (-3.2, 7.8)   (-7, 5, -9)

Properties Objective D

7. If the determinant of a coefficient matrix is zero, then the system has ___?___ solution(s).   **no**

Uses Objective F

8. At the ABC MEDIA, all videotapes, all CDs, and all cassettes have standard prices. One videotape, one CD, and two cassettes cost $27.00. Two of each type cost $47.00. Two videos and three CDs cost $47.75.
   a. Write a system of equations that can be used to find the cost of each item.

   $\begin{cases} V + D + 2C = 27 \\ 2V + 2D + 2C = 47 \\ 2V + 3D = 47.75 \end{cases}$
   b. Use matrices to solve the system.
   video $12.25   CD $7.75   cassette $3.50

ADVANCED ALGEBRA © Scott, Foresman and Company

LESSON MASTER 5-7 A

Vocabulary

1. How do the graphs of $4x + 3y = 24$, $4x + 3y \geq 24$, and $4x + 3y > 24$ differ?

   $4x + 3y = 24$ is a line; $4x + 3y \geq 24$ is line $4x + 3y = 24$ and half-plane above it; $4x + 3y > 24$ is half-plane above line $4x + 3y = 24$.

Representations Objective J

In 2 and 3, write an inequality to describe the shaded region.

2.

   $x > 3$

3.

   $y \geq \frac{4}{3}x - 4$

In 4–7, graph the inequality on the coordinate plane.

4. $x < -2.5$

5. $y \geq 7$

6. $y \geq \frac{2}{3}x + 1$

7. $5x - 4y < 40$

LESSON MASTER 5-8 A

Vocabulary

1. The set of solutions to a system of linear inequalities is called the __?__ for that system.   **feasible set**

Properties Objective E

2. A system of inequalities is graphed at the right. Does the given point satisfy the system?

   a. $(0, 0)$ ___ **yes**

   b. $(-4, 2)$ ___ **no**

   c. $(3, 0)$ ___ **no**

Representations Objective K

In 3 and 4, graph the solution set.

3. $\begin{cases} y \leq \frac{2}{3}x + 5 \\ y \geq -\frac{1}{4}x - 2 \end{cases}$

4. $\begin{cases} x \geq -2 \\ y \leq 4 \\ y < -2x + 3 \end{cases}$

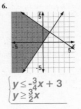

In 5 and 6, write a system of inequalities that describes the shaded region.

5.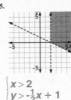

   $\begin{cases} x > 2 \\ y > -\frac{1}{2}x + 1 \end{cases}$

6.

   $\begin{cases} y \leq -\frac{3}{4}x + 3 \\ y \geq \frac{3}{2}x \end{cases}$

LESSON MASTER 5-9 A

Properties Objective E

1. Tell whether the shaded region could be the feasible region of a linear programming problem.

   a. **no**   b. **no**   c. **no**   d. **yes**

Uses Objective G

In 2–5, refer to the following situation: A batch of cookies takes 2.5 cups of flour and 48 minutes to bake. One cake takes 3.5 cups of flour and 75 minutes to bake. Brad's Bakery has 40 cups of flour and can bake for only 7 hours. Brad must make at least two batches of cookies and 3 cakes. Let k be the number of batches of cookies and let c be the number of cakes. The system of inequalities for this problem is at the right.

$\begin{cases} 2.5k + 3.5c \leq 40 \\ 48k + 75c \leq 420 \\ k \geq 2 \end{cases}$

2. Match each inequality in the system with the aspect it describes.

   ii a. number of batches of cookies

   iv b. number of cakes

   i c. total number of cups of flour

   iii d. total cooking time.

   (i) $2.5k + 3.5c \leq 40$

   (ii) $k \geq 2$

   (iii) $48k + 75c \leq 420$

   (iv) $c \geq 3$

3. On the grid at the right, graph the feasible region. Let k be the independent variable.

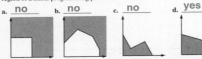

4. List the vertices of the feasible region.

   $(2, 3) \approx (2, 4) \approx (4, 3)$

5. Brad makes $1.25 profit on each batch of cookies and $1.75 profit on each cake.

   a. Write an expression for Brad's total profit in terms of c and k.

   $1.25k + 1.75c$

   b. How many batches of cookies and how many cakes should Brad make to maximize the profit?

   cookies ___ **4 batches** ___   cakes ___ **3** ___

LESSON MASTER 5-10 A

Uses Objective G

In 1–5, use the following situation: Maxine went on a TV game show and won $32,000. She wants to invest that money, some in a savings account which is relatively safe and some in stocks which are somewhat riskier. Maxine wants to put at least $15,000 in savings and at least $10,000 in stocks. The savings account pays 4% and she expects a 6% return on her stocks. Answer the following questions to determine how she should invest the money to maximize her return in a single year.

1. Let s be the amount invested in savings and k be the amount invested in stocks. Write a system of three inequalities to describe this situation.

   $\begin{cases} s + k = 32,000 \\ s \geq 15,000 \\ k \geq 10,000 \end{cases}$

2. Graph the system and determine the feasible region.

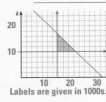

   Labels are given in 1000s.

3. Identify the vertices of the feasible region.

   $(15,000, 10,000)$,
   $(22,000, 10,000)$,
   $(15,000, 17,000)$

4. Write the expression to be maximized.

   $.04s + .06k$

5. a. Explain how you would use the Linear-Programming Theorem to help Maxine invest her money.

   Sample: Evaluate $.04s + .06k$ for each ordered pair in Question 3.

   b. What would be her yearly return? ___ **$1620** ___

6. For his evening meal, Karl plans to eat fish sticks and mashed potatoes. Each ounce of fish sticks contains 5 grams of protein and 0.1 mg of iron. Each cup of mashed potatoes contains 4 grams of protein and .8 mg of iron. Karl wants to have at least 28 grams of protein and 2 mg of iron in his evening meal. If each ounce of fish sticks costs 30¢ and each cup of mashed potatoes costs 69¢, how much of each should Karl eat to satisfy his dietary requirements while minimizing the cost?

   fish sticks ___ **4 ounces** ___   potatoes ___ **2 cups** ___

LESSON MASTER 6-1 A

Questions on SPUR Objectives
See pages 413-415 for objectives.

Skills Objective A

In 1–6, expand and simplify.

1. $(x + 11)^2$
$$x^2 + 22x + 121$$

2. $\frac{1}{3}(3d + 6)^2$
$$3d^2 + 12d + 12$$

3. $\left(6n - \frac{1}{2}\right)^2$
$$36n^2 - 6n + \frac{1}{4}$$

4. $(5y - 8)^2$
$$25y^2 - 80y + 64$$

5. $(c + 5)^2 - (c - 5)^2$
$$20c$$

6. $-7(8z + 12)^2$
$$-448z^2 - 1344z - 1008$$

In 7 and 8, use the rectangles pictured at the right.

7. Write an expression for the area of the shaded region.
$$-x^2 + 19x + 63$$

8. Determine the area of the shaded region if $x = 3$ cm.
$$111 \text{ cm}^2$$

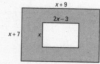

Uses Objective G

9. Cindy has an 11″ by 14″ photograph that she wishes to frame. She wants matting of width w around the edge of the photograph.

a. Give an expression for the total area of the photograph and the matting.
$$4w^2 + 50w + 154 \text{ in}^2$$

b. If $w = 2$ in., what are the inner dimensions of the frame that will hold the photograph and the matting?
$$15 \text{ in.; } 18 \text{ in.}$$

c. What is the total area of the photograph and the matting in Part b?
$$270 \text{ in}^2$$

LESSON MASTER 6-2 A

Questions on SPUR Objectives
See pages 413-415 for objectives.

Skills Objective C

In 1–4, solve.

1. $m^2 = 20$
$$m = \pm\sqrt{20}$$
$$\approx \pm 4.47$$

2. $(n - 2)^2 = 0$
$$n = 2$$

3. $r^2 = 16$
$$r = \pm 4$$

4. $(2p - 4)^2 = 0$
$$p = 2$$

5. $|n - 3| = 8$
$$n = 11 \text{ or } n = -5$$

4. $|2s + 7| = 10$
$$s = 1.5 \text{ or}$$
$$s = -8.5$$

Properties Objective E

7. For what real numbers does $|x| = |-x|$?
all real numbers

8. Simplify $-\sqrt{(2 - 6)^2}$.
-4

9. Describe how the graphs of $y = \sqrt{x^2}$ and $y = -|x|$ are related.
Sample: Both graphs contain (0, 0); the graphs are reflections of each other over the *x*-axis.

Uses Objective G

10. A rectangle measures 6 in. by 12 in. What is the radius of a circle which has the same area as the rectangle?
$$\sqrt{\frac{72}{\pi}}, \text{ or } \approx 4.79, \text{ in.}$$

Representations Objective J

In 11 and 12, graph the equation.

11. $y = |x + 3|$

12. $y + 2 = -|x|$

LESSON MASTER 6-3 A

Questions on SPUR Objectives
See pages 413-415 for objectives.

Uses Objective I

1. The graph of $y = x^2$ is translated 12 units to the left and 6 units up.

a. Write an equation for its image.
$$y - 6 = (x + 12)^2$$

b. Name the vertex of the image.
$$(-12, 6)$$

2. The graph of $y = -5x^2$ is translated 3 units to the right and 7 units down.

a. Write an equation for its image.
$$y + 7 = -5(x - 3)^2$$

b. $(1, -5)$ is a point on the preimage. What is the corresponding point on the image?
$$(4, -12)$$

Representations Objective J

In 3 and 4, assume parabola P is a translation image of parabola Q.

3. What translation maps parabola P onto parabola Q?
$$T_{-5, 12}$$

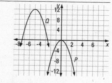

4. Parabola P has equation $y = -2x^2$. Write an equation for parabola Q.
$$y - 12 = -2(x + 5)^2$$

In 6–8, an equation for a parabola is given. a. Graph the parabola and show its axis of symmetry. b. Identify its vertex. c. Write an equation for the axis of symmetry.

6. $y = 3(x + 1)^2$

b. $(-1, 0)$
c. $x = -1$

7. $y + 4 = -3x^2$
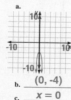
b. $(0, -4)$
c. $x = 0$

8. $y - 5 = (x + 3)^2$
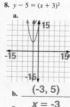
b. $(-3, 5)$
c. $x = -3$

LESSON MASTER 6-4 A

Questions on SPUR Objectives
See pages 413-415 for objectives.

Skills Objective B

In 1–3, write the equation in standard form.

1. $y = 2(x + 5)^2 - 7$
$$y = 2x^2 + 20x + 43$$

2. $y + 5 = -2(x - 6)^2$
$$y = -2x^2 + 24x - 77$$

3. $y - 3 = \frac{1}{4}(x - 2)^2$
$$y = \frac{1}{4}x^2 - x + 4$$

Uses Objective G

4. Suppose a ball is thrown upward from a height of 5 feet with an initial velocity of 30 ft/sec.

a. Write an equation relating the time t in seconds and the height h of the ball in feet.
$$h = -16t^2 + 30t + 5$$

b. Find the height of the ball after 1.5 seconds.
$$14 \text{ ft}$$

5. Suppose a ball is dropped from the top of a 79-foot-tall tree.

a. Write an equation that describes the relationship between h, the height in feet of the ball above the ground, and time t in seconds.
$$h = -16t^2 + 79$$

b. On the grid at the right, graph the height h after t seconds.

c. Estimate how long it would take the ball to reach the ground. Explain your reasoning.
Sample: About 2.2 seconds; this is the approximate value of *t* when *h* = 0.

6. Johanna threw a water balloon upward at a speed of 10m/sec while standing on the roof of a building 12 meters high.

a. What was the height of the balloon after 2 seconds?
$$12.4 \text{ m}$$

b. Assume that the balloon did not land on the roof, and estimate how long it took the balloon to reach the ground.
$$\approx 2.9 \text{ sec}$$

▶

▶ **LESSON MASTER 6-4 A** *page 2*

Representations Objective J

In 7 and 8, graph the parabola for $-3 \leq x \leq 3$.

7. $y = x^2 + x - 6$

8. $y = -2x^2 + 5x + 7$

9. On the graph at the right, the height of a baseball hit upward is shown as a function of time.

   a. What was the initial height of the ball?

   ≈ 5 ft

   b. When did the ball reach its maximum height?

   ≈ 1.8 sec

   c. What was the maximum height?

   ≈ 52 ft

   d. When was the ball 30 ft in the air?

   ≈ 0.3 sec and ≈ 3.2 sec

Answers to Question 9 may vary slightly.

LESSON MASTER 6-5 A

Questions on SPUR Objectives
See pages 413-415 for objectives.

Vocabulary

1. Fill in the blank to make a perfect square.
   $4d^2 - 16d + \underline{\quad ? \quad}$

   16

Skills Objective B

In 2–5, write the equation in vertex form.

2. $y = x^2 - 6x + 10$

   $y - 1 = (x - 3)^2$

3. $y = x^2 + 14x + 5$

   $y + 44 = (x + 7)^2$

4. $y = 5x^2 - 15x - 4$

   $y + \frac{61}{4} = 5(x - \frac{3}{2})^2$

5. $6y = 3x^2 + 30x + 25$

   $y + \frac{25}{3} = \frac{1}{2}(x + 5)^2$

In 6 and 7, find the vertex of the parabola determined by the equation.

6. $y = x^2 - 12x + 24$

   $(6, -12)$

7. $y = -4x^2 + 6x - 7$

   $(\frac{3}{4}, -\frac{19}{4})$

In 8 and 9, write an equation in vertex form equivalent to the standard equation given.

8. $y = 2x^2 - 20x + 57$

   $y - 7 = 2(x - 5)^2$

9. $y = 10x^2 + 10x + 1$

   $y + \frac{3}{2} = 10(x + \frac{1}{2})^2$

10. *Multiple choice.* Which equation is equivalent to $y = 18x^2 + 60x + 45$?

    (a) $y + 3 = 2(3x + 3)^2$ (b) $y + 5 = 2(3x + 5)^2$
    (c) $y + 5 = 2(3x - 5)^2$ (d) $y - 5 = 2(3x + 5)^2$

    b

11. *True or false.* $y = 4x^2 + 4x - 6$ and $y + 7 = 4(x + \frac{1}{2})^2$ have the same vertex.

    true

LESSON MASTER 6-6 A

Questions on SPUR Objectives
See pages 413-415 for objectives.

Uses Objective H

1. The following pictures illustrate the first five numbers in a sequence we shall call the "rectangular numbers."

   2   6   12   20   30

   a. Draw the next rectangular number above at the right.

   b. Find the next three rectangular numbers after 30.

   42, 56, 72

   c. Give a formula for $R(n)$, the nth rectangular number.

   $R(n) = n^2 + n$

   d. Use your formula to find the 100th rectangular number.

   10,100

2. The following table gives the monthly salaries in 1993 for U.S. generals having various years of service.

Years of Service y	Monthly Salary s
2	$6,889.20
4	$6,889.20
8	$7,153.50
12	$7,549.80
16	$8,089.80
20	$8,631.60
26	$9,169.50

   a. On the grid at the right, make a scatterplot of these data.

   b. Fit a quadratic model to these data and plot it.

   $s = 1.3y^2 + 62.5y + 6415$

   c. Fit a linear model to these data and plot it.

   $s = 95y + 6699$

   d. Use either model to estimate the monthly salary of a U.S. general with 10 years of service.

   ≈ $7170 or ≈ $7649

Sample answers are given for 2b–2d.

LESSON MASTER 6-7 A

Questions on SPUR Objectives
See pages 413-415 for objectives.

Skills Objective C

In 1–6, use the Quadratic Formula to solve the equation.

1. $x^2 + 6x - 7 = 0$

   $x = 1$ or $x = -7$

2. $7 = 3x^2 - 4x$

   $x = \frac{7}{3}$ or $x = -1$

3. $m(m + 6) = 36$

   $m = \frac{-6 + \sqrt{180}}{2} \approx 3.71$
   or $\frac{-6 - \sqrt{180}}{2} \approx -9.71$

4. $w^2 = 5w + 3$

   $w = \frac{5 + \sqrt{37}}{2} \approx 5.54$
   or $\frac{5 + \sqrt{37}}{2} \approx -.54$

5. $50d^2 - 12 = -25d$

   $d = \frac{3}{10}$ or $d = -\frac{4}{5}$

6. $(3a + 2)(5a - 1) = 2(5a - 1)$

   $a = 0$ or $a = \frac{1}{5}$

Uses Objective G

7. Juan Torres hit a fast ball thrown by Liz Buckner. Let x be the distance on the ground in feet of the ball from home plate and $h(x)$ be the height in feet of the ball at that distance. Suppose the path of the ball is described by the function $h(x) = -.006x^2 + 2.5x + 4$.

   a. How high was the ball when Juan hit it?

   4 ft

   b. How far from the plate, along the ground, was the ball when it was the same height at which Juan hit it?

   $416\frac{2}{3}$ ft

   c. How far from the plate, along the ground, was the ball when it was 100 feet high?

   ≈ 42.8 ft, ≈ 373.9 ft

   d. The fence is 405 feet away from home plate, and it is 12 feet high. Did the ball go over the fence? Explain your reasoning.

   Yes; when the ball was 405 feet from home plate, it was about 32 feet above the ground.

8. A toy rocket was shot straight up with an initial velocity of 75 m/sec. The platform from which the rocket was shot is 2.3 meters high.

   a. When was the rocket 100 meters above the ground?

   ≈ 1.4 sec, ≈ 13.9 sec

   b. When did the rocket hit the ground?

   ≈ 15.3 sec

Lesson Master 6-8 A

LESSON MASTER **6-8 A**

Questions on SPUR Objectives
See pages 413-415 for objectives.

Skills Objective C

1. Show that $i\sqrt{65}$ is a square root of -65.

$$(i\sqrt{65})^2 = i^2(\sqrt{65})^2 = -1(65) = -65$$

In 2–5, *true or false*.

2. The solution to $x^2 = -5$ are $\sqrt{5}$ and $-\sqrt{5}$. **false**

3. The solution to $g^2 = -13$ are $13i$ and $-13i$. **false**

4. $i\sqrt{31} = -i\sqrt{31}$ **false**

5. $i\sqrt{17}$ is a square root of -17. **true**

In 6–7, solve.

6. $9r^2 + 13 = -12$

$$r = \tfrac{5}{3}i \text{ or } r = -\tfrac{5}{3}i$$

7. $(s + 2)(s - 2) = -8$.

$$s = 2i \text{ or } s = -2i$$

Skills Objective D

In 8–18, simplify.

8. $-5i^2$ **5**

9. $3i \cdot 4i$ **-12**

10. $\sqrt{-361}$ **19i**

11. $\sqrt{15} \cdot \sqrt{-15}$ **15i**

12. $\sqrt{-3}\ \sqrt{-3}$ **-3**

13. $\sqrt{-25} + \sqrt{-64}$ **13i**

14. $-2\sqrt{-4}$ **-4i**

15. $12i - 18i$ **-6i**

16. $\dfrac{\sqrt{-9}}{\sqrt{-36}}$ **$\tfrac{1}{2}$**

17. $(i\sqrt{12})^2$ **-12**

18. $3i(4i + 5i)$ **-27**

65

Lesson Master 6-9 A

LESSON MASTER **6-9 A**

Questions on SPUR Objectives
See pages 413-415 for objectives.

Vocabulary

1. In $\sqrt{6} + \tfrac{3}{2}i$, name the *real* part and the *imaginary* part. real $\sqrt{6}$ imaginary $\tfrac{3}{2}$

Skills Objective D

In 2 and 3, simplify.

2. $(5i - 3i)(5i + 3i)$ **-16**

3. $(5i + 3i) + (5i - 3i)$ **10i**

In 4–13, perform the operations and give the answer in $a + bi$ form.

4. $(6 - i) + (3 + 4i)$ **9 + 3i**

5. $(6 - i) - (3 + 4i)$ **3 − 5i**

6. $(1 + i)(1 - i)$ **2**

7. $\dfrac{2}{1 + i}$ **1 − i**

8. $5(3 - 2i)$ **15 − 10i**

9. $(4 + 2i)(-3 - i)$ **-10 − 10i**

10. $-5(3 - i)$ **-15 + 5i**

11. $\dfrac{2 + i}{3 - i}$ **$\tfrac{1 + i}{2}$**

12. $\dfrac{8 \pm \sqrt{-36}}{2}$ **4 ± 3i**

13. $(\sqrt{2} + i\sqrt{2})^2$ **4i**

In 14–19, suppose $m = 1 + 8i$ and $n = -2 + 3i$. Evaluate and write the answer in $a + bi$ form.

14. mn **-26 − 13i**

15. n^2 **-5 − 12i**

16. $4m + 3$ **7 + 32i**

17. $4m + 3n$ **-2 + 41i**

18. $im - in$ **-5 + 3i**

19. $m^2 + 2m + 1$ **-60 + 32i**

66

Lesson Master 6-10 A

LESSON MASTER **6-10 A**

Questions on SPUR Objectives
See pages 413-415 for objectives.

Skills Objective C

In 1–3, solve.

1. $2x^2 - 7x + 15 = 0$

$$x = \tfrac{7}{4} \pm \tfrac{\sqrt{71}}{4}i$$

2. $3x = 7 + 5x^2$

$$x = \tfrac{3}{10} \pm \tfrac{\sqrt{131}}{10}i$$

3. $-4(2n^2 - 2n) = 3(n + 6)$

$$n = \tfrac{5}{16} \pm \tfrac{\sqrt{551}}{16}i$$

Properties Objective F

In 4 and 5, a quadratic equation is given. a. Evaluate its discriminant. b. Give the number of real solutions. c. Tell whether the real solutions are rational or irrational.

4. $15x^2 - 3x + 7 = 0$

a. **-411**

b. **0 solutions**

c. _____

5. $15h^2 - 11h - 14 = 0$

a. **961**

b. **2 solutions**

c. **rational**

In 6–9, give the number of real solutions.

6. $5z = 12z^2 - 5$ **2**

7. $19w^2 = 7w$ **2**

8. $6c^2 - c + 15 = 0$ **0**

9. $9 - 12t = t^2 - 3$ **2**

Representations Objective K

In 10 and 11, give the number of x-intercepts of the graph of the parabola.

10. $y = 15x^2 + 7$ **0**

11. $y + 14 = -3(x - 2)^2$ **0**

12. Does the parabola with equation $y = -\tfrac{1}{4}x^2 + x - 3$ ever intersect the line with equation $y = -2$? If so, how many points of intersection are there? Explain your reasoning.

Yes; one; the equation $-2 = -\tfrac{1}{4}x^2 + x - 3$ has $x = 2$ as its only solution, so the parabola and the line intersect at the single point $(2, -2)$.

13. The graph of $y = 4x^2$ has one x-intercept. How many x-intercepts does the graph of $y = 4(x - h)^2$ have if $h \neq 0$? Explain your reasoning.

One; the graph of $y = 4(x - h)^2$ will be a horizontal translation image of the graph of $y = 4x^2$.

67

Lesson Master 7-1 A

LESSON MASTER **7-1 A**

Questions on SPUR Objectives
See pages 473-475 for objectives.

Vocabulary

1. In the expression b^n, b is called the __?__. **base**

2. The *identity function* f has the equation $f(x) =$ __?__. **x**

3. If $g(x) = \tfrac{1}{x}$, is g an example of a *power function*? Why or why not?

No; a power function is of the form $g(x) = x^n$, where n is a positive integer.

Uses Objective F

4. In a game with a friend, Felipe has a $\tfrac{4}{7}$ chance of winning a round, and each round is independent. Suppose Felipe and his friend play six rounds. What is the probability that Felipe will win all six rounds? $\left(\tfrac{4}{7}\right)^6 \approx .0348$

Representations Objective I

5. *Multiple choice.* Which of the following could be a graph of an odd power function? **b**

(a)   (b)   (c)

6. The point $(-2, -32)$ is on the graph of an odd power function.

a. What other point must be on the graph? **(2, 32)**

b. Write an equation for this function. **$y = x^5$**

7. a. On the grid at the right, sketch graphs of $f(x) = x^3$ and $g(x) = x^5$.

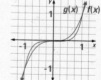

b. For what values(s) of x is $f(x) = g(x)$?

$x = -1, 0, 1$

c. For what values of x is $f(x) > g(x)$?

$x < -1, 0 < x < 1$

68

LESSON MASTER 7-2 A

Skills Objectives A and B

In 1–9, simplify.

1. $(x^5)^6$ ___ x^{30}

2. $(4w^2)^3$ ___ $64w^6$

3. $7y^3 \cdot 8y^5$ ___ $56y^8$

4. $-\frac{c^{12}}{2c^9}$ ___ $-\frac{c^3}{2}$

5. $\frac{z^{18}}{(z^5)^2}$ ___ z^8

6. $\frac{b^4 \cdot 3b^9}{6b^5 \cdot b^6}$ ___ $\frac{b^2}{2}$

7. $\frac{(-9z^4)^3}{9z^{11}}$ ___ $-9z$

8. $\frac{p^6}{p^0}$ ___ p^6

9. $\left(\frac{v}{2}\right)^4\left(\frac{10}{v}\right)^3$ ___ $62.5v$

In 10–13, evaluate.

10. $(15)^0$ ___ 1

11. $(4^3)^2$ ___ 4096

12. $\frac{(12)^3}{(12)^2}$ ___ 12

13. $2^5 \cdot 3^5$ ___ 7776

Properties Objective E

In 14–17, *true or false*. If false, rewrite to be true. **Sample corrections are given.**

14. $(q^4)^6 = q^{10}$
false; $(q^4)^6 = q^{24}$

15. $(m^{10}y^7)^3 = m^{30}y^{21}$
true

16. $r^5 \cdot r^{12} = r^{17}$
true

17. $\frac{z^9}{z^3} = z^3$
false; $\frac{z^9}{z^3} = z^6$

Properties Objective F

18. In 1985, the U.S. population was roughly $2.4 \cdot 10^8$ people, while water usage was approximately $4 \cdot 10^{11}$ gallons per day. Estimate the number of gallons of water used per person daily in the U.S. in 1985.
$\approx 1{,}667$ gal

19. Jupiter's largest moon, Ganymede, is the largest moon of any planet in our solar system, with a diameter of about $5.27 \cdot 10^3$ km. Estimate Ganymede's volume.
$\approx 7.66 \cdot 10^{10}$ km^3

LESSON MASTER 7-3 A

Skills Objectives A and B

In 1–6, write as a decimal or a simple fraction. **Samples are given.**

1. $10^{-3} \cdot 10^{-4}$ ___ .0000001

2. 6^{-2} ___ $\frac{1}{36}$

3. $\left(\frac{2}{5}\right)^{-3}$ ___ $\frac{125}{8}$

4. $(-8)^{-4}$ ___ $\frac{1}{4096}$

5. $\frac{9^{-4}}{9^{-6}}$ ___ 81

6. $(7^{-3})^2$ ___ $\frac{1}{117{,}649}$

In 7–12, simplify the result using only positive exponents.

7. $x^{-6} \cdot x^5$ ___ $\frac{1}{x}$

8. $\frac{y^{-12}}{7y^5}$ ___ $\frac{1}{7y^{17}}$

9. $(4m^{-3})^5$ ___ $\frac{1024}{m^{15}}$

10. $(2^{-1}z^3)^4(4z^{-5}y)^3$ ___ $\frac{4y^3}{z^3}$

11. $\left(\frac{3f}{4h}\right)^{-2}\left(\frac{4f^2}{3h}\right)^3$ ___ $\frac{64h}{27}$

12. $7^{-2}g^5 \cdot 7^6g^{-9}$ ___ $\frac{2401}{g^4}$

Properties Objective E

13. *True or false*. For any positive base b and any real exponent n, $b^{-n} = -(b^n)$. If true, prove the statement. If false, provide a counterexample.
false; sample: $3^{-2} = \frac{1}{3^2} = \frac{1}{9}$; $-(3^2) = -9$; $\frac{1}{9} \neq -9$

Uses Objective F

14. The Law of the Lever states that the distance d of a person from the fulcrum varies inversely as his or her weight w.
   a. Write this variation equation with positive exponents. $d = \frac{k}{w}$
   b. Write this variation equation with negative exponents. $d = kw^{-1}$

15. In Caroline's pinhole camera, the radius of the pinhole is 5.2×10^{-1} mm. Find the area of the pinhole, the region through which light can reach the film.
$\approx .85$ mm^2

LESSON MASTER 7-4 A

Uses Objective G

1. Yu invested $500 in a savings account that pays 3.2% interest compounded annually. How much money will be in his account after 5 years if no deposits or withdrawals take place during the 5 years?
$585.29

2. Debbie invested $5,000 in a 5-year CD (certificate of deposit) that pays 7.8% interest compounded quarterly. The CD matures next February. If no deposits or withdrawals took place during the 5-year period, how much will the CD be worth when it matures?
$7357.23

3. Maria invested $6000 in an IRA (individual retirement account) 25 years before she planned to retire. With a 4% annual yield, if Maria makes no deposits or withdrawals during the 25 years, what will be the value of the IRA when it matures?
$15,995.02

4. Suppose that you plan to put $1000 in a credit-union savings account for two years at 4% interest compounded daily. Shoreline Credit Union compounds 360 days a year; South Side Credit Union compounds 365 days a year. How much more money will you earn if you invest at South Side?
.0066 cent

5. Suppose $2500 is invested for $1\frac{1}{2}$ years. Plan A pays 3.12% interest compounded daily (365 days a year). Plan B pays 3.13% interest compounded quarterly. If the investment is untouched for the entire time, which plan will earn more interest? Explain your reasoning.
Plan A; Plan A earns $119.77 and Plan B earns $119.69.

LESSON MASTER 7-5 A

Skills Objective C

In 1–5, give the first four terms of the geometric sequence described.

1. constant ratio 3, first term -1
-1, -3, -9, -27

2. constant ratio -.1, first term 12
12, -1.2, .12, -.012

3. first term $\sqrt{2}$, second term 2
$\sqrt{2}, 2, 2\sqrt{2}, 4$

4. $g_n = 60\left(\frac{1}{2}\right)^{n-1}$, for $n \geq 1$
60, 30, 15, 7.5

5. $\begin{cases} g_1 = -2 \\ g_n = 3g_{n-1} \text{ for all integers } n \geq 2 \end{cases}$
-2, -6, -18, -54

In 6–9, a sequence is given. a. Tell if the sequence is geometric. b. If yes, give its constant ratio.

6. 12, 36, 108, 324, …
   a. yes   b. 3

7. 3, 6, 9, 12, 15, …
   a. no   b.

8. .5, 5.5, 60.5, 665.5, …
   a. yes   b. 11

9. $\frac{9}{6}, \frac{7}{6}, \frac{5}{6}, \frac{3}{6}, \ldots$
   a. no   b.

In 10 and 11, a geometric sequence is given. a. Give an explicit formula for the nth term of the sequence. b. Give a recursive formula for the sequence.

10. 10, 1, .1, .01, …
   a. $g_n = 10(.1)^{n-1}, n \geq 1$
   b. $\begin{cases} g_1 = 10 \\ g_n = .1g_{n-1}, n \geq 2 \end{cases}$

11. 6, -1.2, .24, -.048, …
   a. $g_n = 6(-.2)^{n-1}, n \geq 1$
   b. $\begin{cases} g_1 = 6 \\ g_n = -.2g_{n-1}, n \geq 2 \end{cases}$

12. Find the sixth term of the geometric sequence whose first term is 7 and whose constant ratio is 2.1.
285.88707

Uses Objective H

13. A car was sold for $22,000. If its value decreases 12% each year, what will be its value after 5 years?
$11,610.10

14. After each bounce, a ball bounces to 80% of its previous height. If it is originally dropped from a height of 6 feet, how high will it bounce after it hits the floor the 6th time?
≈ 1.57 ft

Name

LESSON MASTER 7-6 A

Questions on SPUR Objectives
See pages 473-475 for objectives.

Skills Objectives A, B, and D

In 1–6, write as a decimal or a simple fraction.

1. $64^{\frac{1}{3}}$ 4
2. $64^{\frac{1}{6}}$ 2
3. $100^{\frac{1}{2}}$ 10
4. $(.04)^{\frac{1}{2}}$ .2
5. $-36^{\frac{1}{2}}$ -6
6. $625^{\frac{1}{4}}$ 5
7. Estimate $153^{\frac{1}{2}}$ to the nearest integer. 12

In 8–11, solve.

8. $4z^{\frac{1}{2}} = 36$
   $z = 81$
9. $-4y^{\frac{1}{5}} = 128$
   $y = -33{,}554{,}432$
10. $C^{\frac{1}{8}} + 27 = 30$
   $C = 6561$
11. $2r^{\frac{1}{3}} - 5 = 6$
   $r = 166.375$

Properties Objective E

In 12 and 13, show that the given number is an eighth root of 65,536.

12. $4i$ $(4i)^8 = 4^8 \cdot i^8 = 65{,}536 \cdot 1 = 65{,}536$
13. -4 $(-4)^8 = (-1)^8 \cdot 4^8 = 1 \cdot 65{,}536 = 65{,}536$

In 14 and 15, use the Number of Real Roots Theorem to give the number of real roots possible.

14. 6th root(s) of -41 0 roots
15. 7th root(s) of 68 1 root

In 16–19, write <, =, or > in the blank to make the statement true.

16. $10^{\frac{1}{2}}$ > $10^{\frac{1}{3}}$
17. $16^{\frac{1}{4}} \cdot 81^{\frac{1}{4}}$ = $2 \cdot 3$
18. $34^{\frac{1}{5}}$ > 2
19. $\left(\frac{1}{4}\right)^{\frac{1}{2}}$ = .5

Uses Objective F

20. The equation $P_N = P_0(1 - x)^n$ describes the depreciation value of a car over n years, where P_N is the price of the car now, P_0 is the original price paid, and x is the yearly depreciation rate. If a car costs \$11,453 today and cost \$12,000 four months ago, find the yearly depreciation rate. $\approx 13\%$

Name

LESSON MASTER 7-7 A

Questions on SPUR Objectives
See pages 473-475 for objectives.

Skills Objectives A, B, and D

In 1–9, write as a decimal or a simple fraction. Give decimal answers to the nearest hundredth.

1. $81^{\frac{5}{4}}$ 243
2. $32^{\frac{3}{5}}$ 8
3. $4^{\frac{3}{2}}$ 8
4. $35^{1.5}$ 207.06
5. $3^{\frac{7}{2}}$ 46.77
6. $\left(\frac{27}{125}\right)^{\frac{2}{3}}$ $\frac{9}{25}$, or .36
7. $21^{\frac{4}{5}}$ 11.42
8. $(0.09)^{\frac{5}{2}}$ 0
9. $1000^{\frac{4}{3}}$ 10,000

In 10–12, simplify.

10. $y^{\frac{2}{3}} \cdot y^{\frac{3}{4}}$ $y^{\frac{17}{12}}$
11. $\frac{z^{\frac{5}{6}}}{z^{\frac{2}{3}}} \cdot z^{\frac{1}{3}}$ $z^{\frac{1}{2}}$
12. $\left(a^{\frac{1}{2}}b^{\frac{2}{3}}\right)^2$ $ab^{\frac{4}{3}}$

In 13–16, solve.

13. $y^{\frac{2}{3}} = 25$
   $y = 125$
14. $8x^{\frac{3}{5}} = 27$
   $x = \frac{243}{32}$
15. $32 = k^{\frac{5}{6}}$
   $k = 64$
16. $216 = 64z^{\frac{3}{4}}$
   $z = 5.0625$

Properties Objective E

In 17 and 18, write <, =, or > in the blank to make the statement true.

17. If $a > 1$, $a^{\frac{9}{8}}$ > a.
18. If $0 < b < 1$, $b^{\frac{5}{4}}$ < b.
19. Show that $-7i$ is *not* a fifth root of 16,807.
   $(-7i)^5 = (-7)^5 i^5 = -16{,}807i \neq 16{,}807$

Uses Objective F

In 20 and 21, use the following information: In 1619, Johannes Kepler discovered that the average distance d of a planet from the sun and the planet's period of revolution r around the sun are related by the formula $d = kr^{\frac{2}{3}}$. When d is in millions of miles and r is in days, $k \approx 1.82$.

20. Mercury, the planet closest to the sun, orbits the sun every 88 days. About how far is Mercury from the sun? $\approx$ 36 mil. mi
21. Neptune is about 2796 million miles from the sun.
   a. Estimate Neptune's period of revolution in days. $\approx$ 60,214 days
   b. Estimate Neptune's period of revolution in years. $\approx$ 165 years

Name

LESSON MASTER 7-8 A

Questions on SPUR Objectives
See pages 473-475 for objectives.

Skills Objective A

In 1–6, write as a decimal or a simple fraction. Give decimal answers to the nearest hundredth. Samples are given.

1. $125^{-\frac{5}{3}}$ $\frac{1}{3125}$
2. $36^{-\frac{3}{2}}$ $\frac{1}{216}$, or .00
3. $4 \cdot 16^{-\frac{3}{4}}$ $\frac{1}{2}$, or .50
4. $\left(\frac{64}{125}\right)^{-\frac{4}{3}}$ 2.44
5. $8 \cdot 128^{-\frac{5}{7}}$ $\frac{1}{4}$, or .25
6. $28^{-1.2}$ .02

Skills Objective B

In 7 and 8, simplify, using only positive exponents.

7. $\frac{-15x^7y^{-\frac{2}{3}}}{5x^{-10}y^{\frac{1}{3}}}$ $-3\frac{x^{17}}{y}$
8. $(m^2n^4)^{-\frac{3}{4}}$ $\frac{1}{m^{\frac{3}{2}}n^3}$

Skills Objective D

In 9–12, solve.

9. $y^{-\frac{2}{3}} = 16$
   $y = \frac{1}{64}$, or .015625
10. $w^{-\frac{4}{9}} = 256$
   $w = \frac{1}{262{,}144}$
11. $v^{-5} = 243$
   $v = \frac{1}{3}$, or $.\overline{3}$
12. $p^{-1.6} = 1024$
   $p \approx .013$

Properties Objective E

13. Suppose $x > 1$. Arrange the following from least to greatest: $x^{-3}, x, x^{\frac{5}{4}}, x^{-\frac{1}{2}}$. $x^{-3}, x^{-\frac{1}{2}}, x, x^{\frac{5}{4}}$
14. *True or false.* If $0 < k < 1$, then $k^{-\frac{2}{3}} > k$. true

Uses Objective F

15. Suppose the formula $N = 150{,}000\left(\frac{25}{9}\right)^{-\frac{t}{4}}$, where t is the time in months and N is the number of items sold per month, models the predicted decline in sales of a specific item over the next 24 months. Will the company sell 54,000 items 13 months from now? Explain your reasoning.
   No; in 13 months, the company will sell only 5420 items.

Name

LESSON MASTER 8-1 A

Questions on SPUR Objectives
See pages 527-529 for objectives.

Skills Objective A

1. In the notation $g \circ h(x)$, which function is applied first? h

In 2–8, consider the functions defined by $g(x) = x^2 + 2x + 1$ and $h(x) = 2x - 3$.

2. Find $g(h(4))$. 36
3. Find $h \circ g(4)$. 47
4. Find $g \circ h(-7)$. 256
5. Find $g(g(0))$. 4
6. Find $g(h(x))$. $4x^2 - 8x + 4$
7. Find $h(g(x))$. $2x^2 + 4x - 1$
8. The function $g \circ h$ maps $-\frac{1}{4}$ onto what number? $6\frac{1}{4}$

In 9 and 10, rules for functions f and g are given. Does $f \circ g = g \circ f$? Justify your answer.

9. $f: m \to m + 5$ and $g: m \to m - 5$
   yes; $f \circ g(m) = (m - 5) + 5 = m$;
   $g \circ f(m) = (m + 5) - 5 = m$
10. $f(t) = 4t - 3$ and $g(t) = 4t + 3$
   no; $f \circ g(t) = 4(4t + 3) - 3 = 16t + 9$;
   $g \circ f(t) = 4(4t - 3) + 3 = 16t - 9$
11. Suppose that $r(p) = \frac{1}{p}$ and $s(p) = \sqrt{p}$.
   a. Find $r \circ s(p)$. $\frac{1}{\sqrt{p}}$
   b. State the restrictions on the domain of $r \circ s$. $p > 0$
12. Suppose $c(x) = x^4$ and $d(x) = x^5$. Find
   a. $c \circ d(x)$. x^{20}
   b. $d(c(x))$. x^{20}
   c. $c(x) \cdot d(x)$. x^9

LESSON MASTER 8-2 A

Skills Objective B

In 1 and 2, a function is given. **a.** Give an equation for its inverse. **b.** Tell if the inverse is a function.

1. $f(x) = 3x + 2$ **a.** $y = x/3 - 2/3$ **b.** yes

2. $h: x \rightarrow |2x|$ **a.** $y = \pm x/2$ **b.** no

3. Show that $f: x \rightarrow 5x - 6$ and $g: x \rightarrow \frac{1}{5}x + 6$ are *not* inverses of each other.

Sample: Inverse of $f(x)$ is $y = \frac{x+6}{5} \neq \frac{1}{5}x + 6$;

inverse of $g(x)$ is $y = 5x - 30 \neq 5x - 6$.

Properties Objective F

4. *True or false.* If a function has an inverse which is also a function, then the original function passes the Horizontal-Line Test.   true

5. Let $f = \{(1, 4), (5, 8), (9, 12), (13, 16)\}$.
   a. Give the domain of f. $\{1, 5, 9, 13\}$
   b. Give the domain of the inverse of f. $\{4, 8, 12, 16\}$

Representations Objective I

6. *Multiple choice.* Which graph below is *not* the graph of a function which has an inverse?   a

(a)   (b)   (c)   (d)

7. **a.** On the grid at the right, graph the inverse of the function with equation $y = x^4$.
   b. Is the inverse a function? Why or why not?
   Sample: No; the graph does not pass the Vertical-Line Test for Functions.

LESSON MASTER 8-3 A

Skills Objective B

In 1–4, write an equation for f^{-1}.

1. $f(x) = 2x - 6$ $f^{-1}(x) = \frac{x}{2} + 3$

2. $f(x) = \frac{5}{x}$ $f^{-1}(x) = \frac{5}{x}$

3. $f(x) = \frac{x - 7}{3}$ $f^{-1}(x) = 3x + 7$

4. $f(x) = x^2$, when $x \geq 0$ $f^{-1}(x) = \sqrt{x}$

Properties Objective F

5. Consider the function f defined by $f(x) = -2x + 6$.
   a. Write a rule for $f^{-1}(x)$. $f^{-1}(x) = -\frac{x}{2} + 3$
   b. Find $f \circ f^{-1}(x)$. x
   c. Find $f^{-1} \circ f(x)$. x

In 6 and 7, determine whether the functions f and g as defined are inverses of each other. Justify your answer.

6. $f(m) = m^{\frac{4}{5}}$ and $g(m) = m^{\frac{5}{4}}$
   yes; $(m^{5/4})^{4/5} = m$; $(m^{4/5})^{5/4} = m$

7. $f(m) = m^{\frac{4}{5}}$ and $h(m) = m^{-\frac{5}{4}}$
   no; $(m^{-5/4})^{4/5} = m^{-1}$; $(m^{4/5})^{-5/4} = m^{-1}$; $m^{-1} \neq m$

Representations Objective I

8. Consider the function $f(x) = x^2 + 4$.
   a. Give a restricted domain of f so that there exists an inverse function $f^{-1}(x)$. $x \geq 4$
   b. Write a rule for f^{-1}. $f^{-1}(x) = \sqrt{x-4}$

9. Consider $f = \{(1, 6), (4, 3), (-3, 2), (-2, -1)\}$.
   a. On the grid at the right, graph f^{-1}.
   b. What transformation maps the graph of f onto the graph of f^{-1}? $r_{y = x}$

10. *Multiple Choice.* If $(-3, 0)$ is on the graph of a function, which ____b____ point must be on the graph of the function's inverse?
    (a) $(-3, 0)$ (b) $(0, -3)$ (c) $(3, 0)$ (d) $(0, 3)$

LESSON MASTER 8-4 A

Skills Objectives C and D

In 1–6, simplify. Assume that variables are nonnegative real numbers.

1. $\sqrt[3]{.216}$ .6   2. $\sqrt[6]{64}$ 2   3. $\sqrt[4]{6561}$ 9

4. $\sqrt[3]{343}$ 7   5. $\sqrt[5]{.03125}$ .5   6. $\sqrt[5]{\frac{243}{32}}$ $\frac{3}{2}$

In 7–9, rewrite using a single radical.

7. $\sqrt[4]{\sqrt[3]{c}}$ $\sqrt[12]{c}$ 8. $\sqrt{\sqrt{y^3}}$ $\sqrt[4]{y^3}$ 9. $\sqrt{\sqrt{\sqrt{256u^{16}}}}$ $2u^2$

In 10–12, estimate to the nearest hundredth.

10. $\sqrt[3]{16 + 81}$ 3.14   11. $\sqrt[3]{28}$ 1.95   12. $\sqrt[9]{100}$ 1.67

Properties Objective G

13. Give a counterexample to the statement: For all h, $\sqrt[4]{h^4} = h$.
    Sample: If $h = -2$, $\sqrt[4]{(-2)^4} = 2 \neq -2$.

14. For the radical expression $\sqrt[m]{n}$, what are the possible values
    a. of m?   integers ≥ 2 **b.** of n?   nonnegative reals

15. *Multiple choice.* When $x \geq 0$, $\sqrt[9]{x^4}$ equals which of the following?   a
    (a) $x^{\frac{4}{9}}$ (b) $x^{\frac{2}{3}}$ (c) $x^{\frac{9}{4}}$ (d) $\frac{1}{9}(x^4)$

Uses Objective H

16. A cone has volume $V = \frac{1}{3}\pi r^2 h$. Express the length of its radius.
    a. in radical notation. $r = \sqrt{\frac{3V}{\pi h}}$
    b. with a rational exponent. $r = \left(\frac{3V}{\pi h}\right)^{\frac{1}{2}}$

17. Find the radius, to the nearest tenth, of a cone with volume 1063.8 cm³ and height 9.1 cm.   10.6 cm

18. A sphere has volume $V = \frac{4}{3}\pi r^3$. Write an expression for r using radical notation. $\sqrt[3]{\frac{3V}{4\pi}}$

LESSON MASTER 8-5 A

Skills Objective D

In 1 and 2, find e and f.

1. $\sqrt{600} = \sqrt{e} \cdot \sqrt{6} = f\sqrt{6}$
   $e =$ 100 $f =$ 10

2. $\sqrt[3]{1600} = \sqrt[3]{e} \cdot \sqrt[3]{25} = f\sqrt[3]{25}$
   $e =$ 64 $f =$ 4

In 3–8, simplify. Assume that the variables are nonnegative.

3. $\sqrt[3]{54x^3}$ $3x^2 \cdot \sqrt[3]{2x^2}$

4. $\sqrt[5]{32y^9}$ $2y\sqrt[5]{y^4}$

5. $\sqrt[7]{z^{21}w^{14}}$ $z^3 w^2$

6. $\sqrt[9]{2^{12}x^{14}y^{10}}$ $2xy\sqrt[9]{2^3x^5y}$

7. $\sqrt[3]{4x^2} \cdot \sqrt[3]{2x}$ $2x$

8. $\sqrt[4]{3^6w^7} \cdot \sqrt[4]{3^2w^2}$ $9w^2\sqrt[4]{w}$

9. Recall that the geometric mean of a data set is found by taking the nth root of the product of the n numbers in the data set. Calculate the geometric mean for the batting averages of the 1993 Toronto Blue Jays. $\approx$ .285

Devon White	.444
Paul Molitor	.391
John Olerud	.348
Tony Fernandez	.318
Roberto Alomar	.292
Ed Sprague	.286
Joe Carter	.259
Pat Borders	.250
Rickey Henderson	.120

Properties Objective G

In 10 and 11, *true or false.* Justify your answer.

10. $\sqrt[4]{x} \cdot \sqrt[3]{x} = \sqrt[12]{x^2}$ for $x \geq 0$
    false; sample: $\sqrt[4]{x} \cdot \sqrt[3]{x} = x^{\frac{1}{4}} \cdot x^{\frac{1}{3}} = x^{\frac{7}{12}}$;
    $\sqrt[12]{x^2} = x^{\frac{2}{12}}$

11. $\sqrt[7]{x} \cdot \sqrt[14]{x^2} = \sqrt[14]{x^4}$ for $x \geq 0$
    true; sample: $\sqrt[7]{x} \cdot \sqrt[14]{x^2} = x^{\frac{1}{7}} \cdot x^{\frac{2}{14}} = x^{\frac{2}{7}}$;
    $\sqrt[14]{x^4} = x^{\frac{2}{7}}$

Page 1 (81)

Name _____

LESSON MASTER 8-6 A

Questions on SPUR Objectives
See pages 527-529 for objectives.

Skills Objective D

In 1–6, rationalize the denominator. Assume that all variables are positive.

1. $\frac{7}{\sqrt{3}}$ ___ $\frac{7\sqrt{3}}{3}$

2. $\frac{9x}{\sqrt{25x^5}}$ ___ $\frac{9\sqrt{x}}{5x^2}$

3. $\frac{6}{y\sqrt{y}}$ ___ $\frac{6\sqrt{y}}{y^2}$

4. $\frac{4}{2+\sqrt{5}}$ ___ $-8+4\sqrt{5}$

5. $\frac{x}{\sqrt{x}+3}$ ___ $\frac{x\sqrt{x}-3x}{x-9}$

6. $\frac{5+\sqrt{7}}{5-\sqrt{7}}$ ___ $\frac{16+5\sqrt{7}}{9}$

In 7 and 8, write the expression in radical form with no radical in the denominator. Assume that variables are positive.

7. $z^{\frac{3}{2}}w^{-\frac{1}{2}}$ ___ $\frac{z\sqrt{zw}}{w}$

8. $r^{-\frac{5}{2}}s$ ___ $\frac{s\sqrt{r}}{r^3}$

9. Show that $(\sqrt{37}-6)$ is 12 less than its reciprocal.

Sample: $\frac{1}{\sqrt{37}-6} - 12 = \frac{\sqrt{37}+6}{(\sqrt{37}-6)(\sqrt{37}+6)} - 12$

$= \frac{\sqrt{37}+6}{37-36} - 12 = \frac{\sqrt{37}-6}{1} - 12 = \sqrt{37}-6$

In 10–12, use the triangle at the right. Find the ratio and rationalize the denominator.

10. $\frac{AC}{AB}$ ___ $\frac{\sqrt{3}}{2}$

11. $\frac{AC}{BC}$ ___ $\sqrt{3}$

12. $\frac{BC}{AB}$ ___ $\frac{1}{2}$

81

ADVANCED ALGEBRA © Scott, Foresman and Company

Page 2 (82)

Name _____

LESSON MASTER 8-7 A

Questions on SPUR Objectives
See pages 527-529 for objectives.

Skills Objective C

1. Calculate $(-5)^n$ for the value given.

a. -4 ___ .0016   b. -3 ___ -.008   c. -2 ___ .04

d. -1 ___ -.2   e. 0 ___ 1   f. 1 ___ -5

g. 2 ___ 25   h. 3 ___ -125   i. 4 ___ 625

In 2–7, write as a decimal or a simple fraction.

2. $\sqrt[5]{-243}$ ___ -3   3. $\sqrt[7]{-128}$ ___ -2   4. $\sqrt[3]{-27}+\sqrt[5]{-1}$ ___ -4

5. $\sqrt[3]{-1000}$ ___ -10   6. $\sqrt[3]{-343}$ ___ -3.21   7. $\sqrt[9]{-10,077,696}$ ___ -6

Properties Objective G

8. a. *Multiple choice.* Which of the following is *not* defined? ___ iv

(i) $\sqrt[5]{7776}$ (ii) $\sqrt[6]{7776}$ (iii) $\sqrt[5]{-7776}$ (iv) $\sqrt[4]{-7776}$

b. Explain why your answer in Part a is undefined.
Sample: No real number to the fourth power can result in a negative number.

9. Under what conditions does $\sqrt[n]{x^n} = x$ for all values of x?
Sample: n is a positive odd integer greater than 1.

10. *True or false.* If n is an even integer, $\sqrt[n]{x^n}$ is positive. ___ true

Representations Objective I

11. a. On the grid at right, graph $y = \sqrt[3]{x}$ and $y = x^3$ for $-5 \le x \le 5$.

b. Are the two functions inverses of each other? Why or why not?
Sample: Yes; the graphs are reflection images of each other over the line $y = x$.

82

ADVANCED ALGEBRA © Scott, Foresman and Company

Page 3 (83)

Name _____

LESSON MASTER 8-8 A

Questions on SPUR Objectives
See pages 527-529 for objectives.

Skills Objective E

In 1-4, find all real solutions.

1. $\sqrt[3]{a} = 3$
$a = 27$

2. $\sqrt[4]{c} - 8 = 3\sqrt[4]{c}$
no real solution

3. $19 + \sqrt[5]{e-3} = 18$
$e = 2$

4. $25 - 16\sqrt[3]{f+1} = -7$
$f = 7$

Uses Objective H

5. Find 2 points on the line $x = -5$ that are 10 units from (-3, 2). ___ $(-5, 2 \pm 4\sqrt{6})$

6. The equation $d = 1.82\sqrt[3]{r^2}$ gives the average distance d (in millions of miles) of a planet from the sun where r is the number of days in the planet's revolution. In our solar system, Pluto is the planet with the greatest average distance from the sun, 5899 million miles.

a. Find the number of days in Pluto's revolution around the sun. ___ $\approx 184{,}527$ days

b. Pluto was discovered by Clyde Tombaugh in 1930, based on predictions made by Percival Lowell. In what year will Pluto have completed its orbit around the sun and returned to the point where Tombaugh first found it? ___ 2436

7. A sphere with radius r has a volume of 1131 cubic millimeters. Find the length of the radius, to the nearest millimeter. ___ ≈ 6 mm

83

ADVANCED ALGEBRA © Scott, Foresman and Company

Page 4 (84)

Name _____

LESSON MASTER 9-1 A

Questions on SPUR Objectives
See pages 599-601 for objectives.

Properties Objective D

1. Give the domain and the range of the function with equation $f(x) = 3 \cdot 7^x$.

domain ___ all reals   range ___ positive reals

Uses Objective F

2. In 1991, the population of the metropolitan area of Mexico City, Mexico, was 20.899 million. This population was the second largest in the world. The estimated population for Mexico City in the near future can be modeled by $P = 20.899 \cdot 1.0269^{x-1991}$, where P is the population in millions and x is the year 1991. Estimate the population of Mexico City in the year 2000. ___ ≈ 26.539 mil.

3. In 1991, the population of the Lagos, Nigeria, metropolitan area was about 7,998,000. Use the population growth rate of about 4.06% per year to estimate the population of Lagos in the year given.

a. 1995 ___ 9,378,139   b. 1980 ___ 5,162,492

4. The population of a certain strain of bacteria grows according to the formula $N = N_0 \cdot 2^{1.31t}$, where t is the time in hours. If there are now 50 bacteria, how many bacteria will there be in 2 days? ___ 4.24×10^{20} bac.

Representations Objective I

In 5 and 6, *multiple choice.*

5. Which equation has a graph which is an exponential curve? ___ a

(a) $y = 2^x$ (b) $y = x^2$ (c) $y = 2x$ (d) $y = \frac{x}{2}$

6. Which graph could represent exponential growth? ___ c

7. Locate at least 5 points on the graph of $y = 3^x$ on the grid at the right.
Sample points are:
$(0,1), (1,3), (-1, \frac{1}{3}),$
$(1.5, 5.2), (-2, \frac{1}{9})$

84

ADVANCED ALGEBRA © Scott, Foresman and Company

161

LESSON MASTER 9-2 A

Properties Objective D

1. Give the domain and the range of the function g
with equation $g(x) = 3(.7)^x$.

domain ___all reals___   range ___positive reals___

2. Write equations of all asymptotes of the graph
of the function defined by $f(x) = 5(0.9)^x$.   ___$y = 0$___

3. *True or false.* When a and b are positive and $b \neq 1$,
all exponential functions $y = ab^x$ have the   ___true___
same domain.

Uses Objective F

In 4 and 5, use the equation $P = 14.7(0.81)^h$, which
estimates the atmospheric pressure in pounds per square
inch as a function of the height h in miles above sea level.

4. Estimate the atmospheric pressure at sea level.   ___14.7 lb/in²___

5. Estimate the atmospheric pressure at an altitude of
6.25 miles, an approximate cruising altitude of a jet.   ___≈ 3.9 lb/in²___

6. It is predicted that a new car costing $15,000 will
depreciate at a rate of 11% per year. About how   ___≈ $8376___
much will the car be worth in 5 years?

Representations Objective I

7. *Multiple choice.* Which graph could represent
exponential decay?   ___b___

(a)   (b)   (c)   (d)

8. Locate at least 5 points on the graph
of $y = (\frac{1}{3})^x$ on the grid at the right.

Sample points are:
$(0,1), (1, \frac{1}{3}), (2, \frac{1}{9})$,
$(-1, 3), (-.5, 1.7)$

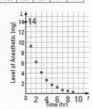

85

LESSON MASTER 9-3 A

Properties Objective D

1. Give the domain and the range of the function
with equation $f(x) = 2e^{4x}$.

domain ___all reals___   range ___positive reals___

2. *Multiple choice.* Which situation does the function
defined by $y = 5e^{2+x}$ describe?   ___b___

(a) constant increase   (b) exponential growth

(c) constant decrease   (d) exponential decay

Uses Objective F

In 3–5, use this information: In 1992, the fastest-growing state of the Union
was Nevada. At this rate, if P is Nevada's population in thousands and t is the
number of years after 1992, then $P = 1336e^{.05t}$.

3. What was Nevada's population in 1992?   ___1,336,000___

4. According to this model, what will Nevada's
population be in the year 2000?   ___≈ 1,993,000___

5. According to this model, what was Nevada's
population in 1990?   ___≈ 1,209,000___

6. If it is assumed that inflation remains constant at 3.44% per year,
then the value V of a dollar n years from now can be modeled
by the equation $V = e^{-.0344n}$. According to this model, what   ___≈ $0.71___
will be the value of the dollar 10 years from now?

Representations Objective I

7. a. On the grid at the right, graph the
equations $y = e^{-5x}$ and $y = e^{.5x}$.

b. *True or false.* $y = e^{5x}$ and $y = e^{-5x}$
are inverse functions.   ___false___

86

LESSON MASTER 9-4 A

Uses Objective G

1. Under certain conditions, algae will grow exponentially
in a pond. Suppose that there are 100 algae in a pond
and that 3 hours later there are 200 algae.

a. Fit an exponential model to these data.

b. Find the number of algae present after
24 hours.

Sample:
$A = 100(1.26)^h$

___≈ 25,639 algae___

2. A pharmaceutical company is testing a new anesthetic.
They injected 14 mg of the anesthetic into the bloodstream
of a laboratory rat and then monitored the level of the drug
every hour. The results are in the table below.

Time (hr)	0	1	2	3	4	5	6	7	8	9
Anesthetic (mg)	14.00	9.38	6.28	4.21	2.82	1.89	1.27	.85	.57	.38

a. Draw a scatterplot of these data
on the grid at the right.

b. Let L be the level of anesthetic
and t be the time. Fit an exponential
model to these data.
Sample: $L = 14(.67)^t$

c. Use your model to find the level
of anesthetic after 12 hours.
___≈ .11 mg___

3. *Multiple choice.* For which set of data below is an
exponential model most appropriate? Explain why.   ___b___

a.
x	0	1	2	3	4	5	6
y	3	18	75	390	1800	10,000	50,000

b.
x	0	1	2	3	4	5	6
y	3	15	75	375	1875	9375	46875

c.
x	0	1	2	3	4	5	6
y	3	6	99	732	3075	9378	23331

Sample: the growth factor is the constant 5.

87

LESSON MASTER 9-5 A

Skills Objective A

In 1–6, write the number as a decimal. Do not use
a calculator.

1. log 1000   ___3___   2. log (0.01)   ___-2___   3. $\log \sqrt[9]{10}$ ___$\frac{1}{9}$, or .$\overline{1}$___

4. log 10⁴⁰   ___40___   5. log 10⁻¹⁷   ___-17___   6. log (-10)   ___none___

In 7–9, find the logarithm to the nearest hundredth.

7. log 9.63   ___.98___   8. log 14,609   ___4.16___   9. log -53   ___none___

Skills Objective C

In 10–13, solve.

10. log $a = 2$ ___$a = 100$___   11. log $b = -3$ ___$b = .001$___

12. log $g = 5.1$ ___$g ≈ 125,893$___   13. log $h = -0.19$ ___$h ≈ .646$___

Properties Objective E

In 14–16, *true or false.*

14. The logarithm of 1 is 0.   ___true___

15. The domain of the common logarithm
function is the set of real numbers.   ___false___

16. The logarithm of -6 does not exist.   ___true___

17. What is an equation of the asymptote to the
graph of the function with equation $y = \log x$?   ___$x = 0$___

Representations Objective J

18. Graph $y = 10^x$ and $y = \log x$ on the
grid at the right.

88

LESSON MASTER 9-6 A

Questions on SPUR Objectives
See pages 599-601 for objectives.

Skills Objectives B and C

In 1 and 2, use the formula $D = 10 \log\left(\frac{N}{10^{-12}}\right)$, which gives the measure in D decibels for a sound with intensity $N = \frac{w}{m^2}$.

1. The sound intensity of traffic on a busy toll road is measured at 5.87×10^{-3} w/m². How intense is this sound as measured by the decibel scale? ≈ 97.7 dB

2. Find the intensity of a sound which has a relative intensity of 73 decibels. $\approx 2.00 \times 10^{-5}$ w/m²

In 3 and 4, use the formula pH = -log C to find the pH of a solution with concentration C of hydrogen ions, H⁺.

3. The concentration of a solution is 3.162×10^{-9} moles of H⁺ per liter.
   a. What is the pH of this solution? ≈ 8.5
   b. Is the solution acidic or alkaline? alkaline

4. A sample of blood has a pH of 7.41. What is the concentration of H⁺ ions in this sample? $\approx 3.89 \times 10^{-8}$

Uses Objective H

5. Elena is speaking at a normal level of 60 decibels, while Ito is whispering at a level of 30 decibels. Elena's normal voice is how many times as intense as Ito's whisper? 1000 times

6. While playing at a relative intensity of 115 decibels, a band was instructed to lower the output to 100 decibels. How many times as intense was the original sound as the softer sound? ≈ 31.6 times

7. What is the measure of a conversation which is twice as intense as a conversation which measures 60 decibels? ≈ 63 dB

8. Bile can range from a concentration of pH 9 to pH 11. The stronger alkaline solution is how many times as concentrated as the weaker alkaline solution? 100 times

9. Hydrochloric acid has pH of 1, and gastric juices have a pH of about 2. The concentration of hydrochloric acid is about how many times that of gastric juices? 10 times

10. Soap A has pH 7.4 and soap B has pH 7.7. How many times as alkaline as soap A is soap B? ≈ 2.0 times

---

LESSON MASTER 9-7 A

Questions on SPUR Objectives
See pages 599-601 for objectives.

Skills Objectives A and B

In 1–9, write the number as a decimal.

1. $\log_4 \frac{1}{4}$ -1
2. $\log_{26} 26$ 1
3. $\log_{16} 4$ $\frac{1}{2}$, or .5
4. $\log_2 8$ 3
5. $\log_{39} 1$ 0
6. $\log_{52} 52^4$ 4
7. $\log_8 4$ $\frac{2}{3}$, or .6
8. $\log_6 7776$ 5
9. $\log_5 25$ 2

In 10–13, solve. Round decimal solutions to the nearest hundredth.

10. $\log_7 4000 = \log_{17} 4000$ $x = 17$
11. $\log_x 8 = 15.2$ $y \approx 1.15$
12. $\log_8 z = 1.75$ $z = 38.05$
13. $\log_{12} w = 2.637$ $w = 701.13$

Properties Objective E

In 14 and 15, write in exponential form.

14. $\log_7 \frac{1}{343} = -3$ $7^{-3} = \frac{1}{343}$
15. $\log_9 27 = \frac{3}{2}$ $9^{\frac{3}{2}} = 27$

In 16 and 17, write in logarithmic form.

16. $6^8 = 1,679,616$ $\log_6 1,679,616 = 8$
17. $x^y = z, x > 0$ and $x \neq 1$ $\log_x z = y$

Representations Objective J

18. Graph the equation $y = \log_5 x$ on the grid below.

19. Graphed below is $y = \log_b x$. Find b. $b = 3$

LESSON MASTER 9-8 A

Questions on SPUR Objectives
See pages 599-601 for objectives.

Skills Objective C

In 1–4, give solutions to the nearest hundredth.

1. $\log(4z) = \log 5 + \log 4$ $z = 5$
2. $3 \log_2 4 = \log_2 m$ $m = 64$
3. $\log_5 625 - \log_5 25 = 2 \log_5 h$ $h = 5$
4. $\log_{19}(15y) = \log_{19} 3 + \log_{19} 5$ $y = 1$

Properties Objective E

In 5–12, write the number as a decimal.

5. $\log_{12} 1$ 0
6. $\log_{27} 27^{13}$ 13
7. $\log_8 4 + \log_8 2$ 1
8. $2 \log_9 27$ 3
9. $\frac{1}{3} \log_6 46,656$ 2
10. $\log_5 5^{-20}$ -20
11. $\log_4 3 - \log_4 48$ -2
12. $\log_{18} \sqrt[5]{18}$ $\frac{1}{6}$, or .16

In 13 and 14, rewrite as a logarithm of a single quantity.

13. $\log x + 5 \log r$ $\log xr^5$
14. $\log_3 4 + \log_3 x - \frac{1}{2} \log_3 d$ $\log_3 \frac{4x\sqrt{d}}{d}$

15. The following is a proof that the equation for determining a decibel measure can be written as $D = \log N^{10} + 120$. Give a reason for each step of the proof.

Proof: $D = 10 \log\left(\frac{N}{10^{-12}}\right)$ Given

$D = 10 (\log N - \log 10^{-12})$ a. Quot. Prop. of Logs

$D = 10 (\log N - -12)$ b. Log_b b^n Property

$D = 10 (\log N + 12)$ Definition of Subtraction

$D = 10 \log N + 120$ Distributive Property

$D = \log N^{10} + 120$ c. Power Prop. of Logs

LESSON MASTER 9-9 A

Questions on SPUR Objectives
See pages 599-601 for objectives.

Skills Objective A

In 1–3, write the number as a decimal. Do not use a calculator.

1. $\ln e^8$ 8
2. $\ln e^{\frac{1}{2}}$ $\frac{1}{2}$, or .5
3. $\ln e^{-\frac{2}{5}}$ $-\frac{2}{5}$

In 4–6, find the logarithm to the nearest hundredth.

4. $\ln 95$ 4.55
5. $\ln (-6.3)$ none
6. $\ln 0.03$ -3.51

Properties Objective E

In 7 and 8, write in exponential form.

7. $\ln 15 \approx 2.708$ $e^{2.708} \approx 15$
8. $\ln 1.5 \approx 0.405$ $e^{0.405} \approx 1.5$

In 9 and 10, write in logarithmic form.

9. $e^{-1.3} \approx 0.273$ $\ln 0.273 \approx -1.3$
10. $e^{15} \approx 3,269,017$ $\ln 3,269,017 \approx 15$

In 11 and 12, give the general property of which the statement is an instance.

11. $\ln e^5 = 5$ Log_b b^n Property
12. $\ln 50 + \ln 10 = \ln 500$ Prod. Prop. of Logs

Uses Objective H

13. The maximum velocity v of a rocket is $v = c \cdot \ln R$, where c is the velocity of the exhaust and R is the ratio of the mass of the rocket with fuel to its mass without fuel. Find R for a rocket if $c = 2000$ m/sec and $v = 2200$ m/sec. $R \approx 3.00$

Representations Objective J

14. *Multiple choice.* At the right is the graph of $y = \log_b x$. Point A has coordinates $(e, 1)$. Give the value of b. b

(a) 2 (b) e

(b) $-e$ (d) 3

Page 93

Name

LESSON MASTER 9-10 A

Skills Objective B

In 1–8, solve. Round solutions to the nearest hundredth.

1. $49^x = 343$
$x = 1.5$

2. $13^y = 28,561$
$y = 4$

3. $16^z = 8$
$z = .75$

4. $19,683^w = 729$
$w \approx .67$

5. $12^{m+5} = 17$
$m \approx -3.86$

6. $4e^n = 24$
$n \approx 1.79$

7. $(1.63)^c = e^3$
$c \approx 6.14$

8. $17^{4d-7} = 25$
$d \approx 2.03$

Uses Objective F

9. Sue Aimi wants to invest some money in a certificate of deposit paying interest at 5.8% compounded continuously. How long will it take the money to double?
$\approx$ **12 years**

10. Maria invested $3000 in an individual retirement account (IRA) which earns annual interest of 4.9%. How long will it take her to have $9000 in her IRA?
$\approx$ **23 years**

11. The population of a certain strain of bacteria grows according to the formula $N = N_0 \cdot 2^{1.71t}$, where t is the time in hours and N_0 is the initial population. How long will it take 50 bacteria to increase to 500,000?
$\approx$ **8 hours**

12. In 1994, the population of the world was about 5.6 billion. The U.S. Bureau of the Census predicts that in the year 2020, the world's population will reach 7.9 billion.
   a. Write an exponential equation to model this situation.
   Sample: $p = 5.6 (1.013)^t$
   b. Use this model to estimate when the world's population will reach 10 billion.
   $\approx$ **45 years**

93

Page 94

Name

LESSON MASTER 10-1 A

Skills Objective A

In 1–4, use a calculator to evaluate. Round to the nearest hundredth.

1. $\sin 28°$ **.47**

2. $\cos 62°$ **.47**

3. $\tan 50°$ **1.19**

4. $\sin 62°$ **.88**

In 5 and 6, approximate the trigonometric ratio to the nearest thousandth.

5. Refer to the triangle at the right.

   a. $\sin \theta$ $\approx$ **.528**
   b. $\cos \theta$ $\approx$ **.849**
   c. $\tan \theta$ $\approx$ **.622**

6. Refer to $\triangle ABC$ at the right.
   a. $\sin A$ $\approx$ **.670**
   b. $\cos B$ $\approx$ **.670**
   c. $\tan B$ $\approx$ **1.108**

Uses Objective F

7. A ship sailed 59 kilometers on a bearing of 25°. How far east of its original position is the ship?
$\approx$ **24.93 km**

8. Juanita used an instrument to sight the top of a building and got an angle measure of 62°. She is 5 ft tall and stood 35 ft from the building. About how tall was the building?

$\approx$ **70.83 ft.**

94

Page 95

Name

LESSON MASTER 10-2 A

Vocabulary

In 1–4, use the labeled angles in the picture at the right. Assume that the dashed line is parallel to the ground and that the buildings have the same height.

1. Name all *angles of elevation*.
$\angle 5, \angle 6$

2. *True or false.* $m \angle 2 = m \angle 5$
true

3. Name all *angles of depression*.
$\angle 2, \angle 3$

4. Name two pairs of *congruent* angles.
$\angle 2$ and $\angle 5$, $\angle 3$ and $\angle 6$

Skills Objective C

In 5–8, give the measure of the acute angle θ to the nearest degree.

5. $\sin \theta = .3$ **17°**

6. $\tan \theta = \frac{\sqrt{3}}{3}$ **30°**

7. $\cos^{-1}(.5) = \theta$ **60°**

8. $\tan^{-1}(3) = \theta$ **72°**

Uses Objective F

9. A ramp is to be built up to a doorway. Its slope is to be $\frac{1}{13}$. What angle will the ramp make with the horizontal?
$\approx$ **4.4°**

10. A plane flying at 31,000 feet begins its descent 125 miles from the airport. If the angle of depression is constant, find its measure.

$\approx$ **2.7°**

11. REGULADCON is a regular decagon. If each side of the decagon measures 10, find the length of $\overline{RG}$.

$\approx$ **19 units**

95

Page 96

Name

LESSON MASTER 10-3 A

Skills Objective B

In 1–3, give the exact value.

1. $\sin 30°$ $\frac{1}{2}$**, or .5**

2. $\cos 30°$ $\frac{\sqrt{3}}{2}$

3. $\tan 45°$ **1**

In 4 and 5, give the exact value.

4.
   a. $\sin 60°$ $\frac{\sqrt{3}}{2}$
   b. x $6\sqrt{3}$

5.
   a. $\tan 30°$ $\frac{\sqrt{3}}{3}$
   b. y $12\sqrt{3}$

Properties Objective E

In 6–9, fill in the blank with the measure of an acute angle.

6. $\cos 37° = \sin$ **53°**

7. $\sin 25° = \cos (90° -$ **25°** $)$

8. $\tan 55° = \dfrac{\sin 55°}{\cos 55°}$

9. $(\sin$ **12°** $)^2 + (\cos 12°)^2 = 1$

10. If $\cos \theta = 0.81$ and θ is acute, then $\sin \theta \approx$ **.586**

11. Without using a calculator, explain why $\sin 45° = \cos 45°$.
Sample: A right triangle with a 45° angle is isosceles with its congruent angles both having measures of 45°. Thus both sin 45° and cos 45° equal $1/\sqrt{2}$.

In 12 and 13, verify the property when $\theta = 60°$.

12. $(\sin \theta)^2 + (\cos \theta)^2 = 1$
$(\sqrt{3}/2)^2 + (1/2)^2 = (3/4) + (1/4) = 4/4 = 1$

13. $\sin(90 - \theta) = \cos \theta$
$\sin(90° - 60°) = \sin 30° = 1/2; \cos 60° = 1/2$

96

LESSON MASTER 10-4 A

Skills Objective B

In 1–12, give the exact value. Do not use a calculator.

1. cos 90° **0**
2. cos 0° **1**
3. sin 270° **-1**

4. cos 180° **-1**
5. sin 180° **0**
6. sin 405° $\frac{\sqrt{2}}{2}$

7. sin 630° **-1**
8. cos (-315°) $\frac{\sqrt{2}}{2}$
9. cos(-330°) $\frac{\sqrt{3}}{2}$

10. cos (-690°) $\frac{\sqrt{3}}{2}$
11. cos (-540°) **-1**
12. sin (-270°) **1**

Representations Objective I

13. To the nearest thousandth, find the coordinates of the image of the point (1, 0) under R_{75}. **(.259, .966)**

In 14–21, refer to the drawing at the right of the unit circle with the given points on it. Give the letter that could represent the value.

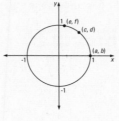

14. sin (-310°) **d**
15. cos 0° **a**
16. cos 80° **e**
17. cos 50° **c**
18. sin 440° **f**
19. sin 1080° **b**
20. cos (-670°) **c**
21. sin 0° **b**

LESSON MASTER 10-5 A

Skills Objective A

In 1–6, use a calculator to evaluate. Round to the nearest thousandth.

1. sin 176° **.070**
2. cos (-1500°) **.5**
3. sin 1802° **.035**
4. cos (-397°) **.799**
5. sin (-255.7°) **.969**
6. cos 223° **-.731**

Skills Objective B

In 7–12, give the exact value.

7. sin 660° $-\frac{\sqrt{3}}{2}$
8. cos (-660°) $\frac{1}{2}$, or .5
9. cos 150° $-\frac{\sqrt{3}}{2}$

10. cos (-1800°) **1**
11. sin 270° **-1**
12. sin (-405°) $-\frac{\sqrt{2}}{2}$

Representations Objective I

In 13–16, use the unit circle at the right. Use your calculator to find

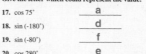

13. the x-coordinate of A. **≈ -.174**
14. the y-coordinate of A. **≈ .985**
15. the x-coordinate of B. **≈ -.940**
16. the y-coordinate of B. **≈ -.342**

In 17–20, use the unit circle at the right. Give the letter which could represent the value.

17. cos 75° **a**
18. sin (-180°) **d**
19. sin (-80°) **f**
20. cos 280° **e**

In 21–24, use the unit circle at the right to find the value.

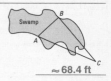

21. cos α **-.391**
22. sin θ **-.970**
23. α **≈ 113°**
24. θ **≈ -104°**

LESSON MASTER 10-6 A

Uses Objective G

1. A baseball infield is determined by a square with sides 90 ft long. In the diagram at the right, home plate is H and first base is F. Suppose the first baseman ran in a straight line from F to catch a pop-up at B, 120 ft. from home plate. If the measure of ∠FHB is 10°, how far did the first baseman run?

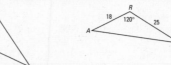

   ≈ 35 ft

2. The air distance from Chicago to Los Angeles is 1745 miles. From Los Angeles to New York the air distance is 2451 miles, and from New York to Chicago it is 714 miles. Two airplanes leave Los Angeles, one heading straight for Chicago and the other straight for New York. Use the Law of Cosines to estimate the measure of the angle they will form.

   ≈ 3°

Representations Objective H

3. Find BC. **≈ 16.94**

4. Find TA. **≈ 37.40**

5. Find m∠K. **≈ 67.4°**

6. Find the measure of the smallest angle. **≈ 41.1° (m∠O)**

LESSON MASTER 10-7 A

Uses Objective G

1. Some students in Advanced Algebra were assigned the task of measuring the distance between two trees separated by a swamp. They determined that the angle formed by tree A, a dry point C, and tree B was 27°. They also knew that m∠ABC was 85°. They found that AC was 150 ft. How far apart are the trees?

   ≈ 68.4 ft

2. Two lookout towers, L and M, are 50 kilometers apart. The ranger in Tower L, Mary Eagle Wing, saw a fire at point C such that m∠CLM = 40°. The ranger in Tower M, Raul Sonoma, saw the fire such that m∠CML = 65°. How far was the fire from Mary?

   ≈ 46.9 km

Representations Objective H

3. Find JM. **≈ 19.30**

4. Find DF. **≈ 25.76**

5. Find PA. **≈ 181.33**

6. Find the length of the shortest side. **≈ 1.18 (OT)**

Lesson Master 10-8 A

LESSON MASTER 10-8 A

Questions on SPUR Objectives
See pages 669–671 for objectives.

Representations Objective J

In 1–3, *true or false*. If false, rewrite the statement to make it true.

1. The range of the sine function is the set of all real numbers.

   false; The range of the sine function is the set of all numbers from -1 to 1.

2. The graph of the sine function has x-intercepts at the even-numbered multiples of 90°.

   true

3. The graphs of $f(\theta) = \cos\theta$ and $g(\theta) = \sin\theta$ are congruent.

   true

4. a. At the right, graph $f: x \rightarrow \sin x$ for $-360° \le x \le 360°$.

   b. Give the y-intercept of the sine function.

   0

   c. Give the period of the sine function.

   360°

   d. What are the x-intercepts of the sine function on this domain?

   -360°, -180°, 0°, 180°, 360°

5. a. At the right, graph the cosine function $g(x) = \cos x$ for $-360° \le x \le 360°$.

   b. Give the y-intercept of the cosine function.

   1

   c. Give the period of the cosine function.

   360°

   d. What are the x-intercepts of the cosine function on this domain?

   -270°, -90°, 90°, 270°

101 ▶

Lesson Master 10-8 A page 2

▶ **LESSON MASTER 10-8 A** *page 2*

6. $y = \sin x$ is the image of $y = \cos x$ under what translation?

   Sample: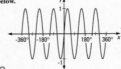

In 7 and 8, fill in the blanks.

7. As x increases from 90° to 180°, sin x decreases from **1** to **0**.

8. As x increases from 180° to 270°, cos x increases from **-1** to **0**.

In 9 and 10, use the graph of $y = f(x)$ below.

9. Does this function seem to be periodic? If so, what is its period?

   yes; 120°

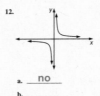

10. Is this function sinusoidal? Explain your reasoning.

   Sample: It appears to be a sine wave that has undergone a size change.

In 11 and 12, a function is graphed. a. Does the function seem to be periodic? b. If so, what is its period?

11.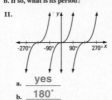

   a. **yes**

   b. **180°**

12.

   a. **no**

   b. _____

102

Lesson Master 10-9 A

LESSON MASTER 10-9 A

Questions on SPUR Objectives
See pages 669–671 for objectives.

Skills Objective C

In 1 and 2, solve for all θ between 0° and 180°. Give θ to the nearest degree.

1. $\sin\theta = .163$ **θ ≈ 9° or 171°**

2. $\sin\theta = -.707$ **no solutions**

In 3 and 4, solve for all θ between 0° and 180°. Give exact values.

3. $\sin\theta = \frac{\sqrt{3}}{2}$ **θ = 60° or 120°**

4. $\sin\theta = \frac{\sqrt{2}}{2}$ **θ = 45° or 135°**

Properties Objective E

In 5–7, fill in the blank.

5. Give the measure of an acute angle. $\sin 68° = \sin(180° - $ **68°** $)$

6. If $\sin\theta = .6$ and $0° < \theta < 180°$, then $\cos\theta = $ **.8** or $\cos\theta = $ **-.8**

7. If $\sin\theta = .7$ and θ is obtuse, to the nearest thousandth, $\cos\theta = $ **-.714**

8. *True or false.* $\cos(180° - \theta) = \sin\theta$. **false**

Uses Objective G

9. Elinor, Juan, and Machiko are playing catch. Elinor and Juan are 59 feet apart, and Machiko and Juan are 46 feet apart. The line from Elinor to Machiko is at a 51° angle with the line from Elinor to Juan.

   a. Find the measure of the angle where Machiko stands. (Hint: There are two answers.) **≈ 85.4°, ≈ 94.6°**

   b. Use your answers to Part a to find the distance from Machiko to Elinor. **≈ 41 ft, ≈ 33 ft**

Representations Objective H

10. Given $\triangle YES$, with $m\angle Y = 30°$, $YE = 6$, and $ES = 4$, solve the triangle and sketch each possibility.

   $m\angle S \approx 131.4°$
   $m\angle E \approx 18.6°$
   $YS \approx 2.55$

   $m\angle S \approx 48.6°$
   $m\angle E \approx 101.4°$
   $YS \approx 7.84$

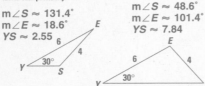

103

Lesson Master 10-10 A

LESSON MASTER 10-10 A

Questions on SPUR Objectives
See pages 669–671 for objectives.

Skills Objective A

In 1–6, evaluate to the nearest thousandth.

1. $\sin\left(\frac{11\pi}{6}\right)$ **-.500** 2. $\tan\left(\frac{3\pi}{10}\right)$ **1.376** 3. $\cos\left(-\frac{7\pi}{24}\right)$ **.609**

4. $\tan(-10)$ **-.648** 5. $\sin(16\pi)$ **0** 6. $\cos(-2.46)$ **-.777**

Skills Objective B

In 7–12, give the exact value.

7. $\sin\left(\frac{\pi}{2}\right)$ **1** 8. $\cos\left(-\frac{\pi}{4}\right)$ **$\frac{\sqrt{2}}{2}$**

9. $\tan\left(\frac{13\pi}{6}\right)$ **$\frac{\sqrt{3}}{3}$** 10. $\cos\left(-\frac{3\pi}{4}\right)$ **$-\frac{\sqrt{2}}{2}$**

11. $\tan\left(-\frac{3\pi}{4}\right)$ **1** 12. $\sin\left(\frac{5\pi}{6}\right)$ **$\frac{1}{2}$, or .5**

Skills Objective D

In 13–18, convert to radians.

13. -45° **$-\frac{\pi}{4}$** 14. 90° **$\frac{\pi}{2}$** 15. 720° **4π**

16. 27° **$\frac{3\pi}{20}$** 17. 1° **$\frac{\pi}{180}$** 18. -18° **$-\frac{\pi}{10}$**

In 19–24, convert to degrees.

19. -2π **-360°** 20. $-\frac{3}{5}\pi$ **-108°** 21. $\frac{3\pi}{8}$ **67.5°**

22. $\frac{7\pi}{12}$ **105°** 23. 1 **$\frac{180°}{\pi}$** 24. $\frac{29\pi}{3}$ **1740°**

Representations Objective J

In 25–28, use the unit circle at the right. Give the letter which could represent the given function.

25. $\sin\left(\frac{\pi}{6}\right)$ **b**

26. $\cos\left(\frac{13\pi}{6}\right)$ **a**

27. $\sin\left(\frac{2\pi}{3}\right)$ **d**

28. $\cos\left(-\frac{2\pi}{3}\right)$ **e**

104

LESSON MASTER 11-1 **A**

Properties Objective E

1. *True or false.* $9x^2 + 4x - 1 + 3x^{-1}$ is a polynomial. ____**false**____

In 2–4, a polynomial is given. **a.** Give its degree.
b. Name its leading coefficient.

2. $m^3 - 3m^7$
   a. __7__
   b. __-3__

3. $4n - 15 - 3n^2$
   a. __2__
   b. __-3__

4. $8p^2 - 1$
   a. __2__
   b. __8__

Uses Objective H

5. Diane Chang invested her savings in an account paying $r\%$ interest compounded annually. Suppose she invests $90 at the beginning of each year for six years. No additional money is added or withdrawn.
   a. Write a polynomial expression for the total amount in Diane's account at the end of the sixth year.

   $90x^6 + 90x^5 + 90x^4 + 90x^3 + 90x^2 + 90x$
   $(x = 1 + r)$

   b. Evaluate how much Diane will have if the account earns 3.9% interest each year. ____**$618.69**____

Representations Objective J

In 6 and 7, graph the function given.

6. $p(x) = x^4 - .2x^3 - 8x^2 - 1.5x + 5$

7. $k(x) = 5x^5 - 3x - 3$

LESSON MASTER 11-2 **A**

Skills Objective A

In 1–4, expand and write in standard form.

1. $(a - 3)(2a^3 - 3a^2)$
   $2a^4 - 9a^3 + 9a^2$

2. $(b + 7)(b - 1)(b + 4)$
   $b^3 + 10b^2 + 17b - 28$

3. $(7 - c)^2 (2 - c)$
   $-c^3 + 16c^2 - 77c + 98$

4. $(-d + 1)(5d^2 - 2d - 3)$
   $-5d^3 + 7d^2 + d - 3$

In 5 and 6, multiply and simplify.

5. $(10e + 2f)(6f - 3g + 1)$
   $12f^2 + 60ef - 30eg - 6fg$
   $+ 10e + 2f$

6. $(2h + j - k)(h - j - k)$
   $2h^2 - j^2 + k^2 - hj - 3hk$

Properties Objective E

In 7–9, an expression is given. **a.** Classify it as a *monomial*, a *binomial*, or a *trinomial*. **b.** Give its degree.

7. $13t^2 + 4t^3$
   a. __binomial__
   b. __3__

8. $384m^6n^2 - m^6n^2$
   a. __monomial__
   b. __8__

9. $r^5t^5u^2 - u - 1$
   a. __trinomial__
   b. __12__

Uses Objective I

10. The largest figure at the right is a rectangle.
    a. What are its dimensions?
    $p + 9, 2p + r + 7$

    b. What is its area?
    $(p + 9)(2p + r + 7) = 2p^2 + 25p + pr + 9r + 63$

11. From a sheet of notebook paper 26.7 cm by 20.3 cm, squares of side x are removed from each corner, forming an open box.
    a. Sketch a diagram of this situation.
    b. Write a formula for the volume $V(x)$ of the box.
    $V(x) = 542.01x - 94x^2 + 4x^3$

    c. Write a formula for its surface area $S(x)$.
    $S(x) = 542.01 - 4x^2$

LESSON MASTER 11-3 **A**

Vocabulary

1. Is $a^2 - 39$ prime
   a. over the set of polynomials with rational coefficients? ____**yes**____
   b. over the set of polynomials with real coefficients? ____**no**____
   c. Explain your answers to Parts **a** and **b**.
   Sample: $a^2 - 39 = (a + \sqrt{39})(a - \sqrt{39})$, so $a^2 - 39$ can be factored over the reals but not the rationals.

2. The Discriminant Theorem for Factoring Quadratics applies to quadratics with __?__ coefficients. ____**integer**____

Skills Objective B

In 3–6, fill in the blanks.

3. $19m^2n - 114mn^2 = 19mn ($ __m__ $-$ __$6n$__ $)$

4. $24p^3t + 60p^3 =$ __$12p^3$__ $(2t + 5)$

5. $5wz + 25w^2z - 35w^3z = 5wz ($ __1__ $+$ __$5w$__ $-$ __$7w^2$__ $)$

6. $(3 - 2h)^3 + (3 - 2h)^4 = (3 - 2h)^3 ($ __1__ $+$ __$3 - 2h$__ $)$
   or $(-2h + 4)$

In 7–12, factor.

7. $a^2 - 12a + 36$
   $(a - 6)^2$

8. $9c^2 + 6c + 1$
   $(3c + 1)^2$

9. $30e^3 - 60e^2 + 30e$
   $30e(e - 1)^2$

10. $g^2 - 64h^6$
    $(g + 8h^3)(g - 8h^3)$

11. $k^4 - 25k^2$
    $k^2(k + 5)(k - 5)$

12. $5r^2 + 9r - 18$
    $(5r - 6)(r + 3)$

13. a. Write $t^4 - 16$ as the product of two binomials. $(t^2 + 4)(t^2 - 4)$
    b. Write $t^4 - 16$ as the product of three binomials. $(t^2 + 4)(t + 2)(t - 2)$

14. *True or false.* $3x^2 - y^2 = (x\sqrt{3} + y)(x\sqrt{3} - y)$ ____**true**____

15. *True or false.* $9a^2 + b^2 = (3a + bi)(3a - bi)$ ____**true**____

LESSON MASTER 11-4 **A**

Representations Objective K

In 1 and 2, estimate the real zeros of the described function to the nearest tenth.

1. $f(x) = 2x^4 - 10x^2 + 3$
   $-2.2, -.6, .6, 2.2$

2. $y = 2x^5 - 5x^3 - 2x^2 + 3x + 1$
   $-.3, .8, 1.5$

In 3 and 4, use the graph of the function to determine its integer zeros.

3. $y = x^3 - 9x^2 + 23x - 15$

$1, 3, 5$

4. $h(x) = 4 - 3x^2 - x^3$

$-2, 1$

5. a. Complete the table of values for the function Q with equation $Q(x) = .09x^3 - 2x + 16$.

x	-10	-8	-6	-4	-2	0	2	4	6
Q(x)	-54.00	-14.08	8.56	18.24	19.28	16.00	12.72	13.76	23.44

   b. Use the table to tell how many zeros the function has. ____**1 zero**____

   c. For each zero, indicate the two consecutive even integers between which the zero must lie. ____**-6 and -8**____

   d. Describe how you could use a graph to justify your response to Part **b**.
   Sample: The graph should show just one x-intercept.

   e. Use technology to find each zero to the nearest hundredth. ____**-6.92**____

LESSON MASTER 11-5 A

Questions on SPUR Objectives
See pages 741-745 for objectives.

Skills Objective C

In 1–3, give the exact zeros of the function described.

1. $A(x) = x(x - 3)(x + 4)(2x - 1)$ $0, 3, -4, \frac{1}{2}$

2. $B(x) = x^2 - 100$ $-10, 10$

3. $C(x) = x^3 - x$ $-1, 0, 1$

Skills Objective D

4. Give equations for 3 different polynomial functions with zeros at $-8, \frac{2}{3}$, and $\frac{5}{2}$. **Samples are given.**

$y = (x+8)(3x-2)(2x-5)$ $y = 2(x+8)(3x-2)(2x-5)$

$y = x(x+8)(3x-2)(2x-5)$

Properties Objective F

In 5 and 6, consider the functions with equations.
$M(x) = x(x-1)(x-2)$ and $N(x) = x^2(x-1)(x-2)$.

5. *True or false.* M and N have the same graphs.   **false**

6. *True or false.* M and N have the same zeros.   **true**

7. *True or false.* 3 is *not* a solution to $(g-3)(g+4) = 7$.   **true**

8. Consider the polynomial $R(x) = 2x^3 - 19x^2 + 35x$.

   a. List its factors. $x, 2x - 5, x - 7$

   b. List its zeros. $0, \frac{5}{2}, 7$

   c. Which theorem allows you to proceed from Part **a** to Part **b** without graphing? **the Factor Theorem**

Representations Objectives J and K

9. At the right, graph the function P with $P(x) = x^3 - 13x^2 + 36x$. Give the real zeros of the function.

   $-3, -2, 0, 2, 3$

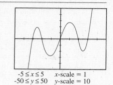

$-5 \le x \le 5$ x-scale = 1
$-50 \le y \le 50$ y-scale = 10

109

LESSON MASTER 11-6 A

Questions on SPUR Objectives
See pages 741-745 for objectives.

Skills Objective B and C

In 1–4, a polynomial is given. a. Factor over the set of *complex* numbers. b. Identify all *real* zeros. c. Check by graphing.

1. $A(r) = 6r^2 + 5r - 4$

   a. $A(r) = (3r+4)(2r-1)$

   b. $-\frac{4}{3}, \frac{1}{2}$

   c.

2. $B(t) = 6t^3 + 33t^2 - 18t$

   a. $B(t) = 3t(t+6)(2t-1)$

   b. $0, -6, \frac{1}{2}$

   c. [graph]

3. $A(x) = x^2 + 5x - 7$

   a. see below

   b. see below

   c. [graph]

4. $T(y) = y - 3y^2 - 4$

   a. see below

   b. none

   c. [graph]

3a. $A(x) = \left(x - \frac{-5+\sqrt{53}}{2}\right)\left(x - \frac{-5-\sqrt{53}}{2}\right)$

3b. $\frac{-5+\sqrt{53}}{2}, \frac{-5-\sqrt{53}}{2}$

4a. $T(y) = \left(y - \frac{1-i\sqrt{47}}{6}\right)\left(y - \frac{1+i\sqrt{47}}{6}\right)$

110

LESSON MASTER 11-7 A

Questions on SPUR Objectives
See pages 741-745 for objectives.

Properties Objective G

In 1 and 2, use the Rational Zero Theorem to factor the polynomial.

1. $L(x) = 30x^3 - 31x^2 + 10x - 1$
$L(x) = (3x-1)(5x-1)(2x-1)$

2. $M(x) = x^4 + 2x^3 + x^2$
$M(x) = x^2(x+1)^2$

In 3–7, a polynomial is given. a. Use the Rational Zero theorem to list all possible rational zeros. b. Find all rational zeros.

3. $P(x) = 7x^5 - 3x^4 - 2$

   a. $\pm1, \pm2, \pm\frac{1}{7}, \pm\frac{2}{7}$

   b. none

4. $Q(m) = 64m^3 - 1$

   a. $\pm1, \pm\frac{1}{2}, \pm\frac{1}{4}, \pm\frac{1}{8}, \pm\frac{1}{16}, \frac{1}{4} \quad \pm\frac{1}{32}, \pm\frac{1}{64}$

   b. $\frac{1}{4}$

5. $R(n) = 3n^2 - 15n - 18$

   a. $\pm1, \pm2, \pm3, \pm6, \pm9, \pm18, \pm\frac{1}{3}, \pm\frac{2}{3}$

   b. $6, -1$

6. $S(x) = 2x^4 - 7x^3 + 5x^2 - 7x + 3$

   a. $\pm1, \pm3, \pm\frac{1}{2}, \pm\frac{3}{2}$

   b. $3, \frac{1}{2}$

7. $T(x) = x^5 + 2x^3 - x^2 - 2$

   a. $\pm1, \pm2$

   b. 1

Representations Objective J

8. Consider $U(x) = 5x^6 + 6x^4 + x^2 + 12$.

   a. Use the Rational Zero Theorem to list all possible rational zeros.
$\pm1, \pm2, \pm3, \pm4, \pm6, \pm12$
$\pm\frac{1}{5}, \pm\frac{2}{5}, \pm\frac{3}{5}, \pm\frac{4}{5}, \pm\frac{6}{5}, \pm\frac{12}{5}$

   b. Graph this polynomial on the grid at the right.

   c. Use Parts **a** and **b** to find all rational zeros of this polynomial.

   Sample: The graph does not intersect the x-axis, so there are no rational zeros.

111

LESSON MASTER 11-8 A

Questions on SPUR Objectives
See pages 741-745 for objectives.

Vocabulary

1. *Multiple choice.* Consider the equation $(x+1)^6(x-2)(x-1) = 0$. Which is true?   **d**

   (a) 1 is a double root.   (b) -1 is a double root.

   (c) 1 is a root with multiplicity 6.   (d) -1 is a root with multiplicity 6.

Properties Objective F

In 2 and 3, use the equation $\sqrt{6}x^3 - 5ix + .4x^2 - 2 = 0$.

2. *True or false.* This equation has at least one complex solution.   **true**

3. This equation has exactly __?__ roots.   **3**

4. Consider the equation $(x-3)^6(x^2-3)(x^2+9) = 0$.

   a. This equation has exactly __?__ roots if multiplicities of multiple roots are counted.   **10**

   b. **3** is a rational root with multiplicity **6**.

   $\sqrt{3}$ is an irrational root with multiplicity **1**.

   $-\sqrt{3}$ is an irrational root with multiplicity **1**.

   $3i$ is a complex root with multiplicity **1**.

   $-3i$ is a complex root with multiplicity **1**.

Culture Objective L

In 5–10, match each mathematician with his contribution toward solving all polynomial equations.

   d 5. Omar Khayyam, 1100s

   a 6. Ludovico Ferrari, 1500s

   c 7. Niccolo Tartaglia, 1500s

   b 8. Karl Friedrich Gauss, 1700s

   f 9. Évariste Galois, 1800s

   e 10. Niels Abel, 1800s

   a. discovered how to solve quartic equations using complex numbers

   b. proved the Fundamental Theorem of Algebra

   c. discovered how to solve all cubic equations

   d. first showed how to solve many cubic equations

   e. proved the general quartic equation cannot be solved using a formula

   f. described method for determining which polynomials of degree 5 or more can be solved with a formula

112

LESSON MASTER 11-9 A

Questions on SPUR Objectives
See pages 741-745 for objectives.

Skills Objective D

In 1 and 2, a function is described. a. Determine whether the function is a polynomial function of degree ≤ 5. b. If so, give the degree of the function.

1. the function(n, a_n) where $a_1 = 2$ and $a_n = a_{n-1} + 3$

   a. _yes_   b. _1_

2.

x	10	20	30	40	50	60	70	80	90
y	-200	-209	-280	-443	-584	-325	1096	4945	13,112

   a. _yes_   b. _5_

3. Suppose the sequence 3, 4, 11, 24, 43, 68, 99, . . . has a formula with degree ≤ 4. Use the method of finite differences to predict the next term.   _136_

4. Can the method of finite differences be used with this set of data? Explain why or why not.

x	1	3	6	10	15	21	28	36	45
y	24	49	74	99	124	149	174	199	224

Sample: No; the sequence of x-values is not arithmetic.

Uses Objective H

In 5 and 6, use the results of an experiment involving rolling a marble down an inclined plane.

Time Passed (seconds)	0	1	2	3	4	5	6
Distance of Marble from Given Point (cm)	10	12.4	14.8	17.2	19.6	22	24.4

5. What degree polynomial would you use to best model these data? Explain your answer.
   Sample: One; the first differences are equal.

6. Use your polynomial to predict how far the marble would be from the given point after 10 seconds.   _34 cm_

LESSON MASTER 11-10 A

Questions on SPUR Objectives
See pages 741-745 for objectives.

Skills Objective D

1. Consider the values in the table below.

x	1	2	3	4	5	6	7	8
y	2	20	50	92	146	212	290	380

   a. This data can be modeled by a polynomial equation of the form $y = ax^2 + bx + c$. List three equations which can be used to solve for a, b, and c.

   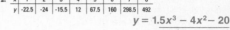 Samples are given.

   $a+b+c=2$ $4a+2b+c=20$ $9a+3b+c=50$

   b. Solve the system to find a formula which models the data above. $y = 6x^2 - 4$

In 2–4, write a formula of degree $n \le 5$ which models the data.

2.

x	1	2	3	4	5	6	7	8
y	-22.5	-24	-15.5	12	67.5	160	298.5	492

   $y = 1.5x^3 - 4x^2 - 20$

3.

x	1	2	3	4	5	6	7	8
y	-3	-16	-27	0	125	432	1029	2048

   $y = x^4 - 4x^3$

4.

x	1	2	3	4	5	6	7	8
y	-2	3	4	-5	-30	-77	-152	-261

   $y = -x^3 + 4x^2 - 5$

Uses Objective H

5. Suppose that Sylvia stacks soccer balls in a triangular pyramid display. That is, one ball is in the top row, three are in the second row, six are in the third row, and so on.

   a. Complete the table.

Number of rows (n)	1	2	3	4	5	6
Total Number of Balls (T)	1	4	10	19	31	46

   b. How many soccer balls are needed for n rows? $1.5n^2 - 1.5n + 1$

LESSON MASTER 12-1 A

Questions on SPUR Objectives
See pages 804-807 for objectives.

Skills Objective B

In 1 and 2, write an equation for the parabola satisfying the given conditions.

1. focus (0, 3) and directrix $y = -3$. $y = \frac{1}{12}x^2$

2. focus (-5, 0) and directrix $x = 5$. $y^2 = -20x$

3. Given $F = (0, -2)$ and line ℓ with equation $y = 2$, write an equation for the set of points equidistant from F and ℓ. $y = -\frac{1}{8}x^2$

Properties Objectives E, F, and G

4. In the diagram at the right, locate five points on the parabola with directrix m and focus F, including the vertex of the parabola.
   Four sample points are given in addition to the vertex.

In 5 and 6, an equation for a parabola is given. a. Tell whether the parabola opens up or down. b. Name the focus. c. Name its vertex. d. Name the directrix.

5. $y = 0.6x^2$

   a. _up_   b. $\left(0, \frac{5}{12}\right)$
   c. _(0, 0)_   d. $y = -\frac{5}{12}$

6. $y = -7(x + 3)^2$

   a. _down_   b. $\left(-3, -\frac{1}{28}\right)$
   c. _(-3, 0)_   d. $y = \frac{1}{28}$

Representations Objective J

7. a. Graph the parabola with equation $y = -\frac{1}{4}x^2$.

   b. Plot and label the focus.

   c. Plot and label the directrix.

directrix

LESSON MASTER 12-2 A

Questions on SPUR Objectives
See pages 804-807 for objectives.

Skills Objective B

In 1 and 2, write an equation for the circle satisfying the given conditions.

1. center at origin, radius 5 $x^2 + y^2 = 25$

2. center at (-3, 7), radius 8 $(x+3)^2 + (y-7)^2 = 64$

Properties Objectives F and G

In 3 and 4, identify the center and radius of the circle.

3. $(x + 3)^2 + y^2 = 26$

   center _(-3, 0)_
   radius _$\sqrt{26}$_

4. $(x - 7.5)^2 + (y + 2.5)^2 = \frac{1}{25}$

   center _(7.5, -2.5)_
   radius _$\frac{1}{5}$_

5. True or false. The distance between any two points on a circle is a constant.   _false_

Uses Objective H

6. A seismograph located 10 miles due north of a recording station detects an earthquake with epicenter 15 miles away.

   a. Write an equation that could be used to describe possible locations of the epicenter. $x^2 + (y - 10)^2 = 225$

   b. A worker was 8 miles due east of the station when the quake occurred. Use your answer to Part a to determine whether the epicenter could have been right below her.   no; $8^2 + 10^2 \neq 225$

Representations Objective J

7. Graph the circle with equation $(x - 3)^2 + (y - 4)^2 = 25$.

8. Write an equation for the circle graphed below.

   $(x+1)^2 + (y-1)^2 = 1$

LESSON MASTER 12-3 A

Skills Objective B

1. What equation describes the lower semicircle of the circle $x^2 + y^2 = 10$?

$y = -\sqrt{10 - x^2}$

2. a. Write a sentence describing all points in the interior of the circle $(x - 3)^2 + (y + 5)^2 = 13$.

$(x - 3)^2 + (y + 5)^2 < 13$

   b. Use your answer to Part a to show that the point (1, -3) is inside the circle.

$(1 - 3)^2 + (-3 + 5)^2 = 4 + 4 = 8$; $8 < 13$, so the point (1, -3) is in the interior of the circle.

Uses Objective H

3. A truck 7 feet high and 4 feet wide approaches a semicircular tunnel which has a diameter of 16 feet.

   a. Will the truck fit through the tunnel? Justify your answer.

Sample: Yes; the equation for the tunnel is $x^2 + y^2 = 64$, and the points (2, 7) and (-2, 7) for the truck are in the interior of the semicircle.

   b. Find the radius of the smallest tunnel the truck could enter.

$\sqrt{53}$, or ≈ 7.3 ft

4. The pilot of a small plane tells an air-traffic controller that he is within a 14-mile radius of a town that is 22 miles north of the airport. Write a sentence that describes his possible locations (x, y) from the point of view of the controller.

$x^2 + (y - 22)^2 < 196$

Representations Objective J

In 5 and 6, graph the inequality.

5. $(x + 1)^2 + (y + 6)^2 \geq 4$

6. $1 \leq (x + 2)^2 + (y - 3)^2 \leq 4$

LESSON MASTER 12-4 A

Skills Objective B

In 1–5, write an equation for an ellipse satisfying the given conditions.

1. foci at (-4, 0) and (4, 0); focal constant 12

$\frac{x^2}{36} + \frac{y^2}{20} = 1$

2. foci at (8, 0) and (-8, 0); focal constant 18

$\frac{x^2}{81} + \frac{y^2}{17} = 1$

3. foci at (0, 3) and (0, -3); major axis length 10

$\frac{x^2}{16} + \frac{y^2}{25} = 1$

4. foci at (-1, 0) and (1, 0); minor axis length $\sqrt{5}$

$\frac{4x^2}{9} + \frac{4y^2}{5} = 1$

5. center at origin, horizontal major axis 8, vertical minor axis 6

$\frac{x^2}{16} + \frac{y^2}{9} = 1$

Properties Objectives E, F, and G

6. Use the conic grid below with centers 10 units apart to draw the set of points P satisfying the condition $PF_1 + PF_2 = 12$.

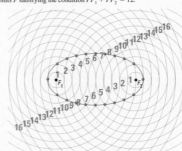

7. Given two fixed points F_1 and F_2 and a focal constant d, give the condition that a set of points P must satisfy in order to be an ellipse.

$|PF_1 + PF_2| = d$

▶ **LESSON MASTER 12-4 A** *page 2*

8. Consider the ellipse with equation $\frac{x^2}{15} + \frac{y^2}{26} = 1$.

   a. Give the length of its major axis.

$2\sqrt{26}$

   b. Name its vertices.

$(\pm\sqrt{15}, 0), (0, \pm\sqrt{26})$

   c. Which axis contains the foci of this ellipse?

y-axis

   d. Find the foci F_1 and F_2.

$(0, \sqrt{11}), (0, -\sqrt{11})$

   e. If P is on this ellipse, find $PF_1 + PF_2$.

$2\sqrt{26}$

Uses Objective H

9. The orbit of Mars around the sun approximates an ellipse with the sun at one focus. The closest and farthest distances of Mars from the center of the sun are 128.5 and 155.0 million miles, respectively.

   a. How far is F_2 from the center of the sun?

≈ 26.5 mil. mi

   b. What is the length of the orbit's minor axis?

≈ 282 mil. mi

Representations Objective J

10. Sketch the graph of $\frac{x^2}{4} + \frac{y^2}{9} = 1$ on the grid at the right.

11. a. The ellipse shown at the right has integer intercepts. Write an equation for it.

$\frac{x^2}{4} + \frac{y^2}{25} = 1$

   b. Verify that the point $(1, \frac{5\sqrt{3}}{2})$ is on the ellipse.

$\frac{1}{4}(1^2) + \frac{1}{25}\left(\frac{5\sqrt{3}}{2}\right)^2 = \frac{1}{4} + \frac{1}{25}\left(\frac{75}{4}\right) = \frac{1}{4} + \frac{3}{4} = 1$

   c. Write a sentence describing the interior of the ellipse.

$\frac{x^2}{4} + \frac{y^2}{25} < 1$

   d. Use your answer to Part c to verify that the point (-1, 4) is in the interior of the ellipse.

$\frac{(-1)^2}{4} + \frac{4^2}{25} = \frac{1}{4} + \frac{16}{25} = \frac{89}{100}$; $\frac{89}{100} < 1$

LESSON MASTER 12-5 A

Skills Objective C

In 1 and 2, find the area of an ellipse satisfying the given conditions.

1. Its equation is $\frac{x^2}{169} + \frac{y^2}{324} = 1$.

234π

2. The endpoints of its major and minor axes are (0, 3) and (0, -3), and (1.5, 0) and (-1.5, 0).

4.5π

3. Which has a greater area, a circle with diameter 10 or an ellipse with major and minor axes of lengths 12 and 8?

the circle

4. Find the area of the shaded region at the right between a circle with radius 4 and an ellipse with major axis of length 16 and minor axis of length 10.

24π

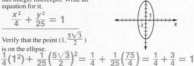

Properties Objective G

In 5 and 6, a scale change is described. a. Write an equation for the image of the circle $x^2 + y^2 = 1$ under the scale change. b. Tell if the image is a noncircular ellipse.

5. $S: (x, y) \rightarrow (8x, 8y)$

   a. $\frac{x^2}{64} + \frac{y^2}{64} = 1$

   b. no

6. $S(x, y) = (3x, 6y)$

   a. $\frac{x^2}{9} + \frac{y^2}{36} = 1$

   b. yes

7. *True or false.* Not every circle is an ellipse.

false

Uses Objective H

8. A jewel shaped like an ellipse is placed on a background that is also an ellipse. The jewel has major axis 4 mm and minor axis 3 mm. The background has major axis 6 mm and minor axis 4 mm. What percent of the background is covered by the jewel?

50%

LESSON MASTER 12-6 A

Questions on SPUR Objectives
See pages 804-807 for objectives.

Skills Objective B

In 1–2, write an equation for the hyperbola satisfying the given conditions.

1. foci at (5, 0) and (-5, 0); focal constant 8 ___ $\dfrac{x^2}{16} - \dfrac{y^2}{9} = 1$

2. vertices at $(-\sqrt{6}, 0)$ and $(\sqrt{6}, 0)$; containing the point (6, 4) ___ $\dfrac{x^2}{6} - \dfrac{5y^2}{16} = 1$

Properties Objectives E, F, and G

3. Use the conic grid below with centers 10 units apart to draw the set of points P satisfying the condition $|PF_1 - PF_2| = 6$.

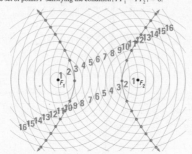

In 4 and 5, the equation for a hyperbola is given.
a. Name its vertices. b. Write equations of its asymptotes.

4. $\dfrac{x^2}{36} - \dfrac{y^2}{16} = 1$

a. ___ (6, 0), (-6, 0)

b. ___ $y = \pm\dfrac{2}{3}x$

5. $x^2 - \dfrac{y^2}{4} = 1$

a. ___ (1, 0), (-1, 0)

b. ___ $y = \pm 2x$

121 ▶

▶ **LESSON MASTER** 12-6 A *page 2*

6. Given two fixed points F_1 and F_2 and a focal constant d, give the condition that a set of points P must satisfy in order to be a hyperbola. ___ $|PF_1 - PF_2| = d$

Representations Objective J

In 7 and 8, sketch the graph of the equation.

7. $\dfrac{x^2}{36} - \dfrac{y^2}{16} = 1$

8. $x^2 - \dfrac{y^2}{4} = 1$

9. Write an equation for the hyperbola at the right.

___ $\dfrac{x^2}{9} - \dfrac{y^2}{4} = 1$

122

LESSON MASTER 12-7 A

Questions on SPUR Objectives
See pages 804-807 for objectives.

Skills Objective A

In 1–4, rewrite the equation in the form $Ax^2 + Bxy + Cy^2 + Dx + Ey + F = 0$.

1. $(x + 5)^2 + (y - 2)^2 = 16$ ___ $x^2 + y^2 + 10x - 4y + 13 = 0$

2. $\dfrac{x^2}{36} + \dfrac{y^2}{49} = 1$ ___ $49x^2 + 36y^2 - 1764 = 0$

3. $y = 2(x - 3)^2 + 5$ ___ $2x^2 - 12x - y + 23 = 0$

4. $3y = \pm\sqrt{2x^2 - 16}$ ___ $2x^2 - 9y^2 - 16 = 0$

Skills Objective B

5. a. Write an equation for the hyperbola with foci at (3, -3) and (-3, 3), and focal constant 6. ___ $xy = -\dfrac{9}{2}$

b. Verify that the point (-0.5, 9) is on the hyperbola.

___ $(-0.5)9 = -\dfrac{9}{2}$

c. Verify that the point (3, -3) is *not* on the hyperbola.

___ $3(-3) = -9 \neq -\dfrac{9}{2}$

Properties Objectives F and G

6. Identify the asymptotes of the hyperbola with equation $xy = 6$. ___ x- and y-axes

7. *True or false.* Every hyperbola has an equation of the form $xy = k$, where $k \neq 0$. ___ false

8. Consider the hyperbola with equation $xy = -18$. Name its

a. foci ___ (-6, 6), (6, -6)   b. asymptotes ___ x- and y-axes   c. focal constant. ___ 12

123 ▶

▶ **LESSON MASTER** 12-7 A *page 2*

Uses Objective H

9. The total cost of n pencils at a price of m each was $15. Write an equation for the conic section which describes all possible combinations (n, m). ___ $mn = 15$

Representations Objective J

In 10 and 11, *multiple choice*. Select the equation that best describes the graph.

(a) $\dfrac{x^2}{a^2} + \dfrac{y^2}{b^2} = 1$ (b) $\dfrac{x^2}{a^2} - \dfrac{y^2}{b^2} = 1$ (c) $y = ax^2$ (d) $y = \dfrac{a}{x}$

10. ___ d

11. ___ b

In 12 and 13, write an equation for the rectangular hyperbola.

12. ___ $xy = 25$

13. ___ $xy = -12$

124

171

LESSON MASTER 12-8 A

Skills Objective D

In 1–3, solve the system.

1. $\begin{cases} y = 2x^2 - 1 \\ \frac{2}{3}x + y - \frac{1}{3} = 0 \end{cases}$

$(-1, 1), (\frac{2}{3}, -\frac{1}{9})$

2. $\begin{cases} (x-1)^2 + (y+6)^2 = 8 \\ 2x - y - 6 = 0 \end{cases}$

$(1.4, -3.2), (-1, -8)$

3. $\begin{cases} ab = -12 \\ 3a - b = 0 \end{cases}$

no solutions

Uses Objective I

4. A rectangular picture has an area of 300 in² and perimeter of 80 in. Find its dimensions.

10 in., 30 in.

Representations Objective K

In 5 and 6, give two equations whose graphs illustrate the situation.

Samples are given.

5. a line intersecting an ellipse in exactly 1 point

$\frac{x^2}{4} + \frac{y^2}{2} = 1$

$x = -2$

6. a line intersecting a parabola in exactly two points

$y = \frac{1}{2}x^2$

$y = x$

In 7 and 8, graph and estimate the solutions.

7. $\begin{cases} y = x^2 + 3 \\ 3x - y + 4 = 0 \end{cases}$

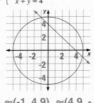

$\approx(-.3, 3.1), \approx(3.3, 13.9)$

8. $\begin{cases} x^2 + y^2 = 25 \\ x + y = 4 \end{cases}$

$\approx(-1, 4.9), \approx(4.9, -.9)$

LESSON MASTER 12-9 A

Skills Objective D

In 1 and 2, solve the system using substitution or linear combinations.

1. $\begin{cases} x^2 + y^2 = 4 \\ 3x^2 + 2y^2 = 10 \end{cases}$

$(\sqrt{2}, \pm\sqrt{2}),$
$(-\sqrt{2}, \pm\sqrt{2})$

2. $\begin{cases} a^2 + (b-2)^2 = 7 \\ a^2 - b + 1 = 0 \end{cases}$

$(\sqrt{3}, 4), (-\sqrt{3}, 4)$

3. $\begin{cases} m^2 + 9n^2 = 36 \\ m^2 - 2n^2 = 3 \end{cases}$

$(3, \pm\sqrt{3}),$
$(-3, \pm\sqrt{3})$

Uses Objective I

4. Temp-O, which manufactures thermometers, made $876,960 in sales last year. This year Temp-O made $888,096 by raising the price for each thermometer by $.04 and selling the same number of thermometers.

a. Write a system of equations to describe this situation.

$\begin{cases} np = 876{,}960 \\ n(p + .04) = 888{,}096 \end{cases}$

b. What was the price of a Temp-O thermometer last year?

$3.15

c. How many thermometers were sold this year?

278,400 therm.

Representations Objective K

Samples are given.

5. Give equations for a parabola and an ellipse that intersect in exactly 3 points.

$y = x^2 - 2$

$\frac{x^2}{9} + \frac{y^2}{4} = 1$

6. Graph $\begin{cases} x^2 + y^2 = 16 \\ xy = -8 \end{cases}$ and estimate the solutions.

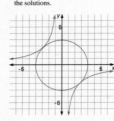

$\approx(-2.8, 2.8), \approx(2.8, -2.8)$

LESSON MASTER 13-1 A

Skills Objective A

In 1–6, evaluate the given arithmetic series.

1. $3 + 6 + 9 + \ldots + 99$

1683

2. the sum of the first 25 terms of the sequence defined by
$\begin{cases} a_1 = 44 \\ a_n = a_{n-1} - 5, \text{ for integers } n \geq 2. \end{cases}$

-400

3. the sum of the first 40 positive integers

820

4. $-16 - 14 - 12 + \ldots + 16 + 18 + 20$

38

5. the sum of the first 20 odd positive integers

400

6. the sum of the first 20 even positive integers

420

7. The sum of the integers $1 + 2 + 3 + \ldots + k$ is 2145. Find k.

$k = 65$

Uses Objective G

8. Mary began each workout with sit-ups, and increased the number of sit-ups she did each week. The first week she did 50; the second week she did 60; the following week she did 70. Each week thereafter, she did 10 more sit-ups than she had done the previous week.

a. How many sit-ups did Mary do in the 19th week?

230 sit-ups

b. In which week did Mary first do 500 sit-ups?

week 46

9. A house of cards is built with 54 cards on the first level, 50 cards on the second level, and 4 fewer cards on each successive level. If the house of cards has 8 levels, how many cards are used in all?

320 cards

LESSON MASTER 13-2 A

Skills Objective B

In 1–6, evaluate the geometric series.

1. $1 + 2 + 4 + 8 + \ldots + 256$

511

2. the sum of the first 10 terms of the sequence defined by
$\begin{cases} g_1 = 50 \\ g_n = .5g_{n-1}, \text{ for integers } n \geq 2. \end{cases}$

≈ 99.902

3. $1 - 3 + 9 - 27 + 81 - 243$

-182

4. $.003 + .006 + .012 + \ldots + .003(2)^{10}$

6.141

5. the sum of the first 13 terms of the sequence defined by
$\begin{cases} g_1 = 2000 \\ g_n = -\frac{1}{4}g_{n-1}, n \geq 2. \end{cases}$

≈ 2666.667

6. $7 - 21 + 63 + \ldots + 7(-3)^8$

34,447

Uses Objective G

7. A ball is dropped from a height of 6 feet and bounces up to 80% of its previous height on each bounce. When it hits the ground for the 11th time, how far has it traveled in the vertical direction?

≈ 48.8 feet

8. On the third of January for eight consecutive years, Ben deposited $2000 in a retirement fund which earns an annual yield of 3.5%.

a. Write a geometric series that represents the value of this investment on January 3rd of the eighth year.

See below. Eighth-year deposit is included.

b. Evaluate the series in Part a.

$18,103.37

8a. $2000 + 2000(1.035) + 2000(1.035)^2 + 2000(1.035)^3 + 2000(1.035)^4 + 2000(1.035)^5 + 2000(1.035)^6 + 2000(1.035)^7$

LESSON MASTER 13-3 A

Skills Objectives C and D

In 1 and 2, a series is given. **a.** Write the terms of the series. **b.** Evaluate the series.

1. $\sum_{n=-3}^{2} (.1)^n$

a. $1000 + 100 + 10 +$ $1 + .1 + .01$

b. $1,111.11$

2. $\sum_{i=0}^{5} (3i - 4)$

a. $-4 + (-1) + 2 + 5 +$ $8 + 11$

b. 21

In 3 and 4, rewrite the series using Σ-notation. **Samples are given.**

3. $1 - 4 + 9 - 16 + 25 - 36 + 49$

$\sum_{n=1}^{7} (-1)^{n-1} n^2$

4. $-8 - 6 - 4 - 2 - 0 + 2 + 4 + 6 + 8$

$\sum_{n=-4}^{4} 2n$

In 5 and 6, evaluate the expression.

5. $8!$ $40,320$

6. $\frac{12!}{9!}$ 1320

In 7 and 8, consider the four digits 1, 2, 3, and 4.

7. a. List all permutations of these digits.

1234	1423	2314	3124	3412	4213
1243	1432	2341	3142	3421	4231
1324	2134	2413	3214	4123	4312
1342	2143	2431	3241	4132	4321

b. How many permutations of four different digits are possible?

24 **permutations**

8. How many four-digit numbers can be created with a 3 as the first digit?

6 **numbers**

Uses Objective H

9. How many different baseball line-ups can be made with a 9-person baseball team?

$362,880$ **line-ups**

10. How many different ways can 7 books be placed on a shelf?

5040 **ways**

129

LESSON MASTER 13-4 A

Skills Objective I

In 1 and 2, a set of grades is given. **a.** Find the mean. **b.** Find the median **c.** Find the mode.

1. 71, 72, 74, 85, 85, 93

a. 80

b. 79.5

c. 85

2. 91, 85, 87, 82, 94, 86, 87, 85

a. 87.125

b. 86.5

c. $85, 87$

3. Data set $A = \{10, 20, 30, 30, 40, 50\}$ and data set $B = \{28, 29, 30, 30, 31, 32\}$. Both sets have the same mean, median, and mode.

a. Calculate the standard deviation of set A. ≈ 12.91

b. Calculate the standard deviation of set B. ≈ 1.291

c. *Multiple choice.* Set $C = \{29, 29, 30, 30, 32\}$. This set has the same mean, median, and mode as sets A and B. Which phrase best describes the standard deviation of set C? **b**

(a) greater than the standard deviation of set A and set B

(b) less than the standard deviation of set A and set B

(c) greater than the standard deviation of set A and less than the standard deviation of set B

(d) greater than the standard deviation of set B and less than the standard deviation of set A

4. The 1994 Statistical Abstract of the United States lists the following data regarding cigarette-smoking habits of people in the U.S. who are 18 years of age or older.

Year	1965	1974	1979	1983	1985	1988	1991
% of population that smokes	42.4	37.1	33.5	32.1	30.1	28.1	25.6

a. Find the mean, median, and standard deviation of the smoking habits of adults in the United States for these data.

mean 32.7% med. 32.1% st. dev. 5.25%

b. Which of these measures *best* describes the data? Why?

Sample: The mean best describes the data because it considers all the percents.

130

LESSON MASTER 13-5 A

Skills Objective D

In 1–8, evaluate.

1. $\binom{7}{2}$ 21 **2.** $\binom{6}{4}$ 15 **3.** $\binom{11}{1}$ 11 **4.** $\binom{35}{0}$ 1

5. $\binom{12}{11}$ 12 **6.** $\binom{8}{5}$ 56 **7.** $\binom{10}{10}$ 1 **8.** $\binom{3}{n}$ $\frac{n!(3-n)!}{}$

Properties Objective F

9. Rows 0 to 2 of Pascal's triangle are given below. Write the next 6 rows.

```
              1                    row 0
            1   1                  row 1
          1   2   1                row 2
        1   3   3   1              row 3
      1   4   6   4   1            row 4
    1   5  10  10   5   1          row 5
  1   6  15  20  15   6   1        row 6
1   7  21  35  35  21   7   1      row 7
1  8  28  56  70  56  28  8  1     row 8
```

In 10–12, use your work above to evaluate the expressions.

10. $\binom{6}{1}$ 6 **11.** $\binom{8}{0}$ 1 **12.** $\binom{5}{2}$ 10

13. $\binom{16}{3}$ represents the 4th element in the 16th row.

14. Verify that for $n = 6$, $\binom{n}{3} + \binom{n}{4} = \binom{n+1}{4}$.

$\binom{6}{3} + \binom{6}{4} = \frac{6!}{3!(3!)} + \frac{6!}{4!(2!)} = 20 + 15 = 35; \binom{7}{4} = \frac{7!}{4!(3!)} = 35$

15. Row 10 of Pascal's Triangle is: 1, 10, 45, 120, 210, 252, 210, 120, 45, 10, 1. Write 45 two different ways using $\binom{n}{r}$ notation.

$\binom{10}{2}, \binom{10}{8}$

In 16–18, *true or false.*

16. $8 \cdot 7! = 8!$

$true$

17. $\binom{65}{10} = \binom{65}{55}$

$true$

18. $\binom{n}{n} = 1$ for all positive integers n

$true$

131

LESSON MASTER 13-6 A

Skills Objective E

1. Fill in the blanks to expand the binomial $(3m + 2n^2)^5$. Let $a = 3m$ and $b = 2n^2$.

a. First, fill in the coefficients.

$(a + b)^5 = \binom{5}{0}a^5 + \binom{5}{1}a^4b + \binom{5}{2}a^3b^2 + \binom{5}{3}a^2b^3 + \binom{5}{4}ab^4 + \binom{5}{5}b^5$

b. Now substitute the values for a and b. $(3m + 2n^2)^5 = (3m)^5 +$

$5(3m)^4(2n^2) + 10(3m)^3(2n^2)^2 + 10(3m)^2(2n^2)^3 + 5(3m)(2n^2)^4 + (2n^2)^5$

c. Simplify.

$243m^5 + 810m^4n^2 + 1080m^3n^4 + 720m^2n^6 + 240mn^8 + 32n^{10}$

In 2–5, expand the binomial.

2. $(x^2 + 1)^8$ $x^{16} + 8x^{14} + 28x^{12} + 56x^{10} + 70x^8 + 56x^6$ $+ 28x^4 + 8x^2 + 1$

3. $(3c - 5)^3$ $27c^3 - 135c^2 + 225c - 125$

4. $(x^3 - y)^4$ $x^{12} - 4x^9y + 6x^6y^2 - 4x^3y^3 + y^4$

5. $(\frac{1}{2} + 2d)^4$ $\frac{1}{16} + d + 6d^2 + 16d^3 + 16d^4$

6. a. Use the first three terms of the binomial expansion of $(1 + .03)^8$ to estimate $(1.03)^8$. 1.2652

b. Find $(1.03)^8$ using a calculator. Do you think the answer in Part a is an acceptable estimate? Why or why not?

≈ 1.26677; **Sample: Yes; the answers are equivalent to the nearest hundredth.**

In 7–9, convert to an expression in the form $(a + b)^n$.

7. $\sum_{r=0}^{n} \binom{n}{r} x^{n-r} 4^r$

$(x + 4)^n$

8. $\sum_{r=0}^{n} \binom{n}{r} (2t)^{n-r} (-u)^r$

$(2t - u)^n$

9. $\sum_{r=0}^{n} \binom{n}{r} z^{n-r} (\frac{w}{2})^r$

$(z + \frac{w}{2})^n$

Uses Objective F

10. Which entry in Pascal's triangle is the coefficient of a^4b^2 in the binomial expansion of $(a + b)^6$?   **row 6, 3rd element**

132

LESSON MASTER 13-7 A

Questions on SPUR Objectives
See pages 880-883 for objectives.

Skills Objective D

1. *Multiple choice.* Which is *not* a subset of {P, E, A, R}? ___ **c**
   (a) {A, E, R} (b) { }
   (c) {P, E, T, R} (d) {R, E, A, P}

2. a. How many subsets of {P, E, A, R}
   have 3 elements? ___ **4**

   b. List the subsets with 3 elements.
   {P, E, A}, {P, E, R}, {P, A, R}, {E, A, R}

3. Suppose a set has 9 elements. What does $\binom{9}{3}$ represent?
   number of 3-element subsets of a
   9-element set

Properties Objective F

In 4–6, *true or false.* If true, verify the statement.
If false, rewrite so that the statement is true.

4. $\binom{6}{0} + \binom{6}{1} + \binom{6}{2} + \binom{6}{3} + \binom{6}{4} + \binom{6}{5} + \binom{6}{6}$ equals the
   total number of subsets of a set with 7 elements.
   false; Change "7 elements" to "6 elements".

5. $\binom{6}{0} + \binom{6}{1} + \binom{6}{2} + \binom{6}{3} + \binom{6}{4} + \binom{6}{5} + \binom{6}{6} = 2^6$
   true; 1 + 6 + 15 + 20 + 15 + 6 + 1 = 64 = 2^6

6. $\binom{6}{0} + \binom{6}{1} + \binom{6}{2} + \binom{6}{3} + \binom{6}{4} + \binom{6}{5} + \binom{6}{6}$ equals the
   sum of row 7 of Pascal's triangle.
   false; Change "row 7" to "row 6."

7. What does the symbol $_8C_4$ represent?
   number of 4-element subsets of an
   8-element set

---

8. *Multiple choice.* Which equation is correct? ___ **a**
   (a) $_9C_7 = \binom{9}{7}$ (b) $_7C_9 = \binom{9}{7}$ (c) $_9C_7 = 7^9$ (d) $_7C_9 = 7^9$

9. a. Evaluate $_5C_0 + _5C_1 + _5C_2 + _5C_3 + _5C_4 + _5C_5$. ___ **32**
   b. What does this have to do with Pascal's triangle?
   32 is the sum of the numbers in row 5.

Uses Objective H

In 10 and 11, use this information: Sam has a collection
of 16 compact discs, five of which are by the group
MATH-MANIA.

10. How many different ways can Sam choose 6 CDs
    from all the discs in his collection? **8008 ways**

11. How many mini-collections of 3 CDs could be
    formed from the *MATH-MANIA* CDS? **10 collections**

In 12–14, use this information: Julie has an extensive
stamp collection with 10 particularly valuable stamps
from Mexico and 8 from Spain.

12. Write an expression to show how many
    ways she can choose 10 of these stamps. **43,758 ways**

13. a. How many possible displays of at least one stamp
    can be made up entirely of Spanish stamps? **255 displays**

    b. How many possible displays of at least one stamp
    can be made up entirely of Mexican stamps? **1023 displays**

14. How many possible displays of five stamps can be
    made with 2 Spanish and 3 Mexican stamps? **3360 displays**

LESSON MASTER 13-8 A

Questions on SPUR Objectives
See pages 880-883 for objectives.

Vocabulary

1. Define *independent events.*
   Sample: events for which the outcome of one
   does not affect the outcome of the other

2. Define *mutually-exclusive events.*
   Sample: events which cannot occur at the
   same time

3. Explain the difference between a *trial* and an *experiment.*
   Sample: A trial is one situation which may be
   repeated; an experiment is a collection of trials.

Uses Objective J

In 4–7, a coin with $P(H) = .8$ is tossed four times.

4. a. Calculate the probability of 0 tails. **.4096**
   b. Calculate the probability of exactly 1 tail. **.4096**
   c. Calculate the probability of exactly 2 tails. **.1536**
   d. Calculate the probability of exactly 3 tails. **.0256**
   e. Calculate the probability of exactly 4 tails. **.0016**

5. In Question 4, which events are mutually exclusive? Explain.
   Sample: All are mutually exclusive, as no two
   of them can occur at the same time.

6. a. What is the probability of getting at least 2 tails? **.1808**
   b. What is the probability of getting at most 2 tails? **.9728**

7. Are the events in 6a and 6b mutually exclusive?
   Why or why not?
   Sample: No; getting 2 tails is a part of
   each experiment.

In 8–10, consider this situation: You answer each
item on a true-false test by guessing. The probability
of correctly answering each question is 0.6.
a. Write the expression to calculate the probability
of the given event. b. Calculate the probability
of the event.

8. 8 questions, 5 correct.
   a. $\binom{8}{5}(.6)^5(.4)^3$
   b. $\approx$ **.279**

9. 8 questions, at least 5 correct.
   a. $\binom{8}{5}(.6)^5(.4)^3 + \binom{8}{6}(.6)^6(.4)^2 + \binom{8}{7}(.6)^7(.4) + \binom{8}{8}(.6)^8$
   b. $\approx$ **.594**

10. Suppose you answer 2 questions correctly on an 8-item test.
    What is the probability you will now get at least 5 correct?
    a. $\binom{6}{3}(.6)^3(.4)^3 + \binom{6}{4}(.6)^4(.4)^2 + \binom{6}{5}(.6)^5(.4) + \binom{6}{6}(.6)^6$
    b. $\approx$ **.821**

11. Suppose a fair coin is tossed 9 times. Give the probability
    of each event.
    a. exactly 3 heads b. exactly 4 tails.
    $\approx$ **.164** $\approx$ **.246**

12. Suppose a fair coin is tossed n times.
    a. How many different ways can r heads occur? $\binom{n}{r}$
    b. How many different combinations of heads and
    tails are possible? 2^n
    c. What is the probability that r of n times a
    head will occur? $\binom{n}{r}/2^n$